World Literature and the Politics of the Minority

World Literature and the Politics of the Minority

Edited by
Jihee Han

RAWAT PUBLICATIONS
Jaipur • New Delhi • Bangalore • Hyderabad • Guwahati

ISBN 978-81-316-0576-9

Published by
Prem Rawat for **Rawat Publications**
Satyam Apts, Sector 3, Jawahar Nagar, Jaipur 302 004 (India)
Phone: 0141 265 1748 / 7006 Fax: 0141 265 1748
E-mail: info@rawatbooks.com
Website: www.rawatbooks.com

New Delhi Office
4858/24, Ansari Road, Daryaganj, New Delhi 110 002
Phone: 011 2326 3290

Also at *Bangalore, Hyderabad* and *Guwahati*

Typeset by Rawat Computers, Jaipur
Printed at Chaman Enterprises, New Delhi

Contents

Preface

World Literature and the Politics of the Minority examines the discursive cartographies of world literature. "World Literature" is often imagined as a unified, homogeneous literary space in which universal aesthetic standards and literary values are shared and comprehensively applied to. For instance, widely-circulated anthologies of world literature such as *The Norton Anthology of World Literature, The Longman Anthology of World Literature,* and *The Bedford Anthology of World Literature* all feature a monochronic vision of world literature following the West-centered timelines of the ancient, the middle, and the modern/contemporary regardless of Space/Time heterogeneity and diversity that exist in the areas of the world. Given this unilinear typology of world literature, the polychronic literatures of minor countries and peoples have had little chance to be properly represented. For instance, the polyphonic voices of minority literatures have often been regarded as unfit for the established time frame of world literature or dismissed as cacophonic noises *vis-à-vis* the more tamed and familiar notes of the Other imagined on the basis of Western Orientalism. Thus, this book revises the conception of the term 'the minority' and explores the ethics of the new minority in the age of global digitalization. As praxis, it aims to draw attention to the minority voices of India, China, and Japan and at the same time the rarely heard voices of Egypt, the United Arab Emirates, and Korea. Ultimately, *World Literature and the Politics of the Minority* takes note of the nomadic digital mode of existence spreading all over the world and suggests the necessity for a new transmutable imagination of 'Becoming' that will enable us to re-imagine the world as we know. Taking a flight from the binary opposition between 'the major, aesthetically superior, and culturally developed Western literatures' and 'the minor, less sophisticated, and regional non-Western literatures' in the discourse of world literature into the political dynamics between the analogue arborescent system and the digital interface system, it also makes an attempt to meditate on the role of new humanists confronting the challenges of the capitalist world economy system.

Last but not least, I'd like to express my deepest gratitude to all contributors and fellow comparatists for showing their great support for the idea that a minority voice needs to be represented by a minority scholar. They not only contributed their precious essays but also put up with the long, snail-paced process with extraordinary generosity and patience. Without their graciousness, this project would have been buried alive somewhere in the heart of one minority scholar.

Contributors

Jihee Han is Associate professor of English at Gyeongsang National University, the Republic of Korea. She has published many essays on modern American poetry and Korean literature and culture. Some of recent publications are Korean translation of *The Fact of a Doorframe by Adrienne Rich* (Moonji 2011), "Korea" in *Cultural History of Reading* (Greenwood 2010), "Korean Novelists and Novels" in *Facts on File Companion to the World Novel 1900 to the Present* (Facts on File 2009), and "Korean Poets and Poetry" in *Facts on File Companion to World Poetry* (Facts on File 2008).

Jasbir Jain is the Honorary Director of the Institute for Research in Interdisciplinary Studies (IRIS), Jaipur. She was Sahitya Akademi Writer-in-Residence (2009), and Emeritus Fellow (2001–2003) both at the University of Rajasthan. Recipient of the SALA Award (2008) and of IACS Award (2003). Jain is deeply interested in indigenous narrative strategies and theoretical positions. Amongst her work are three volumes on the Indian novel covering the period 1860–2000 published between 1998–2006, *Indigenous Roots of Feminism: Culture, Subjectivity and Agency* (2011) and *The Writer as Critic* (ed.) and *Muslim Culture in Indian Cinema* (ed.). Former K.K. Birla Fellow. Jain also writes in Punjabi and has translated from Punjabi into English.

Wang Ning is Professor of English and Comparative Literature and Director of the Center for Comparative Literature and Cultural Studies at Tsinghua University, and Zhiyuan Chair

Professor of Humanities at Shanghai Jiao Tong University. Among his numerous books and articles in Chinese, he has authored two books in English: *Globalization and Cultural Translation* (2004), and *Translated Modernities: Literary and Cultural Perspectives on Globalization and China* (2010). He has also published extensively in English in many international prestigious journals like *New Literary History, Critical Inquiry, boundary 2, Modern Language Quarterly, Comparative Literature Studies, Semiotica, Neohelicon,* and *ARIEL*.

Myles Chilton is Full Professor at Nihon University in Japan. His academic interests are in exploring relationships between contemporary world literature, globalized cultures, and pedagogy. He has published articles on modern Canadian, British and Japanese literary representations of global cities in *Comparative Critical Studies, Studies in the Literary Imagination,* and *The Journal of Narrative Theory*. His current work concerns issues surrounding world literature and language pedagogy.

Marie-Therese Abdel-Messih is Professor of English and Comparative Literature Universities of Cairo, and Kuwait (on secondment). Member of the International Advisory Board and Associate Editors of CLCWeb: *Comparative Literature and Culture*, Purdue University; Member of Board of Trustees: The International Prize for Arabic Fiction (IPAF) supported by the Booker Prize Foundation; Member of the Advisory Board of the National Centre for Translation. Among translations and numerous articles in English and Arabic, she has authored books in Arabic: *A Transcultural Reading of Literature* (1997; 2004); *Visual and Verbal Cultural Representations* (2001); *National Culture: Global or International Options* (2006; 2009).

Santosh Gupta is Professor of English. She is an independent scholar now having superannuated from the University of Rajasthan, Jaipur. She conducted a research Project funded by UGC on Modern Prison Writings. She held senior administrative positions as Dean, Faculty of Arts (2002–2005) and Chairperson of the Department of English, both at the University of Rajasthan, Jaipur. She has worked extensively in the twentieth century fiction, British and Indian,

Postcolonial and Feminist Writing and Theory. She has participated in several international and national level Conferences. She has published papers on R.K. Narayan, Anita Desai and Shashi Deshpande, and is working on the Amitav Ghosh's works.

Saddik Gohar is Associate Professor at United Arab Emirates University in Al Ain. His recent publications include *Singers in the Wasteland: Voices of Protest in Modern Poetry*, "Navigating Myth and Tradition in Feminist Emirati Poetics: An Inter-textual Approach," and "Engaging British Modernist Traditions into Contemporary Arabic Poetry." He is also a contributor to Doris Jedamski's *Chewing over the West: Occidental Narratives in Non-Western Readings*.

Doris Hambuch is Assistant Professor at United Arab Emirates University in Al Ain. Her publications include articles on Derek Walcott, Frank Martinus Arion, and Dionne Brand. She is a contributor to the *Encyclopedia of Postcolonial Studies* and to the *Who is Who of Contemporary Women Writers*. She is currently co-editing a collection of essays titled *In Motion: Caribbean Cinema in the 21st Century and Beyond*.

Hajime Saito is Associate Professor at the University of Tsukuba in Japan. He published *Teikoku Nihon no Eibunhaku* (English Literary Studies in Imperial Japan) in 2006 (published in Japanese).

Liu Hao is Assistant Professor of Department of Foreign Languages at Tsinghua University in China. She published "A Cultural Reading of the New Elements in a Chinese adaptation of *Hamlet*," the 4th Tsinghua-Lingnan Symposium on Translation, Hong Kong, 2010, "On the Chinese adaptations of *Hamlet*," the 7th National Symposium on International Drama and Shakespeare, Hefei, 2009, and "Love and the Image of Distant Place in Shakespearean Drama and Traditional Chinese Drama" in *Shakespeare Our Contemporary: Context, Intertexuality and Perspectives*, ed. by Zhang Chong (Shanghai: Fudan UP, 2005).

INTRODUCTION

Cartographies of World Literature

The Minority Literatures and the Politics of the Minority

Jihee Han

STARTING THE FLIGHT

Edward Said's notion of Orientalism has long been applied to criticize Western [re]presentations of tamed East/East Asia, so that it now almost seems to be a passé to mention it in contemplating the relations between the East and the West. However, Said's perspective still serves as a useful tool to grope for the location of East Asian minority literatures that are rarely recognized in the twenty-first century atlas of world literature. Although postcolonial comparatists have been raising the issues of cultural imperialism and literary hierarchy in world comparative literature, the cognate space of the world is still territorialized according to the notions rooted in the binary oppositions of Western metaphysics. The "world" in the "World Literature" is still divided into Eurocentric blocks: the developed First World/the primitive or tribal Third World, the wealthy Northern Hemisphere/the poor Southern Hemisphere, or the modern and progressive West/the highly civilized but frozen East. The world literary space is still imagined, named, and systemized by postmodern Orientalists who are now equipped with latest theoretical perspectives. When they encounter a new literature of a different style, they tend to explore it in Western intellectual traditions, contextualize it in Western literary influences, and locate it in the boundary of what they have appreciated as aesthetical instead of examining the potentials of the rupture and multiplicity the new literature can provoke and/or add. The recent anthologies of world literature serve good examples of the tendency of West-centered homogenization embedded in the imagination of world literature. Almost like a global tableau vivant of world literatures, the African tribes, the Asian/East Asian exotic peoples, and the pan-European liberal intellectuals inhabit each area and mutually constitute a romanticized ecological vision in the ever-growing volumes of anthologies of world literature. There, all regional non-Western literatures certified and admitted to enter in such an idyllic literary space manifest the notion of 'the diversity of species' in the cultural history of the world. However, the addition of the kind and the number does not change the Western soil of the world literary ecology: the newly added literature is soon to yield its place to another by a literary advisor's call, who is mostly Anglo-European.

On the issue of Anglo-Eurocentrism embedded in the discourses of world literature, Rey Chow had already addressed in her essay "In the Name of Comparative Literature" in 1995. Taking note on the point that Western comparatists presuppose the "world" as mainly composed of Anglo-European countries, Chow indicates the problematic that Charles Bernheimer connotes in his 1993 ACLA Report. Even if Western comparatists deserve credit for their conscious efforts to extend the boundary of world literature by substituting literatures of India, China, and Japan for those of England, France and Germany, such efforts, she argues, would not have an effect on the fundamental shift of their outlook on the "world." She goes on to assert that unless Western comparatists give up "a social Darwinian understanding of the nation," they will only reproduce "Eurocentric, nation-oriented model" of comparative literature (109). In such a metaphysical frame, she points out, non-Western literature will always remain the representatives of, for instance, Asia which has developed its own unique literary tradition distinguished from the masterpieces of "master" nations and cultures (109). She expresses her uncomfortable feelings of such innate social Darwinism of Western comparative perspective by directly pointing out "its false claim to 'universalism'."

> The problems of comparative literature—its 'Eurocentrism' and its false claim to "universalism"—can therefore not be solved simply by strengthening the local versions of the same problems, nor by simply adding emphases to the study of non-European languages and cultures as if such study did not already have a fully implicated and complicit role in the history of the teaching of the humanities in the West. (111)

Now, after about seventeen years of post-structuralism, postcolonialism, multiculturalism, and ethnic/area studies, what kind of change of perceptive has the West's claims to "universalism" produced for the advancement of world literature? Has Korea, one of the marginalized Others, been represented in a recent, more balanced map of world literature? Have major anthologies of world literature innovated themselves enough to evoke a new perception of the world by adding more minority literatures of diverse, say Asian, countries? Disappointingly, the answer is in the negative. As far as I have checked out the big three anthologies of world literature (Bedford, Longman, Norton), Chow's prediction not only turns out to be quite precise but also still sends a clear warning sign to comparatists from marginalized countries. Non-Western literatures such as those of Korea, Taiwan, Vietnam, or Tibet, just as Chow had already suggested, still hold little imagination in Western mind and remain the way they had been seventeen years before as the West's Other and as "the marginalized 'others' to the 'Other' which is 'great' Asian civilizations" such as China and Japan (Chow 109). Korean literature still occupies an almost invisible peripheral space in the global cultural atlas as a literature of lesser prominence and draws a slight interest only in relation to the history and culture of China and Japan in world literature.

Moreover, as Chow had already indicated, Western comparatists still subscribe to a social Darwinian understanding of world literature. Examining 2006 debates between Anglo-European and postcolonial comparatists over the future direction of comparative literature, I still witness the remnants of cultural imperialism and Orientalism in Anglo-European discourses of world literature. Such Western scholars as Charles Braider and Susan Bassnett, responding to Gayatri Spivak's argument of "death of a discipline," turn the direction of the discourse into the debate of the origin. Braider acknowledges that postcolonial scholars such as Spivak, Homi Bhabha, and Anthony Appiah brought in "the genuinely global perspective" of the discipline (161). At the same time he indicates that "much of the original impetus" behind the discipline "came from scholarship on the 'long' European Renaissance" with "the baroque and its neoclassical aftermath" (161). Bassnett also defends the "Eurocentric origins" (3) and "the canonical status quo" (5) of

Western comparatists against the discursive challenge of "Spivak and Southern hemisphere scholars" (5). In a very casual style she indicates the sacredness of Western literature—sacred in the sense that it is not necessary to question or justify its ultimate value—saying, "the stifling weight of the Great European Tradition was such that it is not surprising that there should have been such a violent reaction by postcolonial scholars" (5).

Suppose that the discourses of world literature seem to be stuck in the recurring debate of the origin, I think it is about time to take a flight from the linear speculative paradigm of the homogenous World Literature to Rhizomatic thinking in order to imagine a new global literary space in the face of the increasing socio-political complexities caused by the capitalist world economy system. Actually, be "Southern hemisphere scholars" or "Eurocentric" scholars or "Oriental" scholars or "Occidental" scholars, we all face the crisis of the Humanities and thus feel the need to reflect upon the ways to cope with the capitalist management system that has relentlessly been weeding out so-called impractical, unyielding, and unpromising departments and/or academic programs and further indiscriminatingly been advancing the realignment and merge of different disciplines in the Humanities studies. Down-sized, down-played, and threatened by capitalism and its logic of limitless global competition, it seems that scholars of the Humanities all around the world are situated in the position of the minority. Then, what would be more appropriate than to discuss the function of world literature within the capitalist system of global economy and to meditate on the politics of the minority? Here I, myself belonging to the minority and to the marginalized Other of China and Japan in the current discourses of world literature, try to assess the cartographies of world literature and then to meditate on the new minority and its ethical potentials as a new perspective of world literature.

THE WEST'S PERCEPTION OF THE WORLD: THEN AND NOW

As is widely known by now, we are living in the capitalist world economy, which attempts to measure our minds and behaviors with globally regulated digital codes. One of the leading world-system analysts Immanuel Wallerstein has already called our attention to the necessity for understanding the world as world-system and presented the historiography of the "origins, geography, the temporal development, and the contemporary structural crisis" of the modern world (23). In particular, tracing the origin of the modern world-system, he asserts that in the sixteenth century the "world" had covered only Europe and the Americas and that such a notion of the world had been consolidated up until the nineteenth century by European scholars. According as the modern economic system developed, he describes, philosophers began to distinguish "scientific" approach to the knowledge of the world from "humanist" one. Among them those who defended "empirical 'science'" insisted on the "divorce between philosophy and science," and due to this divorce, the modern university system was born with "full-time, paid professors" who asserted that each department was "the locus of a particular 'discipline'" (Wallerstein 2–3). Presently, the traditional philosophy, too, was divided into two faculties, "science" and "humanities," both of which were in turn subdivided into various modern disciplines. Especially, according to Wallerstein, historians, despite their emphasis on scientific data, thought "themselves as humanists rather than scientists" and chose to be affiliated to the faculty of humanities because they emphasized human will or agency as a crucial factor in human social life (5).

Among many historians, Wallerstein notes, Leopold Ranke made a huge impact on how modern historians came to view the world. In the nineteenth century the "overwhelming majority (probably 95%)" of historians belonged to "only five zone," including "France, Great Britain, the United States, the various parts of what would later become Germany and Italy," and only those countries that had "written documents" were viewed as worthy of being called "historical" and of composing the "world" history (5). Following Ranke's insistence on "written documents," therefore, modern historians studied their own countries first and other "historical" nations secondly (Wallerstein 5). Yet Ranke's obsession with "written documents" also restricted modern European historians to the study of the past and left them "little to say about the contemporary situation of their countries" (Wallerstein 6). Unlike them, scholars of economics, political science, and sociology took upon themselves the study of the present on the basis of "the dominant liberal ideology of the nineteenth century" (Wallerstein 6). They developed three social spheres of the present, which are "the market, the state, and the civil society" (Wallerstein 6).

While modern historians studied the past of the world, and modern social scientists studied the present of the world, Wallerstein indicates, there was a group of scholars called "Orientalists" who came to make a contribution to the understanding of the non-Western world. Given that the nineteenth century in Europe was the age of colonialism as well, it is only natural that those "Orientalists" who had the knowledge of the other parts of the world were in great demand. Anthropologists studied "primitive" peoples or "tribes" who had "a common set of customs, a common language, and in some cases a common political structure," whereas ethnographers practiced philological skills in "deciphering ancient religious texts" of high civilization such as China, India, Persia, and the Arab world (Wallerstein 7–8). Wallerstein then goes on describing how modern economy system as well as political system provoked the changes in the perception of the world from 1914 to 1968 Student Revolution in France to the present. To sum up, Wallerstein's world-system analysis provides a historiography of the West's knowledge of the "world" but coincidentally yields a point of reference to understand Western comparatists's perception of the "world" and "World Literature."

As is implied in Wallerstein's analysis of the modern European understanding of the "world," Western scholars generally operate their outlooks of and approaches to the "world" based upon one of the most important Western intellectual traditions, which is the Enlightenment. According to Richard Gray, the Enlightenment thinking "proclaims its allegiance to the concrete, tangible world while nevertheless building up all knowledge from self-awareness, the certainty of one's own existence" (9). Yet, the Enlightenment logic is, as Bertrand Russell has once asserted, not only objective in that it gives priority to empirical experience and demonstrable evidence but also subjective in that "its criterion of judgment—clearness, distinctness, agreement or disagreement—have an internal, individualistic, subjective basis, so making life contingent upon mind" (Gray 10). Just like modern European historians who held on to written documents and yet restricted the world history to European and American countries, Western comparatists seem to reproduce the essentially binary metaphysical frame of the Enlightenment thinking when they try to present an 'objective' grand narrative of the "World Literature" by using their 'subjective' wit. In Wallerstein's words, they hold the ground firmly that although "all forms of knowledge activity necessarily involve grand narratives," some grand narratives of the world reflect human realities more closely than others (21). Therefore, from the start their anthologies of world literature covered only European countries and America. Later, investigating the overall individual characteristics of world literatures, they inserted their subjective belief, in the making of successive anthologies of world literature, that Anglo-European literatures reflect more 'general' human conditions of living and thus more 'universal' human values. While apparently stressing their objective attitude by often emphasizing the fact that the world we are living now is, in Wallerstein's words, "never the same from one minute to the next" (22), they paradoxically employ a subjective gaze to find what is frozen in time and space when approaching to non-Western countries such as China and India. Oftentimes, they tend to restrict themselves to the study of the past of social lives of human beings in the case of the highly civilized non-Western countries and seem to aim to trace the unconscious 'system' that is already there.[1] Even when examining a minority country's unfamiliar literary work, they show a tendency to take out their subjective reading glasses and trace the familiar origin, the genetic axis, or the law of continuity in order to locate it in their syntagmatic system.[2] Consequently, despite balancing themselves between the discourses of the 'ever-present' Western literary world and the 'classical' non-Western literary world, Western comparatists seem to relegate the task of interpreting the present pulse of the non-Western world to economists, sociologists, anthropologists, and so on, as modern European historians had done. Not regarding time and space as radial or sometimes chaotic and not transforming histories into historiography, they also seem to remain shackled by the objective-subjective conundrum inherited from "the Great European Tradition" (Bassnett 5).

THE WESTERN WORLD REPUBLIC OF LETTERS AND ITS ARBORESCENT SYSTEM

Suppose that Western comparatists operate on the basis of the legacy of Enlightenment shackle of objective universalism and subjective wit and early Orientalists's syntagmatic thinking, the current Western discourse of "comparative world literature" seems to further echo the rhetoric of American westward Frontier myth as well. For instance, when Anglo-European comparatists call for an open road, a boundless future, and universal aesthetics in the world literary space and envision optimism in their grand narrative of "comparative world literature," they seem to put out their desire to maintain their role as the powerful center that regulates the quality of literary goods and the flow of literary currency in the world literary market as capitalist managers would. By calling attention once more to the fact that they are the first who coined the word "world literature" and practiced comparative methodology in understanding world literatures, they try to reinforce the white origin myth of world literature and justify their desire for the single, unified World Republic of Letters where individual writers or countries all around the world can discuss ideal literary topics and at the same time practically negotiate to buy and sell literary products following the standardized procedures they have already set up.

As a matter of fact, it is not difficult for a minority scholar to see the benefits of Western scholars' taking the advantageous position first in the digitalized literary market with the new conception "comparative world literature." Now with such a comprehensive conception Western comparatists can cover both comparative studies and world literary studies and increase their scholarly and critical influence more world-widely. Not only preserving Eurocentric literary traditions, aesthetic values and standards but also consolidating their position as a virtual agency to issue a certification to qualify a local literature to become a world-class literature through the Norton, Longman, or Bedford gates of world literature, Western and Western university-affiliated comparatists continue to wield power at the substantial level. Besides, through the digitally controlled global market system of multinational publishing houses, they can continue to re-strengthen their Eurocentric canon of world literature and contribute to the stable demand of Western literary works and textbooks all around the world as conveniently as possible.

However, Western conception of "comparative world literature" is limited in that it does not reflect the present heterogeneous realities of world literatures properly. In other words, despite trying to be comprehensive, Western comparatists still compartmentalize multiple, diverse, and heterogeneous world literatures into one unified literary whole and in doing so, they cannot but justify cutting corners of their own Anglo-European literatures as well as slashing out minority literatures on a large scale on the principle of the Enlightenment logic of progress. For instance, David Damrosch, leading American comparatist and chief editor of *Longman Anthology of World Literature,* emphasizes the shifting notion of "canon" in world literature as the evidence that Western comparatists support the ideal of multiplicity in the world literary space. He asserts that the canon has never been fixed but progressed reflecting the changes of global literary market. He exemplifies his view by dividing canons into three categories such as "hyper-canon," "counter-canon," and "shadow-canon" (45). "Hyper-canon" includes major Anglo-euro writers that pulled love and respect from critics and readers; "counter-canon" represents a new spectrum of non-Western writers postcolonial critics discovered and promoted such as Borges, Achebe, and Cortaza; "shadow-canon" has past Anglo-European glories that cannot produce any literary meaning pertinent to the contemporary critical horizon such as Hazlitt, Southey, and Rander (45–51). Indicating the consistent progress in the canon formation of world literature, Damrosch stresses that the postcolonial discourse that challenges the established world literary canon is not a new phenomenon but can rightfully constitute the history of the discourses of world literature.

However, in the age of the capitalist world economy system and with the consequential emphasis on the skills of English as a *lingua franca,* such a progressive Anglo-Eurocentric canon model does not satisfy the social needs of non-Western readers. For instance, many East-Asian comparative scholars, who are often affiliated to English department or department of foreign languages, have a hard time inducing students to believe that reading Western writers of "hyper-canon" such as Shakespeare or

T.S. Eliot has validity for them. Most of them have been educated without a chance to develop their cultural taste in literature, and furthermore they enter the university with mistrust of the value of literary or humanities studies. What they want mostly is to enhance their English skills or their TOEIC or TOEFL scores to get a good job. More importantly, as passing through the 1990s with the dominance of US hegemony and neo-liberalism with its token expression, "globalization," many of East-Asian young people have replaced 'the world' with the concept of 'the globe.' Unlike older generations, they view the world not as a West-centered hemisphere but as a global village where they believe they can make connections with peoples all around the globe. Although still interested in the West, they now like to look at different mirrors, to know more about other non-Western cultures, and to read contemporary global writers such as Achebe, Paulo Coelho, and Haruki, as well as Asian-American writers Myungmi Kim, Ha Jin, and so on because they find out more about themselves and the global conditions of living through those writers they think they can relate to. The rapid development of social network services and digital media such as Twitter, Facebook, Kakaotalk and Youtube is also an important factor that has made a huge impact on the change of young people's perspective of the world. Younger generation of people all around the world today interact one another in cyber space, for instance, making digital relationships, enjoying mutually exchanging cultural activities, and reproducing a trend all together globally. Considering such a drastic change in the perception of the world from 'the West-centered world' to 'the globe,' Western distinction of three stages of canon or progressive paradigm of world literature is in need of serious revision.

Pascale Casanova, although showing a more inclusive attitude toward global writers, still carries a Hegelian model of the progressive change in her influential book, *The World Republic of Letters*. First, she points out that world literature is a system of discourses in which comparatists of the world can participate. Then, like Damrosch, she highlights the fact that over a long period of time world literature has formed a process of absorbing revolutionary discourses of various local communities into its world literary system. She traces the origin of the process in the formation of French national literature in the sixteenth century and argues that the world literary system had been formed over four hundred years. Over this long period, she describes, almost all national writers could "earn" their literary presence in the world literary space as "the result of struggles" (177). In other words, she suggests that those writers have overcame the reality that "denied [their creative liberty] in the name of literary universality and the equality of all writers as creative artists" by "inventing complex strategies that profoundly alter the universe of literary possibilities" (177). Likewise, she argues that world writers with little literary currency can also earn their places in the market by wisely using two kinds of methods, which are "assimilation" and "differentiation." Then she indicates that "an almost universal and transhistorical order of development" has governed "what is normally experienced, analyzed, and reported by historians of literature as an inalienable historical and national peculiarity" (179). Finally, what the "cultural centers" should do is, she thinks, to allow "the demands for literary freedom and the revolts to which they have given rise" to "reinvent and defend the structure of world literature through revolution" (179). She also indicates that each national writer's entrance into the World Republic of Letters through assimilation and differentiation has been allowed "in virtually transhistorical fashion" (179). Despite the apparent emphasis on the equal opportunity for world literatures, Casanova's transnational perspective might be viewed as a contemporary version of nineteenth century objective universalism because her model methods of "assimilation" and "differentiation" still resonate with an authoritative view of the Western "cultural centers." For instance, although she even mentions some of Korean writers and encourages good English translations, she reveals not only a lack of discussion on how to lower the barrier to entry but also a lack of information on who to decide which work makes a successful "assimilation" and "differentiation" to and from whose tradition.

Seen from the perspective of Deleuze and Guattari, Western conception of "comparative world literature" seems to reflect a mode of "arborescent" thinking that "is forever imitating the multiple on the basis of a centered or segmented higher unity" (16). According to Deleuze and Guattari, "arborescent systems" are "hierarchical systems with centers of significance and subjectification, central automata like organized memories" (16). In the arborescent system, then, the smallest unit only receives information from a higher unit, which again receives information through pre-established channels that are hierarchically structured. For instance, an individual Korean writer enters the pre-established arborescent system of the Anglo-Eurocentric World Republic of Letters, he/she gets arranged to take an almost already allotted place, which is 'Third World' literature, regardless of Korea's having been out of the Third World status in the world economy. In other words, a heterogeneous literary work of less-known country is highly likely to face an uphill battle with pre-existing prejudices and subjective impressions of so-called "cultural centers," which would set the original literary aesthetics of a minority literature against the established West-centered literary aesthetic standards and in the end assign it to the place of periphery. Besides, most Western comparatists might imagine that certain aspects of universal human conditions of living such as family life, sexuality, work, anger, or jealousy can be carried over from the West to many cultures naturally. Nonetheless, what openly discussed in the West is sometimes never discussed in the East Asia. Thus, a Western novel that deals with those themes that supposedly reflect the general and universal human conditions, if assigned to Asian students, would induce superficial responses from them.[3] And, vice versa is equally true. Considering these heterogeneous and diverse responses of the 'universal' topics, it is hard for a minor writer to compete on an equal footing in the World Republic of Letters or to attempt to execute the methods of assimilation and differentiation as Western "cultural centers" recommend.

Therefore, even if Western conception of "comparative world literature" increases the kind and the number of non-Western literatures in the World Republic of Letters, such increase is not likely to make any fundamental change in its whole arborescent system. The spokes of comparative world literary canon continue to radiate from a single center, and such increase of multiplicity only comprises what Deleuze and Guattari call "the radicale type" because "its ostensibly nonhierarchical presentation or statement in fact only admits of a totally hierarchical solution" (17). In other words, however multiple, heterogeneous, and diverse the comparative world literary canon's branches grow, each of them is connected to a higher segment trunk that comes down to the Anglo-Eurocentric root. As long as the principle of root-trunk-branch-leaf is sustained, the structure of 'Power and Knowledge' in the World Republic of Letters persists, and its hierarchical, radicle solution continues to get re-strengthened.

However, as a matter of fact, Anglo-European languages and literatures came to have taken the position of "cultural centers" not because they are the majority in the number but because they had achieved technological development and industrial revolution earlier and consolidated their languages and literatures as 'the major,' backed up by their countries' politico-economico-military power in the world. As is examined in the discussion of Wallerstein's "modern world-system," modern European scholars had defined the "modernity" in the nineteenth century through differentiating the "pan-European zone" from "high civilizations," such as "China, India, Persia, the Arab world" (8) on the basis of their own 'provincial' histories and prejudiced knowledge of "high civilizations." From this restricted perspective of the world, they had applied their pan-European standards and categories and divided the world into zones: the primitive zone, the pan-European zone, and the highly civilized zone. Later, establishing the university structures, they had naturally regarded their languages as 'the major' languages of 'the world,' created academic journals and literary magazines, and formed national and 'international' associations for themselves. They also spread their knowledge of non-Western "high civilizations" and shared their understanding of the Power to rescue the 'powerless' countries to modernity. Since 1945 when the US university system became "the most influential world-system" and exported its university system to the rest of the globe in combination with the increase of the world-economy system (Wallerstein 9), European scholars in almost all disciplinary areas have prioritized the pan-European world over the old Asian countries and the Third World and maintained the classic binary oppositions of modern pan-European world/old Asian and African world, renovation-leading West/labor-supplying follower non-West, and First World as the major cultural center/Third World as the minor cultural periphery.

Gayatri Spivak, who has already perceived a trace of the stasis embedded in the current Western discourse of world literature, pointed out in her book *Death of a Discipline* (2003) the problematic in the gaze of Anglo-European liberal humanists in the academic field of comparative literature. Even if Western comparatists are preoccupied with difference, diversity, plurality, tolerance, and so on, she asserts, their liberal views reflect the gaze 'from above' and the position of the privileged. She calls their subjective discourses an act of creating specular alterity, indicating that they have been writing the Other palatable and intelligible within the Western ideology of agency and the signifying process. She finds some examples in world feminisms. For instance, she acknowledges that the First World feminism truly made its great contribution to the gender consciousness around the world and the empowerment of Third World women. At the same time, she points out that First World white middle class feminists encouraged Third World women to refashion their lifestyles after Eurocentric ones by setting up schools, providing workshops and designing training programs on their experiences concerning domestic abuses, gender discrimination, and sexual self-determination. Without considering each specific politics, economy history, culture of Third World countries and speculating on the localization of feminisms, she argues, the implementation of First World feminism in Third World countries has a risk of impinging on the process of altering the Other. She suggests that after all, it is Western intellectual desire to become globally engaged centers of knowledge production that has endorsed the birth of a series of disciplines such as Postcolonialism, Cultural Studies, Area Studies, Ethnic Studies, Multiculturalism, and Comparative Literature. In this very respect she maintains that they turn out to be the new names of dead discipline that only reproduce the same old Eurocentric gaze of the West.

As an alternative to the Western gaze, then, Spivak suggests the epistemological frame of "planet-thought" (73). In other words, she argues that if we must take the figure as a guide to understand the other, we "might attempt to figure [our]selves—imagine [our]selves—as planetary rather than continental, global, or worldly" (72). It is because planet-thought opens up to embrace an inexhaustible taxonomy of such names, including but not identical with the whole range of human universals: aboriginal animism as well as the spectral white mythology of postrational science (73). According to her, when we imagine ourselves as "planetary subjects rather than global agents, planetary creatures rather than global entities, alterity remains underived from us" (73). It is not "our dialectical negation" but contains both ourselves and others beyond all difference and otherness (73). Finally, she claims that 'the time for producing historically thin 'theory' describing the feeling of migrants" is over and that "the first phase of the Comparative literature dispute reflected in the Bernheimer collection" is exhausted (84). At the same time, calling "the old postcolonial model—very much "India" plus the Sartrian "Fanon"—will not serve now as the master model for transnational to global cultural studies," she urges that world comparatists should engage in a new kind of comparative literature on the basis of planetary consciousness (85).

However, Spivak's conception of "Planetary Comparative Literature" is, despite being novel, radical, and idealistic, in her own words, "no more than scattered speculations" and does not move away from "the limit of [her] rather conventional US Comparative Literature training" as she frankly admits (84). She still maintains the binary oppositional frame of the Western metaphysics: she calls African, Asian, Hispanic "older minorities" and suggests to add "the new postcoloniality of the post-Soviet sector and the special place of Islam in today's breaking world" along with "Southeast Asia, Micronesia, Polynesia, New Zealand, perhaps Australia, Hawai'i, California—each with different histories of the movements of power" to her new conception of New Comparative Literature (84). Thus, unintentionally, she herself repeats the very practice of those Western comparatists whom she criticized much: she, too, adds the new palatable ones and thus only expands the boundary of West-centered world literature. Moreover, considering the range of diversity and difference in the planet, it seems that Spivak's planetary model can hardly make a substantial impact on how to acknowledge an ever-growing number of the texts of world literatures. The Anglo-Eurocentric World Republic of Letters still remains the most influential world literary system and its assertion of the unified world literary space is interlocked with an incredible global expansion of the capitalist economy system. What to be selected and how to be represented in the world literary market are highly dependent upon the gaze of the established Western and Western university-affiliated authorities of world literature.

THE MINORITY WITHIN THE MINORITY AND THE POLITICS OF THE MINORITY

What is interesting is, after Spivak's discourse of "Planetary Comparative Literature," Western comparatists defended their own views of world literature by striking back the comparatists of "global South" and thus connotatively positioning themselves as 'global North.' In 2006 Bassnett criticized that "Spivak and Southern hemisphere scholars" would politicize important literary issues of Comparative Literature and supported the literary values and traditions of the origin, in other words, Europe (5). In addition, Damrosch, apparently mindful of Spivak's essay, published in the same year an essay entitled as "Rebirth of a Discipline" and defended the objectivity and comprehensiveness of the discipline. He, then, suggested that they should restore the original spirit of "polyglot anticosmopolitanism" and "world-spanning provincialism" of Meltzel and Posnett, each of whom created the expression, "comparative literature" and disciplinary methods from the first (111). Witnessing the globalization of English and its economic effect, he projects positive optimism that Western comparatists have faced not the death of a discipline but a grand chance to invigorate comparative world literature by including new literary works and expanding their influence in world literary market. This way, the discursive debate between Spivak and 'Southern' hemisphere scholars and Bassnett and presumably 'Northern' hemisphere scholars has ended in giving each other a discursive punch and yet confirming each other's discursive position more strongly and consolidating each other's geographic turf more clearly.

Now in 2012, entering the world literary space of World Republic of Letters, I cannot but ask myself the outdated questions, "Who am I?" and "Where am I located?" Given the symbolic space of the South and the North, the East *vis-à-vis* the West refers to Asia or East Asia. Then I am to be viewed as an Eastern hemisphere scholar. Nonetheless, according to OED, the Eastern hemisphere is a geographical term to refer to the east of the Prime Meridian and west of 180° longitude and includes Europe, Asia, Africa, and Australia. In a cultural or geographical sense "Eastern hemisphere" is also a synonym of the Old World. Then, supposedly, Fanon, Spivak, European comparatists and I are all in the same hemisphere and share the similar outlook of the world *vis-à-vis* the Western Hemisphere that includes the Americas. However, I do not see myself as Eurocentric or postcolonial or East Asian. Then I am not an Eastern hemisphere scholar. Culturally situated in East Asia, geographically located in the Eastern hemisphere, and yet discursively excluded in the atlas of world literature as the Other of East Asian China and Japan which are in themselves the Other of the West, I see myself only as a minority Korean who has not given the right to speak out in the symbolic *Polis* of World Republic of Letters.

As is well known, in the ancient Greece, the *Polis,* separate from the *Oikos,* was the ideal space to discuss public policies free from private or economic interests. At the same time, the *Polis* was the limited space in which the minorities were excluded. Only male citizens were given the right to speak out their opinions in the discussions of democratic process, the balance and distribution of power, and so on, whereas women, slaves, and foreigners were silenced. The minorities who were not allowed to participate in the *Polis* could not make their voices heard and thus could not reflect their opinions in the political mechanism that distributes the shares of power.

Likewise, the current discursive space of world literature seems to function as a contemporary *Polis,* in which the established authorities of world literature and some postcolonial literary writers translated in English and certified by the West are given the citizenship to speak up their voices. Generally, in the current symbolic *Polis* called World Republic of Letters as the authorities of world literature Western and Western university-affiliated authorities publish critical essays on world literatures in the academic journals, edit major anthologies of world literature, and produce, circulate, and reproduce the norms and standards that distinguish the aesthetic/non-aesthetic, the literary/non-literary, and the universal/non-universal. They are invited to world-wide conferences as keynote/plenary speakers, attend the reviewing committees for world-renowned prizes as judges/panels, and update the list of world literature canon by certifying new entries to the WRL. In a word, they function as an Ideological State Apparatus (ISA) of the World Republic of Letters, and as such, they stabilize the center-periphery arborescent system of world literature. As such, just like male citizens of the Greek *Polis*, they occupy a privileged position and engage in the political process of exclusion in order to secure their shares in the WRL. And, just like Greek minorities, non-Western minority comparatists, especially when they represent local literary works which are neither written in English nor translated in English, are not given a platform/position/location to speak.

Located in this kind of discursive limbo, then, it is necessary for non-Western minority comparatists to seriously reflect upon the necessity for thinking in the grain of Jacque Ranciere's *Disagreement*. As Ranciere urges, those who have not been given their rightful shares should decide to make strife with those who have not acknowledged them to be rightful counterparts to engage in a dialogue. As he recommends, non-Western minority comparatists need to take special note of the fact that World Republic of Letters is not a purely literary space but inherently a political space in which a wide range of discursive ideas can compete. They also need to realize the dynamics between contriving a new, alternative perspective of world literature and exercising their political right to participate in the discursive space of the symbolic *Polis* of world literature and to speak up their voices of disagreement. Consciously being political, they should start to write critiques and produce their own views and discourses of world literature. Speaking up a voice of disagreement, then, has more significance than asking for acknowledgment in the current World Republic of Letters because it is an act of survival. It is an act of refusing to accept the established assumptions of world literature where non-Western minority literatures are ignored. It is an act of disagreement as to the ways they have been imagined by the West and the ways they have been led to believe their literatures are less universal and less aesthetical in comparison with Western ones.

Starting to disagree at the very border that demarcate the inside and the outside of World Republic of Letters, non-Western minority comparatists can demand a critical scholarship to re-evaluate respectable Western discourses of world literature because the border is the very space where they can raise the issue of the Anglo-Eurocentric arborescent system of current world literature and claim their right to change. While actively participating in the political mechanism of World Republic of Letters, non-Western minority comparatists, conscious of the fact that their speaking up is essentially a political act, can disseminate their alternative discourses without letting them turn into one of the age-old debates over the origin or being reduced to one of the postcolonial challenges to "the Great European Tradition". By way of acting out their agency and claiming their rights, then, non-Western minority comparatists can raise new consciousness to the reality the World Republic of Letters faces in the twenty-first century. After all, both Western majority and non-Western minority comparatists have to revolutionize the old binary center-periphery conceptual framework and reconfigure the world literary space now in order to speak up a voice of disagreement against the immanent threats of the capitalist world economy system.

NOMADIC AESTHETICS AND THE ETHICS OF THE MINORITY

Given the necessity and the political significance of disagreement, it is time to meditate on how to view the World Republic of Letters differently and how to create a new language. First of all, it is necessary to re-view the meaning of the term, 'the minority.' As is widely known, the word 'the minority' started to be used in the late twentieth century as a term that connotes a power relationship in a society rather than literally suggests the number of people that form the lesser half of a group. For instance, women in a patriarchal society are viewed as the minority regardless of the number of their population; African Americans in white-centered American society are also considered the minority regardless of their percentage of the whole ethnic groups. On the contrary, in South Africa white people, who hold less than ten per cent of the whole population, are not the minority because they have more political and economic power than Africans. From an ecological viewpoint, mankind, regardless of the smaller number as a species, is not the minority because men dominate nature and other species. Likewise, although European countries are outnumbered by Third World countries in the world, their literatures hold the position of the majority because they produce and consolidate the literary norms and aesthetic standards of world literature. As evidenced by these instances, the minority as a term reflects the calculations of power and the mechanism of the exclusion.

The minority is also a term that has been confusingly understood as something that is essentially related to the human rights of the powerless. This confusion comes from the general assumption behind the logic of egalitarianism that everyone is equal before God. Thus, when the difference between 'Us' and 'the Other' is acknowledged, two assumptions, that 'the Other' should be respected as the equal creation of God and that their inalienable human rights should be protected, are connotatively implied. In this conceptual frame, thus, the politics of the minority is often either mistaken for or interchangeably used with the politics of humanitarianism, whose emphasis is put on the tolerance of the powerless and the egalitarianism among human beings. However, humanitarian and egalitarian concerns ironically fail to recognize the revolutionary, liberating wave that the politics of the minority can create because the moment the minority is viewed as the powerless to be protected, their political plight, which is originally caused by the systematic and structural process of discrimination, exclusion, and silence, gets naturalized as belonging to part of the universal human plight. In other words, the predicaments of the minority get to be understood as not 'our' pain but 'their' own troubles and categorized as something that needs to be socially taken care of. In this context Giorgio Agamben sarcastically diagnoses of the current society, saying that human rights fell to such a base situation that humanitarian acts now are nothing but a name tag for the acts of casting a compassionate gaze and sending out relief supplies to those who cannot be protected by the state or civil society.

Hence, when the politics of the minority is contemplated within the frame of 'the helpless Other' who should be pitied, rescued, and protected, the minority's language of Difference instantly gets contained in the humanitarian logic and cannot make any political impact on the transformation of the established view. Let's take a relationship between the white and the colored in the USA for example. The white majority may think that even if it is almost impossible for them to understand the difficulties of the colored minority completely, they can relate themselves to the suffering they go through as fellow human beings. On the other hand, the colored, looking back at the compassionate gaze of the white, may insist that the white will never be able to understand specific predicaments they face on a daily basis. In these two different languages, both the white and the colored simplify the complicated contexts of their real lives and compress the multiple layers of what they try to signify into humanitarian lumps, i.e., the conflict between the haves and the have-nots. Both parties thus unconsciously contribute to valorizing each as a fixed position in the binary opposite.

Therefore, what is requisite for non-Western minority comparatists is to de-valorize the simplified conceptual perspective of the binary opposite of the majority West and the minority non-West and instead, to start to imagine the politics of the minority as the politics of a nomad who drops his/her anchor in any political discourses if he/she wishes to speak up his/her disagreement and then leaves to create another innovative space. In other words, it is more effective to conceive the minority as a fluid discursive position that presumes the nomadic gaze rather than as a fixed position that signifies the socially underprivileged and disadvantaged entity. The new minority, as a new language that breaks, cracks, and ruptures the lopsided, astigmatic approach to world literature, may as well be less sophisticated, less artistically developed, and less universal but more political, more historical, and more regional. Re-imagining the minority as such, then, actually opens the potentials of the term because the new minority can activate a generative process that the established authorities of any arborescent system cannot configure. In desiring Difference and making alliances to heterogeneous multitudes, the new minority does not follow the monolinear line of Time/Space of "World Literature" but creates the "line of chance, line of hips, line of flight" in world literatures (Deleuze and Guattari 25). It can "connect any point to any other points" and its traits are not "necessarily linked to traits of the same nature" but only "brings into play very different regimes of signs, and even nonsign states" (Deleuze and Guattari 21). Thus, those who take up the language and the desire of the minority can constantly shift between the established/the revolutionary, the known/the mystery, and the high-brow literature/the low or pop culture. For instance, a white middle class American male belongs to the Western majority but can also become the minority when he takes flight from Western-centered values to Korean Buddhism. Likewise, a Korean working class woman who belongs to non-Western minority can take the position of the Western majority when she puts Western values in practice. Thus, re-configuring the politics of the minority, non-Western minority comparatists can emphasize the nomadic fluidity of the minority and the language of Becoming.

However, it is important for non-Western minority comparatists to be careful about presenting the politics of Difference as well. In other words, they do not just argue for the acknowledgment of their territorial differences including nation, language, history, culture, and religion, but should make a rhizomatic engagement in 'Becoming Difference,' that is, "moving between things, establishing a logic of the And, overthrowing ontology, doing away with foundations, nullifying endings and beginnings" (Deleuze and Guattari 25). While forming alliances with any groups, including the rich/the poor, the disabled/the healthy, the homosexual/the heterosexual, the urban/the rural, the center/the periphery, the white/the colored, the intellectual/the laborer, and so on, it should also refuse any attempts to reproduce a hierarchical relationship. The new minority, in a way, can be viewed as sharing a sense of solidarity with digital collective intelligence in the face of the capitalist world economy system that drives us out to the ever-intensified, limitless competition and degrades us to see ourselves only as consuming subjects in the market.

Further, the new minority, instead of being interested in seizing the power, should be able to put its nomadic imagination into practice and make never-ending flights from the established norms, standards, frames, and orders. It should aspire to freedom and continue to make contacts with the Other and revolutionize the established status-quo. Refusing to be worn out, the new minority should hold up the ethics of Becoming and continue to create the new *modus vivendi* that cannot be categorized and measured by any arborescent system. Getting into this Deleuze and Guattarian rhizomatic direction, non-Western minority comparatists will be able to revolutionize the current Anglo-Eurocentric discourses of world literature. They will be able to shed light on the new *modus literati* that reflects the nomadic mode of existence whose new aesthetics can stimulate the imagination of the established "cultural centers."

Finally, I come back to where I started, that is, the discussion of the capitalist world economy system in which we live. Whether the majority or the minority, all of us humanities scholars are now living in the ever changing capitalist world-system, where criss-crossing movements of the capital and the labor are being accepted as given conditions of Being. The capital moves faster than ever and continues to make an international search for an opportunity to make more profit. When no more yielding is expected, the capital dismisses one place and rummages another place without taking its responsibility for having broken down the ecology of the place. In addition, the mode of production is also getting more global and more digitally managed. Thus the whole process of production, distribution, circulation, and consumption is controlled not within the national territory but transnationally and digitally. As intellectuals, then, we, be either Western or non-Western, should take a full consideration of this phenomenon of deterritorialization in our contemporary globe and need to contemplate our role as a disseminator of knowledge from an ethical point of view. What knowledge do we want to disseminate to contemporary readers/students who will constitute the majority of transnational digital nomads with each national identity?

Clearly, the twenty-first century *modus vivendi* is that of a digital nomad. Contemporary people gather in a virtual agora and form an alliance case by case, but at the same time they easily and unexpectedly disperse in any directions they desire. They just temporarily stay at a particular point and readily move to another point. From a positive point of view, these digital nomads are called "collective intelligence" but in a negative sense they may be just a migrating mass sometimes easily controlled and manipulated by commercialism and capitalism. Thus, it is high time to let us meditate on the ethics of Becoming and lead them to imagine themselves as the new nomadic minority. The nomadic *modus vivendi*, being global without a center, is open to the citizens of the globe and consequentially the nomadic *modus literati*, being plural within the self, is to be explored all around the world. The moment one logs on to the digital space, he/she can get connected globally and become a first-person plural that can make multiple, diverse, and heterogeneous interspaces by using his/her creative Difference. After all, this nomadic mobility is not the ability to move from one place to another but the capacity to move from the self-same gaze of the 'Me' to enter into the strange, constantly shifting energy of the 'Not-Me.' It is the capacity to become the Other, enjoy experiencing Difference, and speak up for a voice of Disagreement for the human rights of any group, race, and nation. It is the capacity to occupy a space temporarily and leave the inertia of the power behind. It is the continuation of repetition of emptying out one's Self and filling it with Difference through becoming the Other. This capacity of having a transmutable imagination can be the base for the new ethics of world literature and the knowledge for scholars of world literature to disseminate in the age of global digitalization.

Given the new approach to the minority, *World Literature and the Politics of the Minority* is composed of nine plateaux that cannot complete an organic whole. Nine essays, overthrowing the logic of consistency and following the principle of contingency, illuminate the nomadic fluidity of the new minority. Jasbir Jain's essay "Minority Discourses in/and World Literature: Dalit and Tribal Writing" critiques "the over-arching concept of world literature" of Western comparatists and investigates "the fall-out of the relationship between a single dominating concept of world literature and the multiplicity of locations and aesthetics of minority discourses." Although Indian literature has been quite extensively exposed to the world and included in most anthologies of world literature, Jain's essay creates the line of flight in the Indian Literature as is imagined by the world through delineating the aesthetics of Dalit and tribal writings which have been ignored so far.

Wang Ning's essay "Chinese Literature as World Literature" provides a comprehensive view of comparative literary studies in China. He addresses the major issues Chinese comparatists have faced and still does in the process of forging the identity of national literature and at the same time promoting Chinese writers up to the level of world-class writers. In particular, he takes an issue of translation and shows examples of how translation determined the destiny of two equally outstanding Chinese writers. Wang Ning's essay is included because it shows the line of 'Chance' in the current WRL system. Any writer belonging to the majority country like China can become the minority in WRL if not translated in English. This fluidity between the majority and minority exemplified in the case of Chinese literature reveals the limit of the arborescent system of world literature and supports the necessity of revision.

Myles Chilton's "Global Englishes, Literary Studies, and the Japanese Academy" looks into the situation of Anglophone literature in the context of English language study in Japanese higher education. Addressing the problems of emphasis on "instrumentalized" English language study, he explores how "Anglophone literary studies will intersect with world literature, global studies, and the global spread of English." Chilton's essay manifests the shifting reality of a nomadic minority who is the majority as an English-speaking Canadian scholar and yet exists as the minority who struggles to promote the spiritual values of English literary study among non-English speaking Japanese majority who pursue only the practical values of English language study.

Marie-Therese Abdel-Messih's "Mutability of Home and Exile: *The Oriental Dance*" introduces a contemporary Egyptian writer Khaled El Beri's novel, *The Oriental Dance*. She explains how El Beri represents "local/global interrelated processes during the

1980s and 1990s and their impact on the lives of Middle-Easterners moving between Europe and the Middle-East." Along with literary analysis of three immigrant laborers, she brings in the religious and political contexts that surround their lives and illuminates how "global events like the Iraqui War" have worsened their local/global displacement. Abdel-Messih's essay provides a rare chance to look inside the psyche of Middle-Eastern people since Egyptian literature has hardly been represented in the anthology of world literature.

Santosh Gupta's "Diasporic Imagination and the Significance of Home in the Novels of Amitav Ghosh" also provides a chance to understand the minority experience called "the Bengal diaspora." Explaining Ghosh's literary career and his major novels, Gupta draws our attention to "the fragmentation of geo-political space of India" and contemplates the burden of Indian intellectuals through Ghosh's question of whether to "remember a postcolonialist map properly, ever to put together a coherent account of a world where histories are mysteriously over-laid?" Gupta's essay is significant since she deals with the dispossession and deterritorialization of nomadic laborers who have to leave their homes either voluntarily as refugees or involuntarily as indentured laborers or slaves. Getting connected to the experiences of subalterns, we will be able to re-view the oppression as well as freedom the global movements of the capital and the labor bring onto our mode of existence.

Jihee Han's "The Burden of History: Ko Un's Poetry as a Political and Philosophical Act" illuminates the complicated historical and political contexts that have affected modern Korean writers. Drawing the reader's attention to the political turmoil of modern Korean history, including the Japanese Occupation, the Emancipation of Korea, the partition of two Koreas, successive military dictatorships, she explains how Ko Un, struggling against political oppressions, creates a dynamic *Hwaeom* literary space for *Minjung* (grass roots) and slowly evolves into a national bard. Han's essay on Ko Un's place in the history of Korean poetry and his unique Korean *Minjung* poetics provides a chance to contemplate *Hwaeom* Buddhist vision of life in the context of nomadic ethics of Becoming.

Saddik Gohar and Doris Hambuch's "Literature of the Arabian Peninsula and Transcultural Literary Exchange in the Post-Oil Era" addresses the minority status of "the Gulf Cooperation Council members," including "Kuwait, Bahrain, Qatar, United Arab Emirates, Oman, and Saudi Arabia," in the anthologies of Middle Eastern literatures and introduces the current situation of comparative studies in the United Arab Emirates. Gohar and Hambuch's essay is pertinent in this book since literature of the United Arab Emirates is one of the minority literatures which have hard time in speaking up their voices in WRL.

Hajime Saito's "Ikezawa Natsuki as a Conscientious Witness to Japanese Society and History" introduces Ikezawa Natsuki who dealt with a theme of clashes between the West and the East and raised a rare voice of resistance to global interventions of the USA, including the Okinawa Military Base and the Iraqui War. Hajime also draws our attention to Natsuki's skillful handling of "the history of the complicated relations of two racial groups in Hokkaido" which are "the Ainu and the Wajin." Clearly, Natuski's case illuminates what an individual can accomplish if he desires for Difference and becoming the minority. Actively pursuing the line of flight, Natuski could unearth the hidden history of Japan, which Japanese world-class writer Murakami Haruki dismissed.

Finally, Liu Hao's "Shakespeare in China: Past, Present, and Future" provides an interesting line of flight, in which we can encounter Easternized Shakespeare. Tracing the history of Shakespeare studies in China, Hao illustrates how Chinese audience have read and used Shakespeare as they like. Hao's essay surely shows how the aesthetics of the minority can create new *modus literati* that Western authorities of Shakespeare cannot imagine.

All the essays in this book share the perception that it will become indispensible part of our lives to learn and understand the Other in the age of the ever-increasing global interactions. They put out the desire to go beyond the territories of national literatures and to meet the challenges of the capitalist world economy system from minority perspectives. Whether to take a ride of Becoming and enjoy filling one's Self with the differences of the Other is solely up to the reader.

NOTES

1. In case of China and India, their classical texts are more seriously treated in most of the anthologies of world literature.
2. In case of Korea, Korean literature is almost always mentioned in reference to the relations with Chinese or Japanese literatures. Korea is, in this respect, imagined as the Other's Other by the West.
3. Likewise, East Asian family values and hierarchical relationships and absolute subordination to the elders might be hard to be crossed over to Western readers.

REFERENCES

Agamben, Giorgio. "Beyond Human Rights." *Means Without End*. Trans. Vincenzo Binetti and Cesare Casarino. Minneapolis: U of Minnesota P.

Anderson, Benedict. *Imagined Communities: Reflections on the Origin and Spread of Nationalism*. New York: Verso, 1991.

Appadurai, Arjun. *Modernity at Large: Cultural Dimensions of Globalization*. MN: U of Minnesota, 1996.

Balachrishnan, Gopal. "The National Imagination." *Mapping the Nation*. New York: Verso, 1996.

Bassnett, Susan. "Reflections on Comparative Literature in the Twenty-First Century." *Comparative Critical Studies* 3.1–2 (2006): 3–11.

——. *Comparative Literature: A Critical Introduction*. Oxford: Blackwell, 1993.

Bernheimer, Charles. *Comparative Literature in the Age of Multiculturalism*. Baltimore: Johns Hopkins UP, 1995.

Casanova, Pascal. *The World Republic of Letters*. Trans. M.B. Devevoise. Cambridge: Harvard UP, 2004.

Culler, Jonathan. "Comparative Literature, At Last." *Comparative Literature in an Age of Globalization*. Ed. Haun Saussy. Ithaca: Johns Hopkins UP, 2006. 237–248.

Damrosch, David. "World Literature in a Postcanonical, Hypercanonical Age." *Comparative Literature in an Age of Globalization*. Ed. Haun Saussy. Ithaca: Johns Hopkins UP, 2006. 43–53.

Dyer-Witherford, Nick. *Cyber-Marx: Cycles and Circuits of Struggle in High-Tech Capitalism*. Chicago: U of Illinois P, 1999.

Featherstone, Mike, et al. *Global Modernities*. London: Sage, 1995.

Giddens, Anthony. *The Consequences of Modernity*. Cambridge: Polity, 1990.

Hall, Stuart. "The Local and the Global: Globalization and Ethnicity." *Culture, Globalization and the World-System*. Ed. Anthony King. MN: U of Minnesota P, 1997.

Hardt, Michael and Antonio Nergri. *Empire*. Cambridge: Harvard UP, 2000.

Leavis, F.R. *The Living Principle: 'English' as a Discipline of Thought*. London: Chatto & Windus, 1977.

——. *English Literature in Our Time and the University*. London: Cambridge UP, 1969.

Narin, Tom. *Faces of Nationalism: Janus Revisited*. New York: Verso, 1997.

Noble, David. "Digital Diploma Mills" (1977–78). <http://www.firstmonday./issues/issues3_1/noble/index.html>. 20 November 2011.

Pearson, Keith A. et al., eds. *Cultural Readings of Imperialism: Edward Said and the Gravity of History*. New York: St. Martin's, 1997.

Saussy Haun, ed. *Comparative Literature in the Age of Globalization*. Baltimore: Johns Hopkins UP, 2006.

Spivak, Gayatri C. *Death of a Discipline*. New York: Columbia UP, 2003.

Wall, Sarah, ed. *The Norton Anthology of World Literature*. Vol. A to Vol. F. New York: Norton, 2002.

Willson, Rob and Wimal Dissanayke, eds. *Global/Local: Cultural Production and the Transnational Imagery*. Durham: Duke UP, 1996.

CHAPTER 1

Minority Discourses in/and World Literature

Dalit and Tribal Writing

Jasbir Jain

In recent years the over-arching concept of world literature has increasingly engaged our imaginaries as it has graduated from academic syllabi, where texts from different cultures were put together, to the formulation of modern historiography. Seen as a natural development of the multiculturalism and postcolonialism and the shift in the direction of comparative studies, World Literature claims its descent from Goethe's vision of *Weltliteratur* floated in 1827. Yet, because of the location of this concept in political power and in western tradition, there is a hesitation in embracing it unquestioningly. This paper is interested in exploring the likely fall-out of the relationship between a single dominating concept of World Literature and the multiplicity of locations and aesthetics of minority discourses.

THE PROBLEM

David Damrosch, one of the leading propagators of this concept is, along with a team of scholars, presently engaged in putting together a history of World Literature in four volumes roughly adhering to historical divisions of time: ancient, medieval, modern and the like. In the "Third S.K. Das Memorial Lecture" delivered at Gandhinagar (Gujarat, India), on 5 March 2011, he elaborated on this scheme hailing Sisir Kumar Das's two volume *History of Indian Literature* as a model for handling complex multilingual literatures.[1] One of the major challenges for both Das and Damrosch remains the matter of periodization which is more than a matter of history because it brings in both economics and politics.[2]

In the twentieth century we have experienced two blanket terms—postcolonialism and globalization—which have attempted to take the whole world under their cover. They offer us examples of what happens to difference, individuality and subjectivity when such all-embracing concepts take over. Those of us who are not so advantaged in terms of visibility, material power, and political control over others have been fretting against both of them. Literature, in its claims on culture, individual histories and psychological inputs over and above the dependence on its own language for rightful articulation and its own embedding in reality, is the most affected. Postcolonialism has been appropriated by western theory. We have critiques of postcolonialism without any reference to Gandhi, or to the Indian questioning of liberal humanism (as defined by the imperial rulers), or the ethical revolution that took place in India in the 1930s.[3] In fact, there has been a serious questioning of all that the European Enlightenment upheld, for those very values such as universalism, rationality, and linear progress came disguised to the colonies as utilitarianism, the white man's burden and the imposition of western epistemologies leading to a subordination of native discourses. The western critic, even the sympathizer, locates herself in a position of power as does the native informant.[4] Literature, in its strong affiliations with culture and local histories, refuses to tailor itself to these demands and thus there is an erasure of all that which is not visible to the West.[5] Hence my concern as to what happens to minority discourses when they are placed within a sweeping concept like world literature and the long term losses (or gains) arising from this association. It is the 'difference' which is turned around to produce a meaning with or without its history or perspective ending up in violence to both—the master narrative and the minority discourse. It is this 'difference' which is my concern.

It is evident that the moment we begin to think of 'difference' a whole range of problems present themselves. It is a category in itself which refuses to be assimilated in its multi-directional hold in terms of aesthetics, religion, history and economics amongst others. At one level it is this force which constructs identity even as it simultaneously contests it.[6] When an overall collectivity is employed individual differences and subjectivities are bypassed. This would as much be applicable to world literature as it has proven itself to be in the case of postcolonialism. Whatever becomes visible is that which meets the eye—the writing of the diaspora framed by marketing techniques and the 'translated' texts, the basis for whose selection are, at best, uncertain acquire greater visibility than the literatures rooted in their own cultural and linguistic heritage. Even locally translated texts go unnoticed. World literature, if it imagines itself as a coming together of multiplicities, is caught between a similar problem of working through sameness or difference. If it is a confluence, it denies subjectivity and erases difference. Or, paradoxically it seeks alterities and alternative aesthetics, which firmly acknowledge one dominant stream of civilizational/philosophical/theoretical discourse. Even history is worked through imperial trajectories. It does not frontally face the Other as an Equal.

Minority discourse is the voice of this 'unequal' Other. It is not a question of numbers but of invisibility, of 'voicelessness,' and lack of power. Referred to variously as subaltern, feminist, margins, dalits, blacks, natives they all come under the category of minorities, people who have lived with oppression and violence for ages. Their kinship patterns and value structures differ considerably from each other. Their relationship to nationhood and constructs such as respectability and sexuality likewise project variations. In fact, they resist the possibility of an overall umbrella being imposed on them.

MARGINS

The term margins can be viewed in a number of ways but we are habituated to see it as a matter of exclusion and view it as a reference to what falls outside the mainstream. This results in a polarization, which merely distances and separates but does not necessarily create communication. Another way of looking at the margin is as in case of the sea waves, which are playful and inconstant and reflect a fluidity. A third way available to us is to look at margins as boundaries that protect and enable harmony and build a collectivity such as the borders of a nation. This definition is one of the essential bases for a collective identity which fosters both identity and a sense of belonging. Thus there is a constant need to view the margins in the context of their fluidity or otherwise and whether they are exclusionary or inclusionary. In fact, it is only when all three perceptions flow together that they forge the strength of their own and begin to feed the center.

The moment we examine the inner multiplicities of the word dalit, caste becomes an important factor and within it food, purity and employment are further identifying categories.[7] Though the history of dalit protest goes further back in history and can be traced through a long lineage, the Bhakti movement which spanned a period of nearly eight or nine centuries in its journey from south to east to north and west, which covered the whole subcontinent as the bhaktas, men and women, traveled across the country, is a good beginning point. It marked a continuing protest when religion was moved out of temples into individual worlds and the devotees defied social restrictions to seek a meaning in their lives. An identifying point for the ideological beginnings can further be located in the nineteenth century writings of Jotiba Phule[8] who carried out a systematic campaign against Brahmin domination both through activism and his writing. His essay "Ghulamgiri" (Slavery) deserves special mention for its analysis of the problem in analytical terms of socio-political power. Later Bhimrao Ambedkar (1891–1956), was in direct line of this movement and led the protest for equal rights. Through his self-projection of an educated man in western dress he offered the oppressed masses a role-model directly opposed to Mohandas Gandhi's identification with the masses in terms of life style and sartorial matters. Ambedkar's influence was largely on the populations of western India and a number of dalit writers from Maharashtra, Gujarat and Uttar Pradesh have evidently been inspired by him.[9] He rose to the level of a national leader and was a leading member of the constituent assembly entrusted with the framing of the Indian constitution (at the time of independence) in 1947. But the writers of South India hardly ever refer to him. Instead, Periyar's Self-Respect movement and conversion to Christianity have been visible influences on them.[10]

Strangely enough, critical explorations of dalit writings, do not necessarily comment on these historical images and the dalit movement which gathered momentum in the 1960s is marked as a modern beginning. These early groups were called Black Panthers and in retrospect it is viewed as parallel in time to the 60s' Black Movement in the USA. This constant placement in parallelism has hindered both an independent development and evaluation of its impact and aesthetics. The movement itself was both initiated by and in turn generated a great deal of autobiographical writing expressed in poetry, essays, short stories and full-length autobiographies. One of the earliest representative anthologies of Marathi Dalit writing in English translation is *The Poisoned Bread* edited by Arjun Dangle.

Dalit writing seeks to voice the experience of as well as the anguish they feel at the social discrimination which treats them as outcastes, with their touch abhorrent to the upper castes. This inhuman treatment is accompanied by both economic and sexual exploitation. The imagery of their writing, rooted in their raw reality, is very striking. Dwarka Bharti defines 'low caste' through physical representation:

> The meaning of low caste is not that
> It appears to be direct and innocent like
> ....
> Its meaning is
> Not to have a head
> On your shoulders
> that is
> Without head
> Without breath
> He who is
> Is low caste. (*The Meaning of Caste* 194)[11]

Dalit poets write about their immediate surroundings and the issues of anonymity and rejection embedded deep in them. Another poem by Keshav Meshram is extremely evocative in its visual image:

> In our colony
> the postman gets bamboozled

teachings get confused
civilization stumbles
The sun—even he is darkened.
Our houses stand
Like footprints of cattle in the mud.
In the midst of it all is a soul
eager to swim along the current. (*The Poisoned Bread* 9)

And as the poet goes on to describe their "country wine" (often spurious liquor that brings them death) and the "chilled pieces of meat" (which becomes another source of discrimination against them by the vegetarian Brahmins), he moves to and fro between the half-fed people and the postman: The postman has a difficult task in tracing the addressee in this nameless, unidentifiable crowd. But learning gives the younger generation a voice and when they write, in Keshav Meshram's expression, "The axes of words fall upon the trees of tradition" (9–10).

The poems express a great deal more than mere prose would do, for they move between the visualization of the author and that of the reader. At times the images are unfamiliar, shocking and take us into zones of our own inexperience in our locations. I'll just quote two more connected examples before I turn to prose. The first poem "Caves" is by a woman poet, Jyoti Langewar, announcing the grounds of her rebellion:

Their inhuman atrocities have carved caves
in the rock of my heart
....
How did we get to this place
this land which was never mother to us?
Which never gave us even
the life of cats and dogs? I hold their
unpardonable sins as witness.
and turn, here and now,
a rebel. (*The Poisoned Bread* 22)

The phrase 'never mother to us' turns the notion of the nation as motherland on its head, dismisses all possibilities of nurture and brings orphanhood into the discourse simultaneously critiquing both society and nationhood. L.S. Rokade in "To be or not to be born" asks his mother whether he should have been born or not:

> I spit on this great civilization
> Is this land yours, mother,
> because you were born here?
> Is it mine
> because I was born to you? (*The Poisoned Bread* 2)

But the poet opts out of 'belonging' to the land. His dispossession has given rise to the need to disown his birthplace and sever all connections.

The title of the volume, *The Poisoned Bread*, aptly suited to the bitterness which comes with the morsels, literally 'thrown' from a distance into a makeshift container, has been taken from a story by Bandumadhav, "The Poisoned Bread." The story offers a comment of the upper caste landowners and the state's affirmative policies. The education the dalits have gained access to is held against them and leads to further discrimination. Caste continues to be the dividing line. Jobs, despite qualifications, are not given, promotions don't bring with them the accompanied power or position.[12] It is not that these conditions of oppression were not noticed, felt or expressed by writers other than the dalits. There is a tradition of the literature of empathy and of going across by writers such as Mulk Raj Anand, Premchand, Rabindranath Tagore, Thakazchi Pillai, and Shiva Karanth amongst others.[13] Throughout the late nineteenth century and the twentieth century it was an issue which received attention at all levels—political, legal and social—but the deep-rootedness of the issue, even as it migrated to converted communities failed to address the problem in its totality. Conversion brought with it its own suspicions and did not greatly affect discrimination.[14]

Though the term 'dalit' has acquired a generic status, one needs to recognize the separate category of the 'tribal' people who have historically been subjected to a different kind of discrimination. While dalits have traditionally occupied peripheral spaces in the village community, tribes have lived outside its boundaries. They were nomadic and artisan tribes, referred to as adivasis or aboriginals. Their exclusion was not governed by the caste system but by their ethnicity. Their traditional professions have been of snake charmers, storytellers, musicians, woodcarvers, professional mourners, blacksmiths, acrobats and dancers. To them goes the credit for traveling from one place to another with their cultural inputs and for contributing to popular cultural performative forms such as "wang" (masquerade) and "nautanki" (dance drama). The exclusion has affected their social status, education levels and access to social mobility even as their art has provided them with some recognition. Their kinship structures have also been marked by their professions. The women of tribes engaged in performing arts do not marry but have a life-long (or as long as it lasts) liaison with a man, bear his children but go on supporting their parental families.[15] Often they have to live as mistresses or second wives and find themselves abandoned (once they have been lured away from their livelihood by their paramour's notion of respectability). Mahasweta Devi's stories such as "Draupadi," "The Hunt," "Fairytale of Mohanpur," "Bashai Tudu," and "Rudaali" all deal with the tribes as do some of Gopinath Mohanty's work.[16] Laxman Gaekwad, Kishore Shantabai Kale and the well-known "nautanki" queen Gulabbai all hail from the tribal society. If they are bracketed together under the category of dalit, the differences in their experiential narratives are bypassed and ignored.

Women's writing within dalit and tribal writing constitutes another category, as it is distinct from the non-dalit women's writing as well as the dalit men's writing. Social exclusion and social mores, kinship patterns and professions are reflected in different nuances. Masculinity and femininity, likewise, are differently constructed. Unemployment, humiliation, inferior job status are all factors which drain masculine perceptions of self, and when these social difficulties are crossed, there is either a note of pride or a moral dilemma with which they are faced. Women on the other hand do not indulge in too much of self-projection. There is an acceptance of their womanly roles. But in recent writing one can sense their need for recognition of their role in political life.

Upward mobility does not provide an escape from caste oppression. Instead, it places the individual in a situation where he has either to hide his origins for a serious relationship like marriage or an ordinary one of renting a house. Om Prakash Valmiki writes about this in his autobiography as to how economic independence and position do not provide a relief from the ostracism of caste, or the camouflage required to get away from it (Valmiki 95, 119, 149 and 153). Religion based location of identity, similarly poses a problem for the dalit whose ancestral ties may be mixed. Upper caste men often had relationship with dalit and tribal women without legitimizing it through marriage. How does the child locate himself within defined patterns? Sharan Kumar Limbale in his autobiography, *Akkarmashi*, wonders:

> My father too was a Lingayat....That makes me a Lingayat. My mother was a Mahar....So I am a Mahar. But I have been brought up as a Muslim....Shouldn't that make me a Muslim? Do claims of heart have no religious sanction?
>
> Am I a caste–Hindu? But my mother is an untouchable. Am I an untouchable? But my father is a caste–Hindu. I have been tossed a part like Jarasandha—half within society and half outside. Who am I? To whom does my umbilical cord join me?[17]

But when men cross these barriers of stigmas of birth, caste and childhood experiences, they experience a sense of achievement and begin to take pride in their early struggles. Laxman Gaekwad, a social activist and writer of tribal origins, opens his autobiography, with a preface–like piece "Reflections," wherein he gives an evaluative judgment of himself: "I—Laxman Gaekwad—am a dedicated social worker" (vii). The first chapter juxtaposes this statement with his almost anonymous beginnings: "No NATIVE PLACE. No birth-date. No house or farm. No caste, either. That is how I was born" (*The Branded* 1).

Similarly, Kishore Shantabai Kale in his autobiography, *Chora Kothati Ka*, is concerned with the formation of the self and the auto/biography which is part a biography of his mother and whose name Shantabai he proudly acknowledges in his own name, also conveys a sense of pride in his having overcome the disadvantages of a fatherless childhood and the loneliness ensuing from his mother being constantly engaged in dance performances in order to support her parental family. The experience of being tossed around from one family to another, of being bullied and without any of the advantages which the fact of his male gender would have given him in an upper caste home also affected his childhood years. The narrative is a success narrative as Kishore Shantabai Kale is now a practicing medical doctor. Women's autobiographies, in contrast, often proclaim their autobiographies as fictional, perhaps hesitant to work in their private space in a straightforward admission as autobiographical experience. Further their autobiographies are hardly ever about the self, they become community narratives more firmly located in family and are more broadbased than men's writings but both equally effectively generate material for anthropological and historical research as they become part of larger resistance movements.

The very act of dalit writing stands in direct opposition to elitist writing in almost everything—motivation and purpose, ideology and aesthetics and in the nature of experiential reality. It is shaped by the absence of power and recognition. Religion, both as an act of worship and the fact of conversion (either to Islam, Christianity or Buddhism), is a central concern for many of them. Their festivals are a temporary holiday from the misery of life and act as liberating forces. Dalit writing with all its variety, locations, languages and histories, and in transference to different literary forms continues to have its base in personal experience and as such it seeks to define itself through experiential aesthetics rather than classical. Experiential writing ordinarily lacks the backing of philosophical heritage of an educational inheritance accumulated through successive generations. Its language, imagery, logic and form are naturally derived from the familiar, based either on observation or on firsthand experience. One finds that the act of writing, even as it empowers, also allows a distancing from self-pity. Writers very often get engrossed in the act of description. This apparent objectivity is paradoxically vested in their subjective experience. As they engage with the task of constructing an identity for themselves from a condition of anonymity, their newly gained subjectivity reverses the mainstream values. Outside of the norm, outside the mainstream, they also often stand outside daydreaming and idealism. It is the survival struggle which constructs their identity and hence is devoid of all myth and tragic heights which writing by non-dalit writers about them may have.[18]

EXPERIENTIAL WRITING, AESTHETICS AND EVALUATION

One is left with several unanswered questions, the main among them are: is experience in itself an adequate base for good writing? If so, does it necessitate different evaluative standards? Can immediacy acquire a status of permanent value? One also needs to consider the existential and the phenomenological reality which is invested in the nature of this representation as well as the oral element which enters this discourse.

Dalit writers challenge the aesthetic concept 'satya, shivam, sunderam' (i.e., truth, good and sublime). Sharan Kumar Limbale seeks to redefine the above concept. Truth for him is being human, and The God Shiva is represented in human freedom and beauty is represented through humanity (*Dalit Aesthetics* 31), thereby moving away from the metaphysically abstract and locating it in actual life of social interaction. Supplementing this, Kancha Ilaiah in *Why I am Not a Hindu* (1996) resents the Hindu appropriation of the dalit into their religion and thus subjecting the dalit identity to a fixed subordination. Pointing out the difference in value systems, in languages, in cultural mores and the gods that dalits worship, he questions the way power dynamics works in society. In order to substantiate this I would like to make brief references to two autobiographies, the first by a woman dalit writer and the second by a tribal male.

Baby Kamble in her autobiography *Aamcha Jeevan*[19] sets herself the task of detailing the community life with all its festivals, celebrations, mystical experiences demonstrated through shamanism and possession (by gods/goddesses). One scene of a woman being possessed by the spirit of a goddess is an experience of ecstasy and of liberation from all hierarchies. From her writing, one learns about their gods and goddesses: Wadjini and Kadjai (9); Laman Pathan and Mark Mata and Laki Mata (23). Politics in the form of Ambedkar's influence enters the discourse and activism forms a major part but in all this the experience of the individual is bypassed. The other writer, a tribal is Dakshin Bajrange Chhara, a writer of activist plays which critique power structures and police atrocities. He stages them, often, right in front of police stations but when it comes to writing about his own experience, he feels limited. He asks, "How does one write about raw reality? Everything turns into a void, the moment I sit down to write about the endless difficulties and happenings which have made my life complex" (Free translation from Chhara, *Budhan Bolta Hai* 3). Subjectivity, inner reflection and direct articulation about one's feelings are difficult to talk about. The form of the play with its dramatic element allows a distancing where the writer becomes a narrator or a coordinator.

India has a long tradition of upper caste/elitist writers, writing about its oppressed categories, but their representation of dalit experiences is an imaginary construct and one is likely to get into the familiar debate about the authentic and the artistic and whether or not the subaltern can speak or one can write for the 'Other.'[20] But these writings do differ markedly from imperial writing about the colonized[21] and at some point the two kinds of writing, of experience and empathy, do find a kind of connectivity through the interpretative act and the catharsis that may be affected by it. It is not possible to dismiss either as less authentic or less aesthetic. The question that remains is: How much of familiarity and acceptance of difference does one require for both the writing and the interpretative act?

Yet, the issue of evaluation, aesthetics, and reception continues to be a thorny one. Colonial and subordinated categories have so often come across resistance to their writing that they have begun to define their aesthetics differently. Writing from the erstwhile colonies has been greeted with suspicion (and disdain). Achebe's *Things Fall Apart* had a somewhat hostile reception (Achebe 18), and western critics similarly, on the average, responded negatively to Tutuola's *The Palm-Wine Drunkard*. Achebe refers to Elspeth Huxley's remarks on the novel which referred to its "macabre humor" and "grotesque imagery" (Achebe 56). This was the kind of reception that the writing of the fifties emerging from Africa and India received. Indian writing in English was only tentatively accepted as one belonging to a mixed breed, a writing requiring legitimacy and perhaps different standards of evaluation.

Now half-a-century later, the scenario has changed. Rather than tailoring the texts to fit in, they are being selectively translated (especially dalit and women's writing) and marketed abroad. Many are included in the syllabi of postcolonial studies. Each translation marks a new discovery.

CULTURAL DENSITY, CANONIZATION, AND WORLD LITERATURE

The role of translation in World Literature is another important aspect which foregrounds selection of texts and the methodologies of translation. Translation perhaps always has been viewed as a necessary evil, one which recognizes our linguistic rootedness alongside our limitations. Now increasingly we accept it as part of our contemporary life. Diasporic writers speak of themselves as "translated" men (Rushdie). But there is also a growing dissatisfaction with translation and with the work of many "translated" men. The latter acquire a myopic view located in their own history and sharpened by distance while the former is full of loopholes as Arun Prabha Mukherjee has pointed out in her essay "On Reading Renu: Text/Language/Culture/Translation" in *Oppositional Aesthetics* as well as in her introduction to *Her Mother's Ashes*. Cultural density of the culture under representation and the cultural laziness of the other culture reader are charted by several things: the long glossaries at the end of many texts as well the prefaces and long "Introductions" that frame these texts (from Indian writing). The popularity charts of the writers who carried across this culture in a more universally understood idiom, one which works within western constructs or smoothens out differences, offers another indication of the domination of western cultural norms.

This brings me back to the question of power dynamics which works in every sphere: globalization, economy, marketing, publicity and fame. Minority discourses are relatively at the toddler stage. Even their canonization is being hijacked or appropriated by Western academics and the Third World intellectual located in First World academics. Selection, evaluation, framing, and awards that attract public notice all are West-centric. Native awards, even if more prestigious, do not get the same hype. News is made abroad, never mind if it doesn't say what we say or think what we think.

Artistic construct, especially literary art, has its origins in a continuity of cultural history, which it simultaneously represents as well as questions. It moves both horizontally across languages and non-linearly across time. The reader who moves alongside these courses gains the most as texts not translated, minor and major classics, and political happenings crowd the space. World literature, on the other hand, focuses more on the one-to-one interaction with a text and its flow in that particular theology or culture. It also looks at its recurrence, repetition, and interpretation, but in crossing over to minority discourses available in translation, it comes across several barriers—of languages, absence of the writer's oeuvre and of the lived reality and episodic view of history—and which is further handicapped by its location in a master narrative. There is a tendency to generalize the rest from these selected examples. One may as well ask: Are we willing to pay this price?

NOTES

1. S.K. Das, a senior scholar of Comparative Literature, was entrusted with the task of writing the history of the multi-lingual Indian Literature. For this task, he depended on a team of scholars of various Indian languages and completed two volumes covering a history of 150 years (1800–1956), across languages and genres. Refer bibliography for details of the volumes.
2. Each literature is embedded in the history of its language and consequently each defines literary periods in accordance with the development in literary forms. No satisfactory solution so far has been worked out to this gritty problem. Further, the state of modernization or otherwise, the attitude towards and the meaning of romance and all other literary approaches depend on economic conditions, sense of space and time, religious and philosophical discourses and a host of other things and cannot be simply anchored in similar journeys of the west.
3. Western liberalism is an offshoot of imperialism and identified with the 'white man's burden.' As such both liberalism and humanism, have worked towards new definitions derived in some measure from religious and emotional discourses. Ethical revolutionaries, such as

Gandhi, are the ones who have prioritized ethical means and considerations in their strategies of change.

4. My reference here is to those thinkers and intellectuals who adopt pro-minority positions. They too find it difficult to identify themselves fully, primarily because their world view and training do not allow them to attain the degree of 'innocence,' necessary for speaking for the 'Other'. I give two examples. The first is Dorothy Figueira, an extremely sympathetic comparatist, more than willing to come across. Fully aware of the western construction(s) of the other and the power dynamics involved in the 'tolerance' extended to multiculturalism, Figueira, in her otherwise very insightful and incisive work *Otherwise Occupied*, yet continues to locate everything within western theory and epistemological traditions. Despite her recognition of alterities, there is a total absence of alternate theories of aesthetics, time or space. The normative structures of western academics and politics persist. 'Native informant' is a very dubious term, and one would hesitate to employ it for a very respected scholar but Spivak's framing and projections of Indian realities are similarly geared to the west. Spivak dwells at length upon the figure of the "native informant" in her *Critique of Postcolonial Reason* (1999), and identifies her as the most destitute south Asian woman. But I would move in a different direction. The term may as well apply to researcher trained in the west and engaged in projecting their native backgrounds to the west. The researcher who invades a tribal area without fully going across to the other and uses it for outward directed purposes could easily fall into this category. Mahasweta Devi's "Pterodactyl, Puran Sahay and Pirtha" (in *Imaginary Maps*) engages with this issue. Spivak's own conscious defense of her prefaces and translations (ref translator's Preface *Imaginary Maps*, pp. xvii–xxii), is part of this attitude. In both cases—Figueira and Spivak—the crossing over is unable to transcend western theoretical formulations and positions, in order to reach across.
5. In this context, the power play of narrative also needs to be recognized, whether it be a literary, historical or theoretical discourse. Chinua Achebe in the three lectures in *Home and Exile* comments upon the way cultures construct the "Other" differently and also on the "innocence" or otherwise of fiction (33). Achebe, commenting upon Joyce Cary's *Mister Johnson*, observes, "There is such a thing as absolute power over narrative. Those who secure this privilege for themselves can arrange stories about others pretty much where, and as, they like" ("My Home under Imperial Fire," *Home and Exile* 24).

6. Refer Mark Currie's *Difference: the New Critical Idiom* for a detailed discussion on the concept of "difference" (12–13). Currie, in order to explore its complexities, attempts to move away from its grounding in both philosophy and structuralism. He locates the real challenge between the 'concrete particularity' and the perception of identity in relational terms, constantly calling upon opposition and polarity. Currie observes, "ll these relational theories of identity effectively deny difference" (*Difference* 13).
7. For further details, refer my essay "Purity as exclusion, caste as division: the ongoing battle for equality" in *The Politics of Social Exclusion in India*, pp. 124–135.
8. Phule was a bilingual writer. Though this essay is written in Marathi, it is prefaced by an introduction in English.
9. B.R. Ambedkar, a Mahar by caste, qualified as a lawyer, led a political movement for dalit rights and equal citizenship, claimed separate electorates and questioned the Gandhian accommodation of the 'untouchables' as 'harijans' (people of God) within Hinduism. Later, in 1947, he as India's first Law Minister was entrusted with the task of drafting the Indian Constitution wherein reservation for the scheduled castes and tribes was included. His influence on the dalits can be traced in most of the autobiographical and political writings of the dalits, especially of Maharashtra.
10. In the 1920s and 1930s Periyar E.V. Ramasamy led a Self-Respect Movement, mainly in Tamil Nadu, which worked for equal human and economic rights. It encouraged the backward castes to overcome the sense of inferiority thrust on them and work against caste barriers.
11. Dwarka Bharti, "Jati Ka Arth" (The Meaning of Caste) in *Bhartiya Dalit Sahitya Ke Vidrohi Swar.* Ed. V. Thorat and S. Badtaya (Hindi) (Jaipur: Rawat Publications, 2008), p. 194. (Translation mine)
12. See "The Poisoned Bread" in *The Poisoned Bread*, pp.147–154, Kumud Pawde's "The Story of My Sanskrit" in the same collection, pp. 96–106 and Arjun Dangle's "Promotion," pp. 168–172.
13. Several of Premchand's and Tagore's writings (1890 onwards) approach this subject. Tagore's play Chandalika is devoted to this and the two of discussed stories of Premchand are "Kafan" and "Thakur ka Kuan" (Thakur's Well). Shivaram Karanth's Choma's Drum is another fine novel.
14. The subject of conversion to Christianity is discussed in Gopinath Mohanty in his novel *Paraja* (1945), Mulk Raj Anand in *Untouchable* (1935) and Bama in *Kurukku* (1992).

15. The British classified them as criminal tribes under the Criminal Tribes Act, 1871 and labeled them as habitual offenders. In 1952 though the Act was repealed but the stigma of criminality continues. More recently another Act: The Scheduled Tribes and Other Forest Dwellers (Recognition of Forest Right Act) has been passed in 2006 as part of the rehabilitation drive.
16. Tribals can be found all over India. A large number of tribals live in Maharashtra, Assam, North-Eastern hill states, Odisha, Rajasthan, Andhra Pradesh and Madhya Pradesh. But on account of their customs and state of economic and educational progress, they do not constitute a homogenous category.
17. Lingayats are caste Hindu and have no social discourse with the lower castes. Jarasandha is a mythical figure, a man born of two different women in two halves because his father divided the fruit a sage had given him for his barren wife, between his two wives. Each woman birthed half a child.
18. For a detailed discussion on this aspect refer my essay "Classical and Experiential Aesthetics" in *Beyond Postcolonialism: The Dreams and Realities of a Nation* (Jaipur: Rawat Publications, 2006), pp. 200–246. Also a new monograph *Working through Experience: Writing, Reception and Evaluation* (CAS monographs, Department of Comparative Literature, Jadavpur University, Kolkata 2012).
19. The title of the original in Marathi. Hindi translation has the title *Jeevan Hamara* (Our Life), while the more recent English translation chose the title *The Prisons We Broke*, which is a major concession to marketing and feminist studies.
20. I draw attention to Gayatri Spivak's essay "Can the Subaltern Speak" and Margaret Fee's "Who Can Speak for the Other?" Also the reader is referred to Mahasweta Devi—Gayatri Spivak interaction "Conversations with a Writer" in *Imaginary Maps*.
21. Refer Chinua Achebe's criticism of Joseph Conrad's *Heart of Darkness* and Joyce Cary's *Mister Johnson* in his *Home and Exile*.

REFERENCES

Achebe, Chinua. *Home and Exile*. New York: Anchor Books, 2000.

Bandhumadhav. "The Poisoned Bread." Trans. Ramesh Dnyate. *The Poisoned Bread*. Ed. Arjun Dangle, 1992. 147–154.

Bharti, Dwarka. "Jati Ka Arth." *Bharitiya Dalit Sahitya Ke Vidrohi Swar* (Hindi). Ed. V. Thorat and S. Badtaya. Jaipur: Rawat Publications, 2008. 194.

Currie, Mark. *Difference: The New Critical Idiom*. London: Routledge, 2004.

Damrosch, David. "Third S.K. Das Memorial Lecture." Delivered at the International Conference of Comparative Literature Association India, 6 March, 2011 at Gandhinagar (Unpublished).

Dangle, Arjun, ed. *The Poisoned Bread: Translations from Modern Marathi Dalit Writing*. Hyderabad: Orient Longman, 1992.

——. "Promotio." Trans. Lalita Paranjape. *The Poisoned Bread*. Ed. Arjun Dangle. 1992. 168–172.

Das, Sisir Kumar. *A History of Indian Literature 1800–1910*. New Delhi: Sahitya Akademi, 1991.

——. *A History of Indian Literature 1911–1956*. New Delhi: Sahitya Akademi, 1995.

Devi, Mahasweta. "Pterodactyl, Puran Sahay and Pirtha." *Imaginary Maps*. Kolkata: Thema, 1993. 95–198.

——. "Author in Conversation with Gayatri Spivak." *Imaginary Maps*. Kolkata: Thema, 1993. i-xvi.

Figueira, Dorothy M. *Otherwise Occupied: Pedagogies of Alterity and The Brahminization of Theory*. Albany: SUNY, 2008.

Gaekwad, Laxman. *The Branded* (1987). Trans. P.A. Kolharkar. New Delhi: Sahitya Akademi, 1998.

Ilaiah, Kancha. *Why I am Not a Hindu* (1996). Calcutta: Samya, 2002.

Jain, Jasbir. "Purity as Exclusion, Caste as Division: The Ongoing Battle for Equality." *The Politics of Social Exclusion in India: Democracy at the Crossroads*. Ed. Harihar Bhattacharyya, Partha Sarkar and Angshuman Kar. London: Routledge 2010. 124–135.

——. *Beyond Postcolonialism: Dreams and Realities of a Nation*. Jaipur: Rawat, 2006.

——. Working through Experience: Writing, Reception and *Evaluation*. CAS monographs II. Kolkata: Department of Comparative Literature, Jadavpur UP, 2012.

Kale, Kishore Shantabai. *Chhora Kulhati Ka*. Hindi translation from Marathi by Arundhati Devasthale. New Delhi: Radhakrishan Paperbacks, 1997.

Kamble, Baby. *Jeevan Hamara* (1995). Hindi translation from the Marathi original *Jina Amacha* (serialized in Stree) by Lalita Asthana. English translation *The Prisons We Broke* by Maya Pandit. Hyderabad: Orient Black Swan Pvt. Ltd. (2008), 2009.

Lanjewar, Jyoti. "Caves." Trans. Shanta Gokhale. *The Poisoned Bread*. Ed. Arjun Dangle. Hyderabad: Orient Longman, 1992. 22.

Limbale, Sharan Kumar. *Dalit Sahitya Ka Sundaryasastra*. New Delhi: Vani Prakashan, 2000.

——. "The Bastard." Extract from *Akkarmashi*. Trans. Daya Agarwal. *The Poisoned Bread*. Ed. Arjun Dangle, 1992. 113–123.

Meshram, Keshav. "In Our Colony." Trans. V.G. Nand. *The Poisoned Bread*. Ed. Arjun Dangle. Hyderabad: Orient Longman, 1992. 9–10.

Mukherjee, Arun Prabha. "Introduction." *Her Mother's Ashes*. Ed. Nurjehan Aziz. Toronto: Isar Publication, 1994.

——. "On Reading Renu: Text/Language/Culture/Translation." *Oppositional Aesthetics: Readings from a Hyphenated Space*. Toronto: Isar, 1994. 56–66.

Pawde, Kumud. "The Story of My 'Sanskrit'." Extract from Antasphot. Trans. Priya Adarkar. *The Poisoned Bread*. Ed. Arjun Dangle. Hyderabad: Orient Longman, 1990. 96–106.

Phule, Jotiba. "Preface to *Ghulamgiri*." Mahatama Jotiba Phule Rachnavali. Ed. L.G. Meshram 'Vimalkirti.' New Delhi: Radhakrishan Publishers, (1994), 1996. 2 Vols. Vol.1. 123–134.

Rokade, L.S. "To be or Not to be Born." Trans. Shanta Gokhale. *The Poisoned Bread*. Ed. Arjun Dangle. Hyderabad: Orient Longman, 1992. 1–2.

Rushdie, Salman. "Imaginary Homelands." *Creating Theory: Writers on Writing*. Ed. Jasbir Jain. Delhi: Pencraft International, 2000. 213–224.

Spivak, Gayatri. "Translator's Preface." *Imaginary Maps*. Kolkata: Thema, 1993. xvii–xxvii.

Valmiki, Om Prakash. *Jhoothan* (Hindi) New Delhi: Radhakrishan Prakashan Ltd. (1997), 1999.

CHAPTER 2

Chinese Literature as World Literature

Wang Ning

To talk about Chinese literature as world literature, we should first of all consider two confronting issues. Historically, Chinese literature has been received as world literature because of the Sino-centrism. Nowadays, Chinese literature is regarded as an important part of world literature although it has been "marginalized" under the dominance of Euro-centric and West-centric critical modes. Under the rubric of this two-way relationship between Chinese literature and world literature, we will be able to address how Chinese literature has been recognized and included in world literature and how it is transforming itself as world literature. Undoubtedly, the advent of globalization has more or less broken through the old-fashioned Eurocentrism, in which process China has probably benefited most. Culturally, globalization has enabled literary scholars to reflect on the old issues of world literature in a new context, that is, a context of global culture, in which world literature certainly means differently and thus should be remapped. As Chinese scholars of comparative literature studies, then, how should we speculate about some new significance of world literature in a new era from our own perspective? This essay tries to contemplate how to overcome the previous Eurocentric mode of thinking and redefine world literature from a Chinese perspective.

DIVERSIFIED FORMS OF WORLD LITERATURE

Like the case of modernity which has already manifested itself in diversified forms in different countries, there is no such thing as the singular form of world literature.[1] The utopian concept

Weltliteratur constructed by Goethe in his talk to Eckermann was later developed by Marx and Engels as a sort of cosmopolitan way of bourgeois intellectual production and as one of the consequences of globalization in culture and literature. Actually, in the co-authored book *Communist Manifest* Marx and Engels already expanded the narrow domain of world literature to incorporate the entire intellectual and cultural production and circulation. From a disciplinary point of view, their conception of world literature is one of the sources of the newly rising discipline of comparative literature in the latter part of the nineteenth century, which aimed to break through the isolation of individual national literature and establish the factual relations between different national literatures. During the past hundred years, however, world literature has been largely colored with certain Eurocentric or later West-centric characteristics. Or, it has been practiced by a few elite comparatists within a very limited sphere. It has neither properly covered the various aspects of world literary studies nor included the various regions of the world beyond Europe and North America. Although world literature was imagined as the early stage of comparative literature, yet, as Franco Moretti points out, "comparative literature has not lived up to these beginnings. It's been a much more modest intellectual enterprise, fundamentally limited to Western Europe, and mostly revolving around the river Rhine (German philologists working on French literature). Not much more" (54). But after all, world literature as a theoretic concept has been traveling across time and space through translation and finally culminated in the current age of globalization. Although in the present era literature and literary studies, challenged by various forms of popular culture and consumer culture, are often reported to be "dead," world literature, on the contrary, becomes more and more flourishing. It has attracted the attention of not only literary theorists and comparatists, but also scholars of national literatures who are not satisfied with the narrow-minded individual national literature studies only. It has more or less helped comparative literature move out of its crisis and helped literary studies in general step into a much broader cross-cultural context. Over 180 years ago, great European thinker and literary master Goethe conjectured this utopian concept *Weltliteratur* out of the inspirations he had got in reading some minor Chinese literary works, but today, with the same term we are discussing issues of literary studies in general.

Undoubtedly it has proved that it has gone not only far beyond the geographical limitation of Europe and North America on the part of Euro-American scholars but also far beyond the boundary of China on that of Chinese scholars. It has become the aesthetic reality of literary studies in the current age of globalization.

Obviously, Goethe's access to literatures of the Eastern part of the world is largely accidental with the help of translation. Although Goethe himself understood many languages, they were exclusively Western languages. Fortunately, he could get access to some Chinese and Indian literary works through English and French translations. Since one cannot necessarily read all the literatures in their original languages, translation plays an indispensable role in reconstructing various versions of world literature. Due to the dynamic intervention of translation, anthologization and critical studies, world literature has already got different versions in different languages and cultural contexts. With the particular intervention of translation, some works of national significance have become world literature, while those that undergo no translation can only remain 'marginal' or even 'dead' in their own languages and cultural contexts. Thus to be viewed as world literature, a literary work of national renown should be first of all transnational and translational. In the process of transnationalization and translation, a literary work may well undergo certain metamorphosis or transformation in another language and cultural context. Its new significance and 'continued life' or 'afterlife' might well be brought about by means of this sort of cultural translation. The same is true of the canonical body of world literature.

Now, one question needs to be raised. Does world literature only refer to literature in its traditional elite sense? If not, what else does it refer to? Just as Moretti sums up, "world literature cannot be literature, bigger .... It has to be different. The *categories* have to be different" (Moretti 55) different people can think in different ways. Then the point is this in Moretti's words, "world literature is not an object, it's a *problem*, and a problem that asks for a new critical method: and no one has ever found a method by just reading more texts. That's not how theories come into being; they need a leap, a wager—a hypothesis, to get started" (55). In today's context, world literature is obviously an issue-driven topic which attracts theoretic discussion and even debate on literature and literary studies. To get it started for further discussion, other scholars, like David Damrosch, have also developed this conjectural theoretic construction in both theory and practice and thereby, enabled it to get closer and closer to literary production and circulation in the whole world.[2] Although they have more or less touched upon literatures outside of the Western world, their critical experiences are largely based on their knowledge and understanding of Western literature. In my previous elaboration of world literature, I classified world literature into two categories: "world literature in general and world literatures in particular, the former referring to a universal criterion by which to evaluate literature of the greatest world significance, the latter to the different representations, including translations, of literatures from all countries."[3] I have, referring very much to the practice of world literature in China, simply developed this conjectural concept coined by my Western colleagues, pushing it into a broader context of East–West literary relations. For the sake of theoretic elaboration, I focused on the singular form of world literature in my previous essay, but here, I will spend more space discussing its diversified forms in different times and regions.

According to Douwe Fokkema who has a remarkable knowledge of both Western literature and Chinese literature, world literature means differently for different scholars. In elaborating the duality of world literature, he emphasizes both universality and relativity: without the former, literary works of any countries can't be regarded as world literature, and without the latter, world literature will become all the more Eurocentric or West-centric.[4] Fokkema, in describing the unfair division of different national literatures in the name of world literature, tells us,

> Raymond Queneau's *Histoire des littératures* (3 vols., 1955–58) devotes one volume to literatures in French, one to Western literatures, and one to ancient, oriental, and oral literatures. Chinese literature is allotted 130 pages and the literatures of India 140 pages, but the literatures in French are given 12 times more space. In his *Weltliteratur* (1989) Hans Mayer ignored the non-European world completely. (1291)

Probably, Eurocentrism, like a specter, haunts the memory of literary historians even in describing world literature. Thus it is certainly right of Fokkema's dual categorization. But here I would rather use the other two terms to describe the dual characteristics of world literature to avoid the ideological bias: canonicity and readability. The former appeals to the aesthetic quality of world literature, and the latter refers to the wide popularity and influence of an individual literary work. That is, in judging whether a literary work should be regarded as among world literature, we must put forward a set of criteria which should be as objective as possible. I certainly agree with Damrosch that literary texts are fictional, valuable and even beautiful, for they are first of all artistic and aesthetic products. On the other hand, literature is also diversified in artistic form and in aesthetic spirit, so it is hard to judge them in an equally objective way. Still, a relatively objective criterion could be agreed upon among literary scholars. In this sense, we should first of all recognize that there is no such thing as singular world literature as it has been constructed and reconstructed by different theorists and practiced in different times and regions. Starting from this point, I will discuss how world literature has been constructed and reconstructed in the Chinese context and in doing so, try to deconstruct the singular form of world literature.

WORLD LITERATURE AND CHINA

Although for a long period of time China had been isolated from the outside world, and Chinese literature before the nineteenth century had seldom been influenced by literatures of other countries, China still had maintained close relations with the rest of the world. As is well known, ancient China developed so fast that in the Tang Dynasty China became one of the most powerful and prosperous countries in the world not only politically and economically but also culturally and literarily. Domestically, Chinese people thereby viewed their country as the "Middle Kingdom," and internationally Tang-China was called a kingdom of poetry. Actually, when the Tang poetry was most flourishing, Europe was still in the "dark" Middle Ages. Such eminent Chinese poets of different dynasties as Qu Yuan, Tao Yuanming, Li Bai, Du Fu, Li Shangyin, Bai Juyi and Su Shi all appeared much earlier than Dante, Shakespeare and Goethe. Unfortunately, due to the later rulers' inability to govern the country well and control the corruption, it was not long after that China became a second-class feudal and totalitarian country. Even so, Chinese literature still inspired Goethe, who first put forward the concept *Weltliteratur* after reading some Chinese literary works of minor importance. Conjecturing his utopian concept of *Weltliteratur*, he says:

> I am more and more convinced that poetry is the universal possession of mankind, revealing itself everywhere and at all times in hundreds and hundreds of men....I therefore like to look about me in foreign nations, and advise everyone to do the same. National literature is now a rather unmeaning term; the epoch of world literature is at hand, and everyone must strive to hasten its approach. (qtd. in Damrosch 1)

It can be said that Goethe himself was most benefited from translation, which helped him enlarge his European and international reputation, transcending Germany to entire Europe and then to the whole world. Even when he was almost "marginalized" in the German critical circles and thought by young critics as "conservative" and "old fashioned," he was regarded as one of the best known European writers due to the translations of his works into the major European languages. In the age of Euro-centric dominance, to be a famous European writer means to be a world renowned writer. In addition, Goethe's interest in "Oriental" literature and translation and reception of his works in the "Oriental" countries, he has indeed remained one of the most famous world writers for a long time.

Despite the above mentioned facts, Chinese literature has largely been marginalized on the map of world literature since the late Qing Dynasty. In order to change this situation and bring China closer to the world, Chinese intellectuals launched a large-scale project of translating Western cultural and literary works into Chinese so that they could contemplate a way to identify China with the rest of the world. Due to this overall process of rapid Westernization, literary translation in China has indeed been rather imbalanced even today: while numerous Western literary works are available in Chinese, very few excellent Chinese works have been translated into other languages, partly due to the absence of excellent translation and partly due to the bias of Orientalism prevailing in the Western literary scholarship. In the current age of globalization, Chinese literature, like literatures elsewhere, is severely challenged by the global rise of popular culture and consumer culture. Literature and literary studies are often reported to be 'dead.' On the other hand, we should realize that globalization has, while homogenizing national cultures, also offered China a precious opportunity to bring its culture and literature to the world. In order for Chinese literature to be part of world literature in the shortest possible time, some Chinese scholars and translators should consider the matter of translation seriously. In other words, we have seldom translated our own literature into the major world languages, especially English, although this may be only part of the reason to account for the current marginalized position of Chinese literature in the world.

Frankly speaking, the current situation of book marketing is far from satisfactory. In any British or American book stores, it is hard to find many books written by Chinese writers even in the English translation, let alone those written directly in the Chinese language. In sharp contrast, in any book stores in China, it is easy to find as many foreign literary works as possible in the Chinese translation. There are quite a few publishing houses, such as *Shanghai yiwen chubanshe* (Shanghai Translation Press), *Yilin chubanshe* (Yilin Press), and *Waiguo wenxue chubanshe* (Foreign Literature Press), which devote almost all their efforts to publish translated foreign literary works, among which Western literary works occupy the most part of their entire titles. Such leading publishers in Beijing as *Shangwu yinshuguan* (Commercial Press) and *Sanlian shudian* (Sanlian Press) also make the most profits by publishing translated books, of which contemporary Western literary works and those of humanities are sold extremely well. In contrast, books of the similar titles authored by Chinese scholars can hardly be circulated widely. Today's young people do admire Western thinkers and writers much more than their Chinese counterparts. Why does such a phenomenon appear in today's China? Does it mean that China has not produced excellent literary works, or China does not have its own literary masters? The answer to these puzzling questions is obviously positive if we have some knowledge of modern Chinese literature and culture. Since the above questions cannot convince us, it is necessary to make some investigations and find the reasons behind this phenomenon. According to my preliminary observations, the following three reasons are critical.

First of all, due to the prevalent ideological intervention of Orientalism, Western audience has had some long-lasting bias against the Orient and Oriental people, including China and Chinese people. To many of them who have never been to China, the country is viewed as both poor and backward even now. Chinese people are regarded as uncivilized and so far from the elegance of Western people that they can hardly be thought to have produced excellent literary works. It is true that despite my own observation, there is a sharp contrast between the image of the West in the eye of Chinese people and that of China in the eye of Western people. It is regarded as a shame for a Chinese high school student not to know about such Western intellectual giants as Plato, Aristotle, Einstein, Shakespeare, Goethe, Mark Twain, Joyce, Eliot, Faulkner, Hemingway and so on. Their books were sold extremely well in China. On the contrary, it is viewed as quite natural for a Western literary scholar, let alone ordinary readers, not to know about Qu Yuan, Tao Yuanming, Li Bai, Du Fu, Su Shi, Wang Yangming, Lu Xun and Qian Zhongshu. I suppose that these literary masters' works are hardly sold well in the English language, let alone in other languages in Western bookstores. Due to such an unbalance in translation, Chinese literature still has a distance from the position of world literature although it has been trying to enter the mainstream of world literary market.

The second reason may be the absence of excellent translation of Chinese literature. As is known, foreign language teaching in China has been a big educational enterprise, out of which great profits are made by quite a few publishing houses. In recent years, along with the world-wide booming of Chinese language, this enterprise has gradually been on the decline. Even so, it has always carried a great importance in China's high schools, colleges and universities, because learning English language is almost compulsory to the majority of university students in China. However, in fact, most of Chinese college students and teachers, including English majors, can only read English books or newspapers and carry simple daily communications with native English speakers. Although a lot of Chinese scholars have the ability to translate literary or theoretic works from foreign languages into Chinese, very few of them could translate Chinese works into excellent and publishable foreign languages. Sometimes, even when they have translated great Chinese literary works into English or other major foreign languages, their versions are either not appreciated by native speakers for the foreignizing elements or viewed as unfit to be circulated in the target book market. Therefore, many of the translated Chinese literary works published by China's Foreign Language Press are chiefly circulated domestically rather than internationally.

Here let's take the two English translations of *Honglou meng* (*A Dream of Red Mansions* by the Yang couple, and *The Story of the Stone* by David Hawkes, et. al.) for example.[5] Judging by the linguistic faithfulness, the former is much better, but judging by the readability and elegance, the latter is far more effective. The former is so far mostly consulted and studied by some scholars of Chinese and translation studies, while the latter is extremely popular among the broad reading public. As Chinese literary scholars and translators, we should solve the problem of how to effectively translate excellent Chinese literary works into elegant and idiomatic English so that these works could reach the broad reading public in the English speaking countries.[6] In speaking of the principles for literary translation, 'foreignization' and domestication should be taken into consideration in a dialectical way. Chinese readers are very tolerant of the foreignizing elements in reading translated foreign literary works, but in the English speaking world, domesticating tendency is obviously more dominant. Otherwise, how could Yang's version of *A Dream of Red Mansions* fail to reach the broad reading public as Yang Xianyi himself was a near-native English speaker and his wife Gladys Yang was a typical native English speaker? The English-language publisher or book market does not even tolerate the foreignizing elements indicated in such an eminent scholar and translator like Lawrence Venuti whose translation of selected Italian poet De Angelis's poetry "has received many rejections from American and British publishers, including two university presses with noted translation series" (300–301) let alone the "foreignizing" translations done by Chinese translators.

The third reason may be viewed as a paradox. Nowadays, we live in a postmodern consumer society, in which serious literature and other highly cultural products are severely challenged by the rise of popular culture and consumer culture. Since classical Chinese literary works of high aesthetic quality are far from the ideals of the current consumer society, they may not be attractive to contemporary readers even if English translations are available. Even if faithfully translated into English or other major foreign languages, they can hardly be appreciated by the broad reading public, let alone commercially successful ones like many of the Western literary or theoretic works in China. As far as modern Chinese literature is concerned, since it has largely been developed under the Western influence, it can hardly be compared to its Western counterpart even when translated into English or other major foreign languages. We Chinese literary critics and scholars often complain that we do not have our own literary masters like T.S. Eliot, William Faulkner, Marcel Proust, James Joyce, Ernest Hemingway, V.S. Naipaul, Garcia Marquez, Milan Kundera, and so on. Thus our age is that of lacking literary and theoretic masters. For many people, what we should do is only to translate as many literary and theoretic masters and their masterpieces from the West. Given the current unbalance in China's literary and critical circles, it is necessary to solve the problems. Otherwise, we cannot expect the real age of world literature to come in China.

THE COMING OF A REAL AGE OF WORLD LITERATURE

Another question is raised: How is the foreign language level of contemporary Chinese writers? This is a very tough question that might well offend most of the Chinese writers in the contemporary era, but it is very important for Chinese literature to become an important part of world literature. Several years ago, there was a severe debate on whether it is necessary for Chinese writers to understand foreign languages. According to a news report published in *Qingnian bao* (*Youth Gazette*), German sinologist Wolfgang Kubin held that contemporary Chinese writers are too poor in foreign languages to read excellent world literary works. Since most of them do not understand any foreign languages, he argues, they cannot learn from foreign literatures. What they could do is only to explore the way of writing by themselves. Of course, Kubin compared these writers' foreign language level with that of their precursors. Many Chinese writers before 1949 were very good at foreign languages, which certainly enabled them to produce excellent literary works. Lu Xun and Guo Moruo were very good at Japanese, and Lin Yutang's English was so idiomatic that he even wrote his own creative works in excellent English.[7] What Kubin said is absolutely true, but his remark still aroused severe debates among contemporary Chinese writers. Those who are against Kubin's attitude tried to refute: although the writers mentioned by Kubin could read foreign literary works in the original, it was Lin Yutang only who could write excellent English and publish his works in the English speaking countries. All the others only grasped the language on the level of reading rather than writing, or translated foreign literary works into Chinese rather than vice versa. Even so, they pointed out, it did not prevent them from being recognized as world renowned literary masters. In this sense, Kubin's ideas were viewed too radical to convince ordinary people although he might mean well.

Perhaps ordinary people are not aware of the fact that the starting point from which Kubin criticizes contemporary Chinese writers is not Chinese literature but rather world literature. That is, he observes these Chinese writers in a broad context of world literature and evaluates their achievements. Thus he largely offends the writers whose educational background cannot be compared with those of the 4th of May Period chiefly due to the Chinese educational system during the Cultural Revolution when many of them were not even able to study well at high school. Despite that, these Chinese writers have tried their best to pursue as much knowledge as possible by reading extensively excellent foreign literary works through translation as well as canonical Chinese works. Some of them, such as Yu Hua, Mo Yan, Han Shaogong, Wang Anyi, and Jia Pingwa, following suite of their Western masters, dealt with some fundamental issues of human concern and have already attracted wide critical and academic attention from Western sinologists. With the help of translation, their works have become among world literature which can hardly be denied by Kubin. Previously, I mentioned the case of two modern Chinese writers: Ba Jin and Ye Junjian who both studied Esperanto. The former could only read the artificial language, and the latter even wrote literary works in it. Obviously, Ye's Esperanto is much better than Ba Jin's. However, Ba Jin's works have become world literature with the help of excellent translators, while Ye Junjian is remembered by contemporary readers merely as an excellent translator of Hans Christian

Andersen's fairy tales.[8] This undoubtedly proves that any valuable work of art written in any language could become world literature only through translation. The same is true of another two Chinese writers: Lu Xun and Lin Yutang. The former could only read and translate foreign literary works into Chinese, while the latter could write in excellent English and publish in the English speaking world. Yet Lu Xun's international reputation and influence are much wider than Lin Yutang's although Lin's English level is close to a native speaker. For Lu Xun, Guo Moruo, and Ba Jin, their foreign language knowledge and writing skill were still far from enough to produce their literary works. Thus they would rather write in their native language, Chinese. They were fortunate enough to have some excellent sinologists who have translated their works into various major foreign languages and became important world literary masters. Judging from these cases, I think that Kubin does not want these Chinese writers to write in foreign languages, but instead, he sincerely hopes that they could read excellent world literary works in the original so that they could benefit directly from these canonical works both in literary content as well as language style. And in this sense, I think that Kubin really means well.

Obviously, it is not so difficult for contemporary Chinese writers to grasp a foreign language, especially English on the level of reading, but it will certainly influence the quantity of their literary production. From a long-term point of view, it will help them produce excellent literary works, so that they will be among world-class writers. Here, I would like to quote another German theorist and thinker Walter Benjamin, whose ideas on translation and world literature are indeed very insightful and influential even in the Chinese context:

> Just as the manifestations of life are intimately connected with the phenomenon of life without being of importance to it, a translation issues from the original—not so much from its life as from its afterlife. For a translation comes later than the original, and since the important works of world literature never find their chosen translators at the time of their origin, their translation marks their stage of continued life. The idea of life and afterlife in works of art should be regarded with an entirely unmetaphorical objectivity. (72–73)

Truly, Benjamin's literary life is not long but he has got a much longer "continued life" or "afterlife" largely through the English translation of his major works. Such an afterlife will continue through the translation and re-translation by the new generations of translators in different languages. It is also true and necessary for an excellent writer who is very strict with himself to know as much as possible what his domestic and international peers have achieved and are doing now. For in the past, as Benjamin says, "the important works of world literature never find their chosen translators at the time of their origin," he himself was not able to read the translated versions of his own works. Although as an excellent translator himself, Benjamin co-translated French literary master of stream of consciousness Marcel Proust's masterpiece *A la recherché du temps perdu* into German and wrote a short preface to it, he never expected that the German version on which he spent much time and effort has long been surpassed by several new versions. Nonetheless, the short preface entitled "The Task of the Translator," after being translated into French and English, were greatly appreciated by such deconstructionist theorists as Jacques Derrida and Paul de Man and extensively interpreted by them, enabling him to become one of the pioneering figures of deconstructive translation theory. In this sense, if a writer could read excellent world literary works in the original and get aesthetic nourishment and creative inspiration, he will certainly produce an outstanding work.

What I would like to emphasize first of all is this: are Kubin's comments on contemporary Chinese literature facts? If the answer is yes, what shall we do? Secondly, as writers, especially as serious writers of wide international horizon, contemporary Chinese writers should also question themselves: do they write for all the readers of the world or merely for his native fellow readers? If they just want to restrict their writings to domestic reading public as some of the writers expressed, we will not be able to go on our discussion. If a writer not only writes for his own contemporary readers but rather for all the readers of the world, he will at least think over whether the subject matter he deals with is his own initiative and whether it is of certain universal significance. If not, he will not be thought of being original although he might not deliberately repeat or even plagiarize others. In this aspect, I would like to indicate what Henrik Ibsen has experienced in his writing career.

As is well known, Ibsen is now recognized as the "father of modern drama" of world significance, and many of his plays have already been recorded in literary and theatrical history. Yet in his lifetime, he was incompatible to his contemporary critical circles, largely due to his striking individualism and his avant-garde experimental consciousness. Some of his plays, such as *Ghosts* and *An Enemy of the People,* were not well received by his contemporary readers and audience. When he published his *Ghosts,* he was severely criticized by his contemporary critics. Confronted with these malicious attacks, he never gave up but proudly declared that his writing was pointed to the future.[9] It is certainly true of his affirmation that he was writing for the future, which has been proved true by literary history. In other words, Ibsen's art is by no means short-lived. It is open for future interpretations and reinterpretations. Therefore, it is of eternal artistic value. Although Ibsen died over a hundred years ago, his plays are still performed in different countries, attracting not only dramatic critics and scholars but also ordinary readers and audiences. We should say, Ibsen's works are certainly among world literature, while many of his contemporaries, including some Nobel laureates, have been forgotten. The same is true of Goethe. He put forward the utopian conjecture of world literature and was later benefitted from the wide reception of his works in the world. In this respect, Goethe has got a "continued life" and "afterlife" not only in his own country but also in the whole world. Today, both Goethe and Ibsen are most famous and canonical European writers in China, who constantly inspire one generation after another of Chinese writers in their creative writing.

Some Chinese writers might as well raise another question: Goethe did not understand Chinese but could only read Chinese literary works in translation. However, the point is that Goethe read almost all the oriental literary works he could get access to through the English and French translation. Since most of the excellent literary works of world significance are available in English translation, today's Chinese writers, through reading the original works, could at least get aesthetic nourishment and creative inspiration directly rather than wait for the Chinese translation. In this sense, Chinese writers had better at least master the English language, which is considered the lingua franca in the present era. In addition, more and more excellent Chinese literary works should be translated into the major world languages, especially English. Through the joint efforts to be made by us in collaboration with our Western sinologists and publishers, we will most effectively translate excellent Chinese literary works into English and promote them in the world. Given the fast economic development of China, I think that Chinese literature and literary studies can make a great contribution to the remapping of world literature. In the process we may well hope to meet a real age of world literature.

NOTES

1. As far as the modernity of different forms, especially the so-called alternative modernity of Chinese characteristics is concerned, see my book *Translated Modernities: Literary and Cultural Perspectives on Globalization and China*, pp.13–20.
2. I am particularly indebted to Damrosch's threefold definition of world literature focused on the world, the text, and the reader. See David Damrosch's *What Is World Literature?* p. 281.
3. Wang Ning, "World Literature and the Dynamic Function of Translation," *Modern Language Quarterly* 71. 1 (2010), p. 4.
4. See Douwe Fokkema's "World Literature" in *Encyclopedia of Globalization*, pp. 1290–1291.
5. *A Dream of Red Mansions*, trans. Yang Xianyi and Gladys Yang, 4 vols. (Beijing: Foreign Languages Press, 2001) was first published in 3 vols. in 1978–1980; *The Story of the Stone* (Bloomington: Indiana UP) (first eighty chapters translated by David Hawkes and last forty by John Minford) was published in 5 vols. in 1973–1980.
6. See Wang Ning's "Zhongguo wenxue ruhe youxiao di zouxiang shijie?" (How Chinese Literature Effectively Moves toward the World?), *Zhongguo yishu bao* (*China Art Gazette*), 19 March 2010.
7. As for Kubin's comments on contemporary Chinese literature and its writers, please see *Qingnian bao* (*Youth Gazette*), 17 September 2008: "Deguo hanxuejia gubin tui xinshu: bu ti 'laji lun,' 'Zhongguo dangdai wenxue zuida wenti shi yuyan" (German sinologist Kubin published a new book: not mentioning the idea of "garbage," "the biggest problem in contemporary Chinese literature is language).

8. Cf. Wang Ning, "World Literature and the Dynamic Function of Translation," *Modern Language Quarterly,* 71. 1(2010), p. 12.
9. Cf. Einar Haugen, *Ibsen's Drama: Author to Audience* (Minneapolis: U. of Minnesota P, 1979), p. 3.

REFERENCES

Benjamin, Walter. "The Task of the Translator." *Theories of Translation: An Anthology of Essays from Dryden to Derrida*. Ed. Rainer Schulte and John Biguenet. Chicago and London: The U of Chicago P, 1992. 71–82.

Damrosch, David. *What Is World Literature?* Princeton, NJ: Princeton UP, 2003.

Fokkema, Douwe. "World Literature." *Encyclopedia of Globalization*. Ed. Roland Robertson and Jan Aart Scholt. New York and London: Routledge, 2007. 1290–1291.

Moretti, Franco. "Conjectures on World Literature." *New Left Review* 1 (January–February 2000): 54–68.

Venuti, Lawrence. *The Translator's Invisibility: A History of Translation*. New York and London: Routledge, 1995.

Wang Ning. *Translated Modernities: Literary and Cultural Perspectives on Globalization and China*. Ottawa and New York: Legas, 2010.

——. "World Literature and the Dynamic Function of Translation." *Modern Language Quarterly* 71. 1 (2010): 1–14.

——. "Zhongguo wenxue ruhe youxiao di zouxiang shijie?" (How Chinese Literature Effectively Moves toward the World?). *Zhongguo yishu bao* (*China Art Gazette*). 19 March 2010.

CHAPTER 3

Global Englishes, Literary Studies, and the Japanese Academy

Myles Chilton

The globalization of English and the attendant spread of academic attention to world literature and global Anglophone literature indicate how traditional Anglo-American conceptions of English literary studies have opened up under pressure from several sources. The more notable of these include the spread of global English language studies, postcolonial studies, and perhaps most important of all, economic globalization. Yet, despite the nature of this opening up, it has had very little impact on Japan. A turn inward on the part of Japanese students is exacerbating enough in terms of the instrumentalization of English studies in Japan: the less interest there is in foreign cultural products, and the more attention is paid to the prosaic, functional aspects of the English language.

This essay will use the present situation of Anglophone language and literary study in Japan stands as the provocation for a series of related meditations on how to improve the situation, predicated on the belief that studying literature in *any* language is a good thing, and that if one is going to engage with the world's lingua franca, one might as well do it in a way that maximizes returns (to use the argot of global business English). Some of the motivation for these ruminations indeed comes from the business sphere: several high-profile Japanese companies have declared English their official language, meaning that even in offices in Japan among a totally Japanese workforce, English will be the sole language of communication.[1] Another crucial motivation comes from literary world, how its attention to world literature, major and minor literatures on a global scale, and the workings of colonialisms and imperialisms past and present serves to enliven the field, deepen our knowledge, and yes, supply us with the tools to live in a world in which we are closer to and more aware of others than ever before.

To establish my framework, I will first give an overview of the situation of English study in the context of Japanese higher education; its history, consequences, and how the global spread of English has spawned a renewed emphasis on English language study. Despite the perceived need for greater ability in spoken English, the result seems to indicate a more instrumentalized use of English, meaning the language will function as a tool. What that means for the study of Anglophone literature and literary study in Japan is a sense of stasis, or resignation. Moreover, because Anglophone literature is still pursued with a sense of equivalency with the Anglo-American literary academy, that is, with little or no attempt to offer Japanese context to scholarly and critical work on Anglophone literature, there remains a deep divide between Anglophone literary education and the teaching of English as a foreign language. I will also examine the trend to 'internationalizing' Japanese higher education, spurred by Japan's falling birthrate and competition from Asian universities. Part of this 'internationalization' is an increase in courses and programs in English. Conspicuously missing from this internationalization agenda is Anglophone literary study.

In conclusion, I will offer solutions that work with the domination of English language global studies, and steer toward the world literature paradigm to reassert the significance and benefits of literary study. Based on an example of teaching Jamaica Kincaid's novel *Annie John* in comparison with a Japanese novel, *No Longer Human* by Dazai Osamu, I will discuss how world literature's pedagogical attention to localization and to recognizing alterity—alterity in the text and in the reader of the foreign text—can be the opening to a more reflexive and inclusive subjectivity. Thus Anglophone literary studies will intersect with world literature, global studies, and the global spread of English.

ENGLISH IN JAPAN: LANGUAGE AS A TOOL

In order to appreciate what's at stake, it's important to understand both the situation of higher education in Japan, and the place of English language and literary studies. In short, as Brian McVeigh argues, higher education in Japan is perhaps best understood as a system that has moved from serving the political interests of the State to a system that, while not totally abandoning that function, and insofar as these functions can be separated, has been reformed to support the economic interests of the State. Of course all national university systems do these things, but in Japan the degree of involvement with statist projects is considerable. Given the attention to the instrumental, the useful and the relevant, the Humanities have tremendous difficulty in justifying themselves to prospective, and even current students. Moreover, the entire education system is structured around entrance examinations at each major step up the ladder, with difficult entrance examinations to university standing as the final, ultimate test of a student's academic abilities. This system relies on these sorts of memory-based evaluations in order to create a sense of dependency. "Examinations," in the words of one critic, "have become not merely formalized methods for testing an individual's mastery of a body of facts; rather, they have become a key means of forging linkages between being a good Japanese ... official versions of knowledge ... and being a diligent worker" (McVeigh 87). By thus combining the objectives of statism, nationalism, and capitalism, entrance examinations have enormous symbolic capital. Unfortunately, their academic effect is to render knowledge "sliced, disconnected, disjointed, stored, packaged for rapid retrieval, and abstracted from immediate experience" (McVeigh 87). Education in Japan, to quote another critic, "works, 'provided one thinks of it as an enormously elaborated, very expensive intelligence testing system with some educational spin-off, rather than the other way round" (Dore, qtd. in McVeigh 87).

To sum up, I turn to the words of Teruhisa Horio, emeritus professor of education at the University of Tokyo, one of the most trenchant, penetrating, and respected figures in the Japanese educational world, and one-time arch enemy of the Ministry of Education:

> Both colleges and upper secondary schools lost their previously cherished individual character as students devoted all their efforts to preparing for the severe entrance examination competition. When these students finally enter university, they are placed in a situation where they can enjoy a four-year moratorium on living and thinking, by virtue of their special status as candidates being groomed for positions as ordinary salaried workers within the Japanese industrial leviathan. (308)

This is somewhat extreme, and there are key exceptions, but Horio's work is at the pinnacle of a considerable literature on the systematic shortcomings of the Japanese higher education system, to which I could add my own anecdotal reflections and those I hear from colleagues, both Japanese and non-Japanese.

One prominent symptom of the weakness of Japanese higher education can be seen in the teaching of English. In Japan students are subjected to six years of arduous, grammar-and-translation based English study from middle through high school, which leaves them with little practical ability in English and all too often a loathing for the language. Those who have somehow preserved their motivation will have made the best of a very bad situation. But as their English education will have been based on preparing them for the difficult university entrance examinations, the bulk of their knowledge and skill will be in grammatical analysis and translation. The reason for studying in this mode springs from two main factors. The first is that the creation of a skilled work force depended on the ability to process large amounts of data efficiently and swiftly. The second reason concerns the emphasis on translation, and this emphasis has deep historical roots.

The deepest roots concern the Japanese language itself. The Japanese writing system is based on the importation of Chinese characters, though not the Chinese phonetic system, grammar or syntax. The characters, thus, were translated into the existing Japanese language, as were the classic texts of the Chinese tradition, which formed the basis of Japanese philological learning. A similar approach to importing English was therefore natural to the Japanese.[2] English first came to Japan in the 1850s, in the wake of American Commodore Perry's gunboat efforts to open up Japan to trade with the United States. When the Tokugawa government realized that learning English was going to be a necessity in dealing with the Americans, in 1856 they established a program in—the name says it all—the *Bansho Shirabe Dokoro*, that is, the Institute for Research on the Barbarian Books (Western diplomats did protest this name, and it was eventually changed to *Kaiseisho* or the Institute for Open Development). The presence of these institutes shows, how as Masao Miyoshi puts it, "English studies, in short, arose in response to the needs of the state" (276). In order to counter the Western threat, the Tokugawa and later the Meiji governments believed Japan had to catch up technologically, scientifically, linguistically, and culturally. Thus they imported teachers from the West, and many subjects, including literature, were taught in English.

Initially foreign faculty members were granted freedom to teach what they wanted in the way they wanted because Japan believed the need to learn from the West was urgent. Thought control was also relatively benign in the early years of the Meiji era. Another key reason was that government education bureaucrats, like so many others in Japanese officialdom at the time, were eager to emulate Britain. Emulation would in time create a sense of parity and equivalence between Japan and the great imperial power.

The rapid modernization of Japan had to be controlled, as opposition was arising in amidst foreigners' influence and the continued threat of imperialism. In 1890 the Meiji government issued the Imperial Precept on Education, which centralized education and steered it towards the goal of unifying Japan under the emperor. In order to ensure control, the state phased out the system of foreign instructors, with Japanese educated abroad replacing them. Thus a direct source of spoken English disappeared, along with the ideas and opinions those mostly British teachers might have given.

In other words, the emphasis in English education was moving away from actual interaction with the language to translation, as the latter was seen as politically vital. It was vital because the Meiji oligarchs were anxious to establish a one-to-one equivalency between Japanese and English. This linguistic equivalency would suggest cultural equivalency with the British Empire, which served both to legitimize Japanese culture and to further Japan's nascent imperialist project. "The idea of cultural compatibility," as Miyoshi puts it, "was inextricable from the basic quid pro quo principle of international diplomacy. The fact that an English text could be translated into Japanese, and vice versa, was seen at least partially as an act of demonstrating Japan's cultural compatibility with Britain at a time when the British Empire ruled the world" (277–78). Because Japanese could say all the things that English did, it would be a fitting symbol of imperial status.

Literature was also pressed into state cultural service. The Japanese came to settle on the term *bungaku* for literature and conceived of literature in roughly the same way as the West—as a way to unify national consciousness. But as with its Western counterpart, the exact definition remained loose for many decades, as did the institution of literary studies. At the outset of English literature education, foreign teachers reprised what they had learned, reciting facts and names and utterly neglecting to connect any of this information to their Japanese students.

And really, the absence of a Japanese context remains true of English literature pedagogy today. Terry Caesar writes that "in a very real sense the teaching of literature in English in Japan resembles the teaching of Latin literature in the provinces under the Roman imperium" because subjects of Rome, in order to function, much less thrive, needed to learn the language of the master (300). For Japanese, a correct, careful study of the language comes first [or] nothing else of cultural value (from anyone's point of view) will follow. Therefore, it is vital that the provinces adhere to the hegemony of the center, granting the space of the native—native speakers, native sources—final authority in all things. With respect to English, the rest of the world is in the position of provinces to the two major English-speaking nations, England and the United States. Japan is typical of a country that has no vested interest in challenging this state of affairs (Caesar 300–301).

Thus, in Japanese universities there are basically two approaches to English education: that offered by a native speaker of English, who functions as a kind of native informant and speaks from his position as a (usually) white, Anglophone male. The other approach is offered by a Japanese faculty member, who will domesticate an English language text, say, a novel by teaching it in

Japanese (although it will most likely be read in English). Another way of characterizing this situation is by seeing the class with the native English faculty member as a limited engagement with Otherness, while the class with the Japanese faculty member as a moment in the domestication of the Other.

The upshot is that like all other academic fields in Japan, English education is Japan-centered (criticism by academic critics, on the other hand, is poignantly bereft of Japanese orientation—although, as I will discuss later, this paradoxically reaffirms Japaneseness), thus the consciousness of Japanese students is accordingly national. Any discussion of culture is framed by the national, and the foreign enters the discussion in comparison with Japan and in a nationally essentialized framework. English, as the language of modern Japan's most significant foreign interlocutors, is a key medium for comparison: indeed, English functions as a pole of comparison in itself—as when teachers of Japanese, or the National Language as it is called, use the supposed directness of English as a means to illustrate the contextual subtlety of Japanese.

I realize that I'm painting a pretty dire picture. It's not as bad as this necessarily thumbnail sketch suggests, but nevertheless there is truth to it. Let me stress that there are exceptions. There are plenty of Japanese like Teruhisa Horio who are critical of these tendencies and are committed to reforming all education not just in the tertiary sector but to open up critiques of Japaneseness and to mobilize the critical thinking abilities of Japanese students in general. I also want to stress that academic work does happen, that there are dedicated faculty who combine world-class research with an eagerness to teach, and that there are interested motivated students. To narrow things down for the sake of this discussion, those students who enroll in a program like the one in which I teach—called the Division of International Languages and Literatures, in which we teach English, French, German, and Spanish—are interested in, to put it somewhat vaguely (as entering students are wont to do), learning about other cultures, broadening their horizons, improving their foreign-language skills (usually English), and making themselves more employable in what they see as a rapidly internationalizing Japan.

However, it also must be said that student interest in literature as literature or any other cultural product is minimal. Often students enter university without having read much in the way of literature, Japanese or foreign, much less a foreign work in its original language. Their interests reflect institutional and social pressures to view university education as socialization with a measure of skills training in subjects like engineering or design. In this sense English-education motivations actually match the instrumentalized nature of 'global English,' in which the language is stripped down to function somewhat like a code, and any poetic considerations is viewed as a distraction from the business of direct, unambiguous communication. Attitudes like this are conspiring to intensify corporatized reforms planned for Japanese universities. "Japan's thirteen best research universities" and industry leaders recently devised a project to reverse what "corporate executives warn is a growing mismatch between the needs of industry and academe, which is damaging Japan's ability to compete abroad" (McNeill). The aim of the project, according to the education ministry, is to "foster a pool of workers with specialized skills and the ability to think creatively" (McNeill). Despite the nod to creative thinking, the needs in question are expressly economic—"Corporate bosses are increasingly critical of universities for not providing specialized skills" (McNeill)—and Japanese higher education, if these reforms actually come to pass, will have an even more pronounced corporate agenda.

Another recent trend in the Japanese academy not only furthers the corporate agenda but has been partly responsible for keeping Japanese students in Japan. It is a trend that, moreover, sustains the view of English as a tool for communication. The trend I am addressing is the plethora of new 'global studies' programs that feature instruction in English. The impetus for these programs is changing demographics: Japan's falling birthrate, coupled with the gradual aging of the population, is pushing Japanese universities to look abroad, mostly to China, to make up for shortfalls in admissions. In looking abroad, they have noticed the rise in English as a language of instruction in Asian universities and recognized that if the competition is using English, then Japanese universities would have to follow suit. The competition also seems to favor business and economics oriented education, as these are seen as the most useful and relevant to a rapidly globalizing Asia. But it's not all numeracy and formulae: these programs all seem predicated on the notion that globalized education requires a high degree of cross- and multi-cultural knowledge and sensitivity, and thus one can take courses in comparative economics, law, human rights, as well as introductions to socio-linguistics, and cultural anthropology. Alas, the idea that literary study or for that matter study of any other cultural artifact might contribute something to this culturally sensitive turn in education seems not to have occurred to anyone. One can take courses in these things, but they are usually treated as secondary to the more important matters at hand.[3]

This trend toward global studies programs also echoes discussions on education reform. Prominent in these discussions have been the terms *kyō*iku no kokusaika (internationalization of education) and *daigaku no gurō*baruka (globalization of universities).[4] This internationalization or globalization of Japanese higher education has really meant 'Asianization,' as the largest foreign contingent has come from Asian countries. Moves towards accommodating these non-Japanese speaking students have led to an increase in the promotion of English-language bridging or content courses. Internationalization in Japanese higher education has been interpreted as "'Japanization' of Japanese learners of English, the 'development' of Japanese citizens who are able to use English as an instrument or tool to promote, enhance, and defend Japanese interests and independence in an age of globalization" (Burgess et al. 466). This is seen by some Japanese commentators as "a form of resistance to English language imperialism" (Burgess et al. 466). Seen from the globalization perspective—in which Japan is being forced to reposition itself—English language education, though unnecessary for the vast majority of Japanese, is an indication of how strong the global pressure to use English has become. In other words, it is a general idea that Japan is a victim of the spread of global English and must maneuver itself to comply in order not to be left behind.

THE WORLD LITERATURE SOLUTION

Given these constraints, is there any future for Anglophone or any literature in Japanese higher education? Perhaps it is worth looking to another emerging global trend, that of world literature. As

English solidifies itself as a global language, there is a need both to cast the linguistic net wider to recuperate languages and literatures that may be sidelined. In addition, there is a need to relativize or better yet provincialize Anglophone literature to better reflect the differences and diffusions of the language. To put it another way, a global Anglophone component of the world literature project could act both to apply the brakes to runaway English and to enrich the study of Anglophone literature by casting it in a comparative light.

Definitions of world literature start in the early nineteenth century with Goethe's concept of *Weltliteratur* being granted original status. When Goethe declared in 1827 that "a world literature is forming, and that all nations are inclined towards it and therefore take favorable steps" (qtd. in Hoesel-Uhlig 34), he did not mean that *Weltliteratur* should be thought of as a collection of the world's great books. Rather, he was invoking a way of accounting for and understanding the increasing availability of literary texts. John Pizer points out that an acknowledgment of a "subnational-transnational dialectic" (7) in Goethe's thinking leads to a new kind of cultural awareness, one that helps the native understand the other by accounting for otherness, and for the ways in which we can deploy our own perspectives to create comity. One sense of this comity comes in a subsequent articulation of world literature by Marx and Engels. Their belief was that a world literature had been produced out of the constant revolutionizing of bourgeois production, which would then spread world literature across national and cultural boundaries:

> In place of the old local and national seclusion and self-sufficiency, we have intercourse in every direction, universal inter-dependence of nations. And as in material, so is also in intellectual production. The intellectual creations of individual nations become common property. National one-sidedness and narrow-mindedness become more and more impossible, and from the numerous national and local literatures, there arises a world literature. (476–77)

In this view, one of the first globally linked elites—socially as much as imaginatively—was the literary elite able to sample literary texts produced outside of their original national and local contexts.

Contemporary discussions of world literature develop Goethe's thinking to focus on how and why certain works circulate beyond their original culture and of the ways they are received at different sites. The most probing recent discussion of the significance of world literature as a mode of circulation comes from David Damrosch. In his book *What Is World Literature?* Damrosch refines the idea of circulation by maintaining that world literature should not only refer to, in his words, "all literary works that circulate beyond their culture of origin, either in translation or in their original language," but also should consider that, again in his words, that "a work only has an *effective* life as world literature whenever, and wherever, it is actively present within a literary system beyond that of its original culture" (4). Those references to a work's effective life and its active presence in a different site are important, not the least because they open up more questions as to how and why a work can be considered effectively and actively present.

Establishing a work's effective and active presence depends to a great extent on how it is presented to students, and the way Damrosch fleshes out his explanation of world literature lends itself well to the classroom. World literature, he argues, "is an inherently more detached mode of engagement" that calls on the "discipline of distance and of difference." From an epistemological distance we "observe ourselves seeing the work's abstraction from its origins," a meta-vision that "gains us a new vantage point on our own moment" (300). Foreignness is kept fully in view, along with our situatedness, as we let the work and our store of influences and reading strategies combine to create meaning.

These ways of reading utilize a strain of Wolfgang Iser's reader-response theory. Damrosch maintains that "literary narratives work less by communicating fixed information than by creating suggestive gaps that the reader must fill in" (292). But when a book is read 'outside' of its original cultural context (particularly, but not necessarily, in translation), the text does indeed change. When a text circulates from one place to another, it calls upon different frames of reference and language. This circulation, however, does not result in "the loss of an unmediated original version but instead a *heightening* of the naturally creative interaction of reader and text" (Damrosch 292). Damrosch explains how readers in Seville and Berlin may cover Thomas Mann's magic mountain in different flora, "but so may two different readers in Berlin itself" (292), imbuing the meaning of a literary text with the reader's imagination, itself resonating with images, ideas, memories, all produced in accordance with or despite ruling ideologies.

Franco Moretti offers a similar meta-theoretical framework for reading world literature, although rather than the works themselves, his focus is on ways of reading, and on world literature "as a problem in the study of literature across borders, regardless of whether the individual works have been received by other cultures" (Rosendahl Tomsen 16). Moretti maintains that the best way to approach this problem of understanding texts from various places and traditions is to recognize the scope of this analytical ambition; with the scope of this ambition understood, "the greater must the distance be" between text and reader (151). Moretti's hypothesis is that "distant [as opposed to close] reading" of texts within and without narrowly constructed canons will allow us to "focus on units that are much smaller or much larger than the text: devices, themes, tropes—or genres and systems" (151). Enlarging our analytical distance will force us to transcend national canons, and their necessarily circumscribed notions of history, making larger historical and spatial networks and trajectories more visible.

Both approaches contribute to conceiving of literature as non-essentialized speech acts. That said, this renewed attention to world literature comes largely from the Anglo-American academy, leading world literature scholars to express reservations about the Anglophone or Western provenance of this discourse.[5] Thus, I want to stress that I am not suggesting that the teaching of world literature in Japanese universities is necessarily bound up with the teaching of English or that only a non-Japanese native English-speaker could be responsible for handling the world literature brief. In the Japanese context, however, the influence of English would certainly bias Japanese conceptions of world literature because the teaching of English in Japan is bound up with the notion of exposure to the other, to the foreign. Thus, institutionalization of world literature would, to a large extent, involve the participation of English department faculty, both Japanese and non-Japanese.

One of the biggest challenges world literature would face in Japan is that foreign-language programs tend to cover the ground of broadening horizons, albeit in a national framework that sets Japan as one pole of comparison. This leads to a further challenge, one that moreover presents a paradox: while students take courses in English or German or some other foreign literature in order to learn the language and about that culture, one underlying goal is to maintain a sense of Japaneseness. Students are rarely conscious of this objective—although I have heard students articulate that this is their motivation. In any case, one reason behind learning about other cultures and their languages is to keep 'the Other' other, 'the Exotic' exotic, so that differences remain differences—all in the name of preserving a sense of how Japanese culture remains Japanese in the face of globalized culture. The national, and nationalist, paradigm is important in Japan because of how Japan sees itself in the world. In short, when Japanese students think of the world, it is an American-dominated one, with China emerging from the edge. Japan, however, remains solidly in the center. This isn't just the result of dewy-eyed patriotism or narrow nationalism. The Japan-centered aspect of the Japanese imaginary comes out of a long, complex history in which a small island nation nurtures its language, culture, economy, and—perhaps most importantly—its security in the face of threats from all around.

Japan-centeredness also reflects a popular notion that a cultural form—say, the realist novel, jazz, Italian food, among other notable examples one could offer—once imported into Japan, is then mixed and melded with indigenous literary forms, styles, content, and themes, thus somehow becoming 'Japanified.' This process, in the eyes of Japanese scholars and critics, is peculiar to Japan and pervasive but has led to the creation of a Japanese culture as a uniquely porous entity that can consciously, even willfully, absorb an element of a foreign culture and then fruitfully 'Japanify' it to the point where not only the cultural artifact but also the culture as a whole strengthen Japanese identity. This absorption, runs the argument, allows the Japanese to enjoy the cultural fruits of the world, and permits points of entry into foreign consciousnesses, fostering greater mutual understanding and appreciation. Syncretism, hybridism, the mixing and melding play a part in the development of all cultures—these occur in Japan but on Japanese terms.

While in sober moments many would acknowledge that this kind of cultural borrowing and assimilating happens everywhere, this absorption nevertheless figures both as the history and genius of Japanese culture. This dynamic of cultural assimilation and blending furthermore creates a sense of cultural self-sufficiency, which world literature must address. To quote Japanologist Leith Morton,

> [E]thnocentric or indigenous discourse ... is the logical outcome of a context-rich culture and intellectual environment where, to a larger degree than elsewhere, conceptualizations of culture look inwards to indigenous formulations, and share a common set of assumptions about the nature of the society that produced this culture ... [this] insider discourse is part of a process of contestation and debate where different views of culture are challenged, and new views proposed—but rarely do these proposals originate wholly from, or point to paradigms of culture that are explicitly comparative or universal in nature. (255)

Outside views are not ignored—they are a staple of literary criticism—but as Morton asserts, Japanese theorists 'tend to limit their conclusions and applications to Japan alone' (255). This Japan-centered view is true even in the paradoxical case of the practice of English literary criticism in the Japanese academy. As Masao Miyoshi says in reflecting on the content of recent Japanese-produced literary scholarship, 'What is absent in all of the articles ... is any indication of the awareness of the meaning of these critics and theorists [meaning the likes of Eagleton, Jameson, Greenblatt, Showalter, and other heavy hitters] in the context of both English studies in Japan and Japanese society/culture itself' (285). The underlying motive in this case, Miyoshi argues, is to maintain a sense of cultural equivalency with Western culture, now centered in the US as much as Britain.

This tendency seems to totally contradict what I just said about the 'Japanification' of a cultural artifact. In fact, it does not.

The sense of equivalency is a function 'Japanification.' There may be nothing noticeably 'Japanese' about an analysis of a Shakespearian sonnet or a novel by Dickens, but that is the point—and that is what marks it as Japanese. Thus the Japanese conversation about a foreign text, by trafficking in Western theoretical and critical terms, stands as an example of how the Japanese academy maintains a sense of being separate but equal.

Thus, Japanese English literature scholars see themselves as operating within the Anglo-American sphere, while the native literary sphere functions more or less separately from the English and indeed from other European literary spheres. There may be overlap when it comes to the application of critical trends and theory—both the native and Anglo spheres import Western literary theory and put it to work in equal amounts. But there is little interaction between the two spheres. Part of the reason for this divide is the usual gulf between academic departments. It is also a result of the belief that the Western novel and the Japanese novel, or *shosetsu,* though superficially alike, differ in fundamental ways (something that will be touched on later). Lastly, this divide also reflects the separation of things foreign and things domestic which organizes Japanese culture. The effects of this on literary education in Japan reach back to the middle of the nineteenth century; since that time, "for the general reading public in Japan" as Waka Ishikura indicates, "there has been a tendency not to discriminate/differentiate among European literatures, but, rather, to regard them as constituting a univocal *gaikoku bungaku* (outside countries' literature)."[6] Ishikura traces this tendency back to the Japanese importation of "Chinese characters and vocabulary," which carried with them the influence of Chinese literary traditions, which "inevitably made the people keenly aware of the existence of the other." As a result, Ishikura argues that "the sense of difference between 'ours' and 'the other' tended always to remain well defined." "This idea of a dichotomy in literature," he goes on to say, "seems to have been fundamental to the process of accepting European literatures" and they were likely to "establish a unified code, the 'other' of Japanese literature."

In such an academic context with inside and outside firmly fixed and the national the main pole of comparison, how could world literature gain traction? John Pizer suggests what I take to be the best place to start: in the world literature classroom, the instructor should view his or her role "as that of enabling students simply to 'perceive' patterns of cultural alterity and how they interact with a text's universal elements. In other words, my primary role is to inculcate the habit of reading texts, particularly foreign ones, using the technique of the Weltliteratur dialectic" (145). The dialectic calls upon the recognition of cultural baggage, or more to the point, as Damrosch puts it, that literary "works continue to bear the marks of their national origin even after they circulate into world literature" (281). But "these traces are increasingly diffused and become ever more sharply refracted as a work travels farther from home" (Damrosch 281). To resolve the knowledge gap, the world literature framework promotes "an elliptical refraction of national literatures" (Damrosch 283). To explain this, let me quote Damrosch at some length. "This refraction," he begins

> [m]oreover, is double in nature: works become world literature by being received *into* the space of a foreign culture, a space defined in many ways by the host culture's national tradition and the present needs of its own writers .... World literature is thus always as much about the host culture's values and needs as it is about a work's source culture; hence it is a double refraction, one that can be described through the figure of the ellipse, with the source and host cultures providing the two foci that generate the elliptical space within which a work lives as world literature, connected to both cultures, circumscribed by neither alone. (283)

Thus, the interests of the Japanese need not be overlooked in the selection of texts for a world literature course. Indeed, another way to characterize Damrosch's ellipse would be to call it localization with a twist. It is a localization that requires a meta-vision that constantly asks why a foreign literary text should matter, where its foreignness lies (and not just in the matter of nation of origin), and how its meanings can be shared across cultural divides.

This mode of localization moreover dilutes the authority of the 'native,' while reflecting a more multilingual approach. This would not only be more theoretically satisfying but also timely. As it is, many in other Asian sites already contest the idea of native authority. This "perception is not tenable," writes Flora Deborah Floris, an Indonesian English professor, because "English has grown to be a world language. As a universal language it is not only used to communicate with people from other nations (international) but even within EFL and ESL countries" (44). The weight of so much Anglo-American alterity is a reason that "many EFL/ESL learners in Asia undergo laborious and frustrating learning experiences and react to the native literary texts context without full comprehension" (Floris 46). A preferable approach is to use texts from their culture of origins which will allow students to "enhance their local and regional cultural identities and value systems while learning the language" (Floris 47). The goal is not parochial; rather it should be seen as a part of facilitating the development of local and regional cultural awareness, and understanding and empathy with other cultures (Floris 47). Using texts from other Asian cultures of origin would also serve to expand a somewhat Western bias in world literature, which despite the well-meaning efforts of people such as Damrosch, Moretti, and Pizer, remains an issue.[7]

Teaching world literature in this way would require us to note one more caveat, but then of course to use that caveat as a pedagogical strategy. As world literature scholars John Pizer and Sarah Lawall have noted, world literature as a pedagogical site is largely an American phenomenon, having been a part of American literary higher education since the late nineteenth century. World literature courses have been, for the most part, designed to introduce young Americans to the world beyond their borders, to sensitize them to cultural differences. Pizer in his book *The Idea of World Literature* traces the development of world literature as a uniquely American pedagogical practice in order to argue how the meta-theoretical teaching of world literature can be positioned to enhance the cosmopolitan perspective of young Americans in this age of Americanized globalization.[8] This American focus, though of immense value, is of course not entirely applicable to other sites. We can, however, take something from this American history and teach it meta-theoretically. Citing the American provenance would prove stimulating to Japanese students, attuned to and still fascinated by America and its cultural forms as they remain, while simultaneously being wary of the political and historical influence that the United States has had over Japan throughout its modern history. Discussing the Western origins of the idea of world literature would moreover provide a chance to address Japan's ambiguous relationship with the West. Specifically, by bringing into the open the ways that literature is conceived in Japan and the West, we could invite interrogations of just what literature is assumed to provide in the context of education.

For instance, as in the West, literature in Japan has come to be seen as a means of cultural understanding and discovering national identity. One of the key attractions of world literature is that it provides a way of analyzing texts outside of national frameworks and their essentializing notions of national identity. On this level, world literature pedagogy would be tricky but rewarding, given the long and deep hold of national paradigms in Japanese higher education.

Thus, I believe world literature pedagogy would have to foreground the national-subnational dialectic Pizer speaks of and the relevant histories. This foregrounding can begin by announcing that these paradigms are going to be put under interrogation. Let me illustrate this through a consideration of how Jamaica Kincaid's novel *Annie John* could be taught in this framework. *Annie John* tells the story of how a young girl, Annie John, growing up in Antigua struggles to establish some sort of identity free of her rather overbearing mother. Her mother's influence and that of Annie John's school, playmates, and extended family are all complicated by Antigua's colonial history. The novel does a masterful job of representing how personal taste, morality, manners, as well as social convention are shaped by the British colonial influence. Given the postcolonial diegesis of the novel, it is hard to slot *Annie John* into a national category. It is, in one sense, an Antiguan novel. But we can also call it a Caribbean novel—but then Jamaica Kincaid lives and works in the United States. The question becomes even more complicated when we analyze the novel and see that the novel itself forces us to think through the matter of national and other forms of identification in its central problematic. *Annie John* argues that the very thing that Annie John is trying to achieve is a sense of self beyond the influence of her mother, her schooling, her social and cultural milieu. At the end of the novel, Annie John affirms her selfhood: "'My name is Annie John.' These were the first words that came into my mind as I woke up on the morning of the last day I spend in Antigua" (Kincaid 130). She is set to sail to England to become a nurse, something she does not want to do, "but I would have chosen going off to live in a cavern and keeping house for seven unruly men rather than go on with my life as it stood" (Kincaid 130). Her life as it stood has been dominated by her parents, "[a]nd now they are together and here I am apart .... The bitter thing about it is that they are just the same and it is I who have changed, so all the things I used to be are as false as the teeth in my father's head" (Kincaid 133). Annie is angry with herself for not realizing that she has become as hypocritical as her mother about love and filial relations: both her and her mother while professing their love were "at the same proposing separation after separation, including this one, which unbeknownst to her, *I* have arranged to be permanent" (Kincaid 133). The motive for this final separation is to become the sovereign self of Western Enlightenment, the one promised by Western humanism, and withheld from its colonial subjects.

This is also a version of selfhood that has no cognate in Japanese cultural or social history, but like the former Western colonies, Japan has been struggling with the influence of this version of selfhood ever since it learned about it from the West. So, the first move in teaching this text is to point this out—that *Annie John* is more than just a story of a young girl trying to struggle free from the bonds of her mother.

To highlight the impact of Annie John's struggle with selfhood and to really bring it home to Japanese students, the text could be paired with Japanese writer Osamu Dazai's novel *No Longer Human*, which sets up a sharp contrast in terms of the locatability of a central organizing consciousness. *No Longer Human* tells the 'story' of a young man's struggle with every imaginable aspect of human existence: familial relations, social interactions, love and sex, holding a job, being a student, and three suicide attempts. Each of these (and more) presents the narrator (always unnamed) with a painful set of moral and psychological adjustments, which he faces with abandonment, alcohol, sex, drugs, or suicide. The effect of this plot-less narration is to show there is no central organizing consciousness even though there is something like a self struggling mightily against forces comparable to those in *Annie John*. Moreover, like *Annie John, No Longer Human* has a first-person narrator, and the latter text's three main sections are presented in the form of diaries. In *Annie John,* the main character fights the influence of her mother whereas in *No Longer Human* the narrator fights the influence of his father, seeking and failing to find some sort of existential stability in the face of larger social and cultural pressures. Not unlike *Annie John* but in an essential way it is totally unlike *Annie John*.

The comparison of these two novels could serve to open up considerations of self, and non-self and how each corresponds to key moments in Japanese cultural and political history. The contested selfhood of the Western novel *Annie John* is based on a Cartesian, pre-cultural self while the self in *No Longer Human* reflects the shifting nature of narrative perspectives in the face of social pressures. For instance, as a student the narrator drifts into a group of Marxists, not out of any political convictions but because "[f]or such a person as myself the atmosphere of an underground movement was curiously soothing and agreeable" (Dazai 68).

Other instances of this passivity accumulate, revealing competing motivations and moral and psychological inconsistencies. Accompanying these moments is a thematic refrain. Lines from *No Longer Human* including "I can't even guess myself what it must be to live the life of a human being" (21), and "I was congenitally unable to refuse anything offered to me by another person, no matter how little it might suit my tastes" (30), and "I felt so much more relaxed in this irrational world than in the world of rational gentlemen that I was able to do what was expected of me in a 'sound' manner" (69) all underscore the absence of a self organizing impressions, ideas, and narrative structure of responses as in a novel. The concern rather is with narrative flow, externalities, shifting social roles, and awareness of the inability of the self to collect and order experience in an artistic way. In short, these two texts demonstrate key differences between the Western novel and the Japanese *shosetsu*.

The Eurocentric reading of *No Longer Human* struggles to see its first-person narrator as an alienated self. Yet the Japanese reading, as we see, goes down quite another path. If we can map these readings back on to *Annie John,* we get a clearer illumination of what is different between Japanese and Western novelistic representation and also how to bridge these gaps. The really critical engagement in this example of critical world literature pedagogy is that we can utilize these opposed readings to open up questions as to the social utility of this kind of learning. Literature suddenly becomes a project that confers not enlightened consciousness and a sense of the worthiness of our culture but also a process that interrogates how social, political, cultural, and philosophical concepts structure our social lives, how we represent them in literature, and how we read them.

Affirming these literary values—among others—in the face of globalized pressures against prescriptions for higher education to be 'useful' is a tall order, but it is something that those of us in the profession must do, if we are to have a future. We need not engage in the advocacy of particular ideas or values. Indeed, one of the strengths I see in world literature is that such advocacy must ultimately be historically and geographically located, thus diluting some of its pathos. In return, we get an enhanced and enlarged field of literature, one that challenges us a teachers and scholars to engage our students as future citizens of a globally intensified world. The language may be English, and the history may be Japanese, but literature need not petrify itself in the space between.

NOTES

1. These companies include Fast Retailing and online retailer Rakuten. The announcements that these and other companies would conduct all business in English—even in Japanese offices among Japanese workers—has, not surprisingly, met with some resistance. See the article "Rakuten's Decision on English Not Welcomed by Everyone" at <http://www.japantoday.com/category/features/view/rakutens-decision-on-english-not-welcomed-by-everyone>.
2. This short history is heavily reliant on Miyoshi's essay "The Invention of English Literature in Japan."
3. It would be impossible to list them all, so a few examples will have to suffice. One is the Meiji Gakuin University Global & International Studies Program, which is offered in cooperation with the University of California Education Abroad Program. To quote the

program website, "[s]ubjects include politics and security, comparative politics, economic themes, peace and conflict, development and environment, Japanese culture and society—all in an Asian perspective. Curriculum is in English." The University of Tokyo Komaba campus has English-language undergraduate programs on Japan in East Asia, and Environmental Science (<http://www.c.u-tokyo.ac.jp/eng_site/admissions/our-courses/index.html>). Tama University's School of Global Studies offers mainly English-language majors in Hospitality Management, International Development, and Global Business. The website blurb for each major stresses the need for intercultural or cross-cultural knowledge and understanding (http://www.tama.ac.jp/english/ sgs_majors.html.).

4. Burgess et al. describe the difference between the terms *kyō*iku no kokusaika (internationalization of education) and *daigaku no gurō*baruka (globalization of universities). Basically, *kyō*iku no kokusaika emphasizes the active preservation of Japanese unity, economic power, culture and tradition in the face of foreign pressure, and promoting a proper understanding of Japan. The latter term, *daigaku no gurō*baruka indicates a passive compliance with outside events that cannot be controlled. See Burgess et al. pp. 462–465.
5. On this point, it would do well to heed Gayatri Chakravorty Spivak on the complicity between global Anglophone literature and world literature. As Mads Rosendahl Thomsen writes, while Spivak emphasizes "studies of world literature in a global context as a more viable way out of the Eurocentric comparative literature," she warns "against the monolingual triumph of English" (25). Rosendahl Thomsen also notes "how few authors from China, Japan, non-English-speaking India or non-Commonwealth Africa have made their way into the Western world's circulation of literature" (7).
6. Waka Ishikura's "The Reception and Translation of Wordsworth in Japan" can be accessed on *CLCWeb: Comparative Literature and Culture* 8.2 (2006). <http://docs.lib.purdue.edu/clcweb/vol8/iss2/6>. Ishikura describes a knock-on effect of this division of the literary world into Japan and non-Japan, which served to solidify the gap. Foreign texts were "for most readers ... presented in Japanese, regardless of whether they were translated or adapted texts. It follows that possible conflicts with European ideas were likely to be neutralized, partly obscured by the huge gap between Western cultures and the culture of the Japanese and partly dismissed through Japanese translations in which the otherness expressed in the original languages was likely to be blurred or dissipated" (Ishikura).

7. Expanding the range of world literature texts would have another benefit, as Floris explains: "Literary texts have richer and more varied language because they are not created for the specific purpose of teaching. Therefore, students are exposed to natural standard and non-standard forms of the variety of English. They can enjoy and experience the wealth of the language varieties while reading the text. At the same time, they develop their awareness to appreciate all English varieties. To merely teach a standard variety of an English variety would, in many ways, withdraw our learners of enjoying and experiencing the wealth of the new varieties of English" (46).
8. See Pizer, *The Idea of World Literature*, passim.

REFERENCES

Burgess, Chris, Gibson, Ian, Klaphake, Jay and Selzer, Mark. "The 'Global 30' Project and Japanese Higher Education Reform: An Example of a 'Closing in' or an 'Opening up'?" *Globalisation, Societies and Education* 8.4 (2010): 461–475. <http://dx.doi.org/10.1080/14767724.2010.537931>. 19 April 2011.

Caesar, Terry. "Anthologies, Literature, and Theory in Japan." *On Anthologies: Politics and Pedagogy*. Ed. Jeffrey R. Di Leo. Lincoln, NE: U of Nebraska P, 2004. 298–325.

Damrosch, David. *What Is World Literature?* Princeton: Princeton University Press, 2003.

Dazai, Osamu. *No Longer Human*. Trans. Donald Keene. New York: New Directions, 1958.

Floris, Flora Deborah. "Using English Literature Written by Asian Authors in EFL/ESL Classrooms in Asia." *K@ta: a Biannual Publication on the Study of Language and Literature* 7.1 (2005): 43–53. <http://puslit.petra.ac.id/ journals/letters/>. 12 May 2011.

Hoesel-Uhlig, Stefan. "Changing Fields: The Directions of Goethe's *Weltliteratur*." *Debating World Literature*. Ed. Christopher Prendergast. London: Verso, 2004. 26–53.

Horio Teruhisa. *Educational Thought and Ideology in Modern Japan: State Authority and Intellectual Freedom*. Trans. Steven Platzer. Tokyo: U of Tokyo P, 1988.

Ishikura Waka. "The Reception and Translation of Wordsworth in Japan." *CLCWeb: Comparative Literature and Culture* 8.2 (2006). <http://docs.lib.purdue. edu/clcweb/vol8/iss2/6>. 13 May 2011.

Kincaid, Jamaica. *Annie John*. 1983. New York: Farrar, Straus and Giroux, 1997.

Marx, Karl, and Frederick Engels. *Manifesto of the Communist Party. The Marx-Engels Reader*. 2nd Edition. Ed. Robert C. Tucker. New York: Norton, 1978. 469–500.

McNeill, David. "Japan's Top Industrial and Academic Leaders Join in Effort to Stop Global Slide." *The Chronicle of Higher Education Online* 25 Jan. 2011. < http://chronicle.com/article/Japans-Top-Industrial-and/126053/a>. 1 February 2011.

McVeigh, Brian J. *Japanese Higher Education as Myth*. Armonk, NY: M.E. Sharpe, 2002.

Meiji Gakuin University Global & International Studies Program. < http://www.meijigakuin.ac.jp/~kokusai/mgucep/>. 12 May 2011.

Miyoshi, Masao. "The Invention of English Literature in Japan." *Japan in the World*. Ed. Masao Miyoshi and H.D. Harootunian. Durham NC: Duke UP, 1996.

Morretti, Franco. "Conjectures on World Literature." *Debating World Literature*. Ed. Christopher Prendergast. London: Verso, 2004. 148–162.

Morton, Leith. *Modern Japanese Culture: The Insider View*. Melbourne: Oxford UP, 2003.

Pizer, John. *The Idea of World Literature: History and Pedagogical Practice*. Baton Rouge: Louisiana State UP, 2006.

Rosendahl Thomsen, Mads. *Mapping World Literature: International Canonization and Transnational Literatures*. London: Continuum, 2010.

CHAPTER 4

Mutability of Home and Exile

The Oriental Dance

Marie-Therese Abdel-Messih

The post-independence period witnessed several waves of fiction writing in Egypt. The first wave fiction writing in the mid 1950s and 1960s responded to the prevalent socialist theoretical thought calling for the 'representation of reality' in literature and art. Writers were seen as prophets of the nation, art as an epiphany debunking falsehood. 'Realistic' fiction was in line with the socialist claims for an independent unified nation under a military regime, with strong allegations challenging the nation's enemies. However, the military defeat in the 1967 war with Israel unveiled a totalitarian military regime that had baffled the public with the "macho male triumphalist language," to borrow Saghieh (247) which could be no longer believed. Public opinion held the military state patriarchal policies responsible for the 1967 defeat, and claims for 'national' unification were rejected on grounds that they have been masked strategies for censorship and outlawing difference. Resistance to standard values came with the second wave of fiction writing in the 1970s and early eighties in various forms of experimentation in fiction. However, one should add that some major Egyptian novelists did not conform to the socialist discourse prevalent in the sixties, and had introduced several forms of innovation, during that time.

Meanwhile, governance by absolute power has not changed during the 1980s and 1990s under Sadat's and Mubarak's dictatorships. Their allegations that replacing military socialism by 'open door' economic policies would implement democratic governance proved inconsistent in practice. The first post-independence government that was previously formed by high-ranked military became as from the 1980s run by venturing entrepreneurs steering politico-economic processes away from the 'national' to the transnational, which aroused public concern about 'national' identity. Furthermore, public resistance to mushrooming corruption was met with new forms of repression and censorship. To avoid more sophisticated modes of censorship during dictatorship, the third wave of fiction writing in the 1980s and 1990s became most of the time allegorical, satirical, or a form of parody.

In response to public anxiety about questions of 'identity' and 'nation' threatened by economic processes of transnationalization, state media cultural products mobilized a standardized cultural identity of the male 'Egyptian' in an attempt to confer a sense of equilibrium amongst growing social divisions. Towards the 1990s, media cultural products constructed stereotyped cultural essences of the 'Egyptian' that satisfied traditional standards promoting more parochialism to establish a group identity (Abu Lughod 159). Conversely, fabrications by state media policies were countered, on the one hand, by post-national Islamism calling for a global Islamic community *umma*, and on the other, by secular cultural activists seeking to undermine local and global policies mobilizing reductionist nationalism or elitist transnationalism, respectively. Most fiction writers of the fourth wave rejected the constructed identities by state media or reductionist ideologies, consolidating mainstream values informed by a patriarchal discourse. Moreover, the ongoing socio-economic crisis owing to totalitarianism has nurtured existential conflicts leading to eventual dislocations, with youngsters immigrating in search for alternatives in other geographical locations. This is a brief introduction to the socio-political backdrop, against which the fourth wave of post-independence fiction emerged, at the outset of the third millennium. Khaled El Beri (b. 1972, Sohag, Upper Egypt), whose *Oriental Dance* (2010) is the subject of this paper belongs to the latest generation of fiction writers in Egypt.

El Beri lives in London since (1999), and his *Oriental Dance (OD)* is written in his maternal language: Arabic. However, *OD* challenges stigmatization, and cannot be regarded as a 'national configuration.' The novel goes beyond national affiliations as it shows gaps in the national construct; moreover, despite being written in Arabic, the book cannot be read within classical Arabic aesthetics. Unlike classical Arabic formal rigidity, the imagined realities configured in *OD* are subjective and vested in the "experiential," everyday to borrow Jain's term (203). By subverting mainstream values *OD* becomes outside the norm—'minor' in the homeland as well as its host country. The narrative events reveal that the construction of identity is not free-willed but a form of becoming in the process of survival. Against the backdrop of competing identity constructions, and within local/global shifting landscapes, the mutability of home and exile can be discerned, or as Andreas Huyssen notes in another context: "in terms of their memory formation, diaspora and nation, rather than being in opposition to each other, may have more troubling affinities than visible at first sight" (05).

OD represents local/global interrelated processes during the 1980s and 1990s and their impact on the lives of Middle-Easterners moving between Europe and the Middle-East. Rapid change and growing anxieties in the West were initially evoked by AIDS, followed by the desert storm, with George W. Bush emerging in full faith of his Christian Puritanism. Likewise, a growing fundamentalist community was developing in the Middle East, stirring instability and identity problems. News headlines intrigued the West the way mystery movies provided entertainment (*OD* 15). Conversely, in the Middle-East, global events like the Iraqi war have had their impact on the general economic status as well as the subjects' private lives, causing geographical local/global displacements.

The three male protagonists, Ibrahim, Hussein and Yasser travel to London during dictatorship in Egypt in search for alternatives. Ibrahim follows his British wife in search for better job opportunities; Hussein earns a scholarship to obtain a doctorate in law, while Yasser returns to London, his birthplace to make up for his recurrent defeats in Egypt. Wherever they go, the three protagonists remain 'resident aliens,' constantly fleeing from local and global atrocities trapping them in a closed circle of masculinity. They are perpetually wrestling within and among themselves raising unsettled questions of identification and solidarity at home and in the host country. Competitive challenges, duplicity in relationships, secretive schemes in the course of events parody detective fiction, while the search for *an* assailant remains undetermined. The fierce battle for power is experienced among compatriots and aliens alike, whether in Egyptian cities or London. The combatants cannot contain difference nor show an understanding of paradoxical relationships in order to reach each other. The final condition of withering or death awaiting the protagonists at the end of the novel is metaphorical of wreck instead of a landing. As such, *OD* becomes a critique of oppressive masculine practices, as well as ostracism in Western metropolises, thus relating the politics of dislocation in the First and Third Worlds.

My paper will focus on masculinity as represented by the three protagonists, Ibrahim, the potential narrator, Yasser, and Hussein. Until the 1970s, Egyptian fiction abounded with male characters defined by traditional attributes of masculinity, such as internal and external power, regardless of being benevolent/gracious or malevolent/reserved. The former 'hegemonic masculinity' is deconstructed in *OD;* instead of holding a unified manhood, the three male subjects are carriers of histories of frustration, and are weighed down by internal and external stress factors that mark their motivations. Part of their frustrations are due to their subscription to a traditional history in which political and social norms are governed by masculine ideals, unaware of—or unheeding a growing local/global cultural environment undermining 'hegemonic masculinity.' My aim is to trace the mutability of power male-female relationships at home and in the host country, with no change marked as a result of geographical displacement.

The discourse of masculinity is reflected in everyday speech. The narrator sardonically comments, in the opening pages that underwear garments have become of vital importance in private and public spheres. In the private sphere, they are associated with sexual fantasies/intimacies—life giving forces: whereas their importance in the public sphere is marked by their display by top stars in fashion magazines and other media which bears its impact on global economy (*OD* 16). Subsequently, the protagonists pay great attention to the quality of their underwear, and are keen on upgrading it every time they move from their provincial location to metropolitan cities. However, upgrading underwear quality does not change the-once-thought-of-timeless anachronistic masculinity the three males hold on to, and even in the new global context of the sexual revolution and feminist movement they view women as 'love objects.' Ibrahim interprets punctuation marks and digital figures in terms of the female body:

> The sign of the question mark is a woman indeed. Its suppleness in no way bears a semblance to male bodies created in the shape of the stiff English numbers—1, 7, and 4. Women resemble the remaining numbers: 2 is a penitent woman; 6 and 9, a woman tossing restlessly in bed; 5 is an expectant woman apprehending the future; whereas 3 is a corroded femininity, 8 is the fully matured woman-willowy, rounded, playful, without being shrewd or malevolent. (*OD* 239)

Contrary to the early and mid-twentieth century fiction concept of love as a liberating, self-fulfilling force, sexual desire in *OD* is no more a celebration or affirmation of life. Instead, sexual attraction is a blend of fantasy and sordid intentions, identifying women as "teats and buttocks" (*OD* 223). Men's dialogues reflect a view of sexuality based on maliciousness, false promises and baited traps. Ibrahim confesses: "'I've always loved touching women's behinds surreptitiously, in dim or crowded places" (*OD* 492). Men form a male bonding stigmatizing women as either wives or whores: "All women are skank" (*OD* 223). These males gain their sense of masculinity through sexist sniggering, while most of their talks revolve on male sexual performance; Ibrahim would describe a woman as such: "There was this gal that came to the bar with sensational panties on." Hussein comments: "Are you discrediting what panties can do? What's a human but the outcome of two panties slipped off same time and place?" *(OD* 121) By reducing partnership to a sheer physical performance, these men fail to relate to their partners, or families, their failure in private life in line with a communication failure in the public domain. The objective of their relationships at home or in the host country was not to stage a dialogue with the Other but, rather, the search for better opportunities to confirm maleness.

Masculinity determines the three protagonist's male-female relationships. It is noticeable in Ibrahim and Margaret's marital relationship since its incipience. With the decline in the tourism industry in Egypt, owing to terrorist attacks, Ibrahim, the tourist guide strikes a marriage bargain with Margaret, in the hopes of finding more job opportunities in London. Margaret is a senior British woman he inadvertently meets in downtown Cairo. In London, his failure to integrate in public life is coupled with a gradual breakdown of his conjugal relationship. His carefree attitude clashes with Margaret's uncompromising uprightness, and her patronizing attitude is confronted by cynicism on his part. Although his marital decision may have been a marker of oedipal desire, Margaret being older than his mother, as he notes, he safeguards his masculinity by resorting to physical and psychological violence to subdue her. As an Egyptian young man married to an elderly British wife, Ibrahim can only confirm his male authority within domestic space through sexual performance. In return, his wife upholds her power by castigating him physically and psychologically, by willfully declining his physical solicitations or inviting his friends without consulting him. He reacts violently when she does not heed his presence and in one situation he threatens her by sexual signaling with an iron stud. Ibrahim recounts:

> I held Margaret by the hair, and pointed the ice-breaker's tip between her thighs: "You, bitch, you think that I'm not to be respected? You're mistaken." I twisted her body bending it twofold reaching the lower kitchen cupboards. I flung the ice-breaker on the floor having it fall with a sonorous bang. I pulled up her dress and grabbed her cunt. "'I'm the man over here." I pressed it firmly, "'I'm the man over here you bitch. Out you go, do as you may." (*OD* 210)

Being 'homeless' in his home, jobless in the adopted 'promised land,' London, and at the same time finding it hard to integrate socially, Ibrahim seeks for extramarital sexual relationships to salvage his lost male power. His domestic frustrations drive him to flirt with other women he picks on London streets. He can only relate to women through his penis, but finds himself subdued, when snubbed off by their rejection. His cultural assumptions that male power is irrefutable are not tolerated by women who have managed to change the meanings attached to sexuality. The concept of "male sexuality as predatory and overpowering" (Segal 109), shaping male masochistic fantasies have been undermined by Western females braced by a feminist discourse. Ibrahim only succeeds in having an affair with Katia, a Lebanese divorced woman who returns to London to learn to master "oriental/belly dance," a recent fad in London nightclubs. He eventually becomes her victim, not the victimizer, when Katia inflames a rivalry between him and Hussein to take advantage of both.

Similarly, Hussein—the second protagonist—sustains his institutionalized subjectivity through male sexuality. Being physically handicapped he is marginalized in his hometown, and being non-Western, he is marginalized in London. Paradoxically, Hussein comes from a rural background that traditionally confers upon him supremacy for being the bread winner, the household macho, protector of the compliant wife. However, Hussein has to strive hard to sustain this traditional masculinity, a role that denies him male vulnerability. Moreover, the unbalanced marital relationship between him and his wife—Hussein being a doctorate student while Zeinab, semi-illiterate, not only drives him to bully her but also to fantasize on Katia, the Lebanese woman he meets in London: "He'd try to free his mind from dwelling on her body but failed. She's became his ultimate desire" (*OD* 89). His romantic yearning may be the "desire for the passive experience of 'domination'" (Segal 106) to make up for the socially enforced authoritative role being the man of the house. Conversely, Katia is introduced by the narrator as the wily *harem,* the sex kitten who has the upper hold on men, unlike the vulnerable wife. The following passage detects her inner thoughts.

> So what if she would get hooked to a man who wants to sleep with her, provided that he'd take her to London where she'd have the chance of becoming a belly dancer, a chance her parents denied her. So what if she'd sleep with the night-club owner who would sneakily give her flexible working hours. So what if she sleeps with the business man... who promises to lease her one of his restaurants five years exclusively. (*OD* 82)

Subsequently, Katia undermines male sexuality by subjecting men to her power. Unlike Zeinab, Hussein's wife who is subjected to his male power, Katia has her hold on him. While Zeinab is ordered back home with their children, Hussein remains subjected to two pursuits in London: his doctorate, and Katia. He tries overcoming his marginalization in London by football betting, another endeavor to prop up his masculinity.

The third male protagonist—Yasser was born in London, and returns to Egypt with his parents after his father and mother attain their doctoral degrees. During his final university academic year, Yasser develops an intimate love relationship with Marianne, a Christian girl. However, the relationship is disrupted by the death of Yasser's father, a traumatic experience that had a negative impact on his love relationship: "He leaves this flat—the flat where he was visited by love's female messenger ... in pursuit of the love of God, whereby his soul would be enveloped in solemn tranquility that cleanses ennui" (*OD* 28).[1]

The father's loss was first recompensed by a life of physical abstention, and his existential conflict eventually leads him to join a fundamentalist group. Yasser and Marianne's former inter-sectarian relationship, which signified a rapprochement with the other, bore prospects of destabilizing the supremacy of the dominant religion, as the reinstatement of 'one' sect requires the demolition of the 'other.' Once he becomes a member of a fundamentalist group, Yasser jilts Marianne during her pregnancy. He later realizes that this choice does not retrieve the sense of belonging, the now-lost maleness once sustained by his father's protection. Instead of mobilizing identification and solidarity, the fundamentalists' hierarchical organization is based on a discourse of segregation and stratification applied to all aspects of life, ranging from gender to religion. Yasser gradually discovers that his affiliation to the group does not satisfy his yearning for belonging, and he becomes physically and psychically dismembered. He becomes distanced from the group and is eventually distanced from his self: failing to find ways of being and relating, he flees to London. His constant escape problematizes the dichotomy between homeland and host country. All three male protagonists are in a perpetual condition of migrancy.

The three male protagonists' contradictory sexual pursuits become a site of politics between the vulnerability of machismo and women's resistance. Existential and political anxieties arise, machismo becoming a brace to identity and a resistance to alterity, while feminism becomes a brace to women power. The complexity of sexuality, contradictions in male-female relationships are due to differences in the constructions of social roles. Although males and females are subjects in a shared geographical location, differences ensue owing to the oppressive manner males and females relate to their bodies. As Alexander perceptively indicates, vilification and abuse in sexual relationships is on a par with a process of colonization—"a set of exploitative practices in political, ideological, and aesthetic terms, but also lined in minute ways to dualistic-hierarchical thinking" (98). The erotic and the political are closely connected: accordingly a sexuality based on masculinity establishes hierarchical thinking responsible for duality in dealings, and above all the dichotomy between the spiritual and political.

Conflicts arising from double dealings and deception are not confined within the private sphere but extend to the public sphere in the form of petty or serious crimes, fraudulent dealings and treacherous scheming. The events parody the detective genre and the reader has to trace connections to reconstitute the fragmented accounts. The book combines police and medical reports, press releases and a fictional rendition of events. Additionally, the fluctuation between fictional and non-fictional keeps the reader uncertain as to the identity of the narrator. In the book's final piece entitled "Doubt," decoding the signs in the process of reading is fraught with uncertainty for the difficulty in charging the culprit/s responsible for Ibrahim's drowning. "Doubt" is a one page document—a press release issued by a London based Arabic newspaper reporting a proclamation made by British activists about the disappearance of two British citizens, Ibrahim and Yasser in Venice. Ibrahim was found drowned on New Year Eve, while Yasser, committed suicide in an Egyptian mental clinic, shortly after. The death of both potential narrators makes the whole issues raised by the fictitious renditions or the fragment documents irresolvable.

Towards the book's end, the surface stories of a male-female relationship sink into the abyss of an age-old relationship between the West and the Middle East. The labyrinthine entanglement of events shows how the protagonists act as victims and accomplices in local and global schemes. Yasser remains subject to Middle-Eastern fundamentalist groups, as well as British and Italian secret agencies. Likewise, the reader is unable to determine whether Hussein is entangled with devious British Muslims, or a member of British espionage. As narrator, Ibrahim is the uniformed mediator, experiencing events while being unable to decode them. Ibrahim's lack of agency as subject renders him an unreliable narrator, and makes it difficult to verify the culprits involved in his final assassination by drowning. It is also difficult to determine whether the three protagonists are friends or foes, Hussein being involved in Yasser's arrest, and Yasser partly involved in Ibrahim's death. Ibrahim cheats on Margaret, his British wife, and eventually sues her when she decides on a divorce. He plays off Hussein against Yasser, and Katia against Hussein. Katia never manages to become the belly dancer she has longed to be. However, she succeeds in another domain: she knows how to pull the strings while males jerk their knees.

Eventually it becomes clear that the mutability in male-female relationships is encoded in the very title of the book *Oriental Dance.* Among the multiple insinuations of the 'oriental/belly dance'—in the Middle East—is that of 'feminine solicitation and masculine virility,' 'plotting and 'counterplotting,' 'taking risks' or 'walking on tightropes.' These significations are configured by the flow of events, where history is treated as detective fiction, and politics as spectacle. Ironically, belly dance, traditionally associated with the 'Orient' is being trained and staged in London, another sign of local/global mutability. The oriental/belly dance consecrates male-female iconic roles, enacting a game where both partners become 'subject-to' and 'subject-of' role models implementing a discourse of masculinity, and, correspondingly in *OD,* the mutability of the West and the Middle East. The oriental dance reveals that masculine discourse is not confined within a certain geographical location. The closing events are metaphorical of a hegemonic masculinity extending across First and Third Worlds, with all subjects equally involved in its making.

To recapitulate, *OD* deals with the complexities of subject relationships, gendered bodies, among Middle Easterners and

Westerners. It draws attention to the fluidity of geographical boundaries, and language barriers despite translation inaccuracies, slippage being at the heart of language. In his final visit to Rome Ibrahim comments,

> Humans share the same blood despite language divergences. We're not given the choice of whose children to be or our place of birth. Here, [in Rome] that parrot reminds me of Maria, she's also "more of a parrot: teach her Italian she'd speak it; teach her Arabic, she'd speak it"; nevertheless she remains a stranger here and there, incomprehensible to birds, and unacknowledged by one and all. (*OD* 479)

Conversations with British citizens are markers of language fluidity, being written in anglicized Arabic conveying the sense of the language, and the potential for interchangeability. Likewise, Egyptian Arabic has assimilated some Western words used in everyday speech, owing to the spread of technoculture. Potential interchangeability between languages may also be a sign of being alienated from the mother tongue and 'alien' in the host culture. Huyssen's remarks are relevant in this context: "A further point needs to be made pertaining to the changing nature of nationhood and of diaspora under global conditions. One may even suggest that whole nations are becoming diasporic in relation to their past under the pressures of global media and the maelstrom of the postnational" (60). Dividing lines between the West and the Middle East or gendered positions become imperceptible due to mutability in power roles. Power relations established by a military regime in the 1950s and 1960s, consolidated by dictatorships allied to transnational capitalism as from the 1980s have set boundaries hampering the realization of a global wholeness due to local masculinism and global colonialism. However, they have instigated new modes of resistance by the marginalized in the homeland as well as the host country, whose minority writing can deconstruct established masculinities.

NOTE

1. All translations from Arabic are mine.

REFERENCES

Abu-Lughod, Lila. *Dramas of Nationhood: The Politics of Television in Egypt.* Cairo: American UP, 2005.

Alexander, M. Jacqui. "Remembering *This Bridge,* Remembering Ourselves: Yearning, Memory and Desire." *This Bridge we call Home: Radical Visions for Transformations.* Ed. Gloria Anzaldua and Analouise Keating. NY: Routledge, 2002. 81–103.

El-Beri, Khaled. *Oriental Dance.* Cairo: Dar El-Ein Press, 2010.

Ghaill, Macan and Chris Haywood. *Gender, Culture and Society: Contemporary Masculinities and Femininities.* Hampshire: Palgrave Macmillan, 2007.

Jain, Jasbir. *Beyond Postcolonialism: Dreams and Realities of a Nation.* Jaipur: Rawat Publications, 2006.

Huyssen, Andreas. "Diaspora and Nation: Migration into Other Pasts." *New German Critique* 88 (Winter, 2003): 147–164. <http://www.jstor.org/stable/3211163>. 24 May 2011.

Saghieh, Hazim. "'That' how I am, world!' Saddam, Manhood and the Monolithic Image." *Imagined Masculinities: Male Identity and Culture in the Modern Middle East.* Ed. Mai Ghoussoub and Emma Sinclair-Webb. London: Saqi Books, 2000. 236–248.

Segal, Lynne. "Sex as Male Domination?" *The Masculinities Reader.* Ed. Stephen M. Whitehead and Frank J. Barett. Cambridge: Polity, 2001. 101–111.

CHAPTER 5

Diasporic Imagination and the Significance of Home in the Novels of Amitav Ghosh

Santosh Gupta

Amitav Ghosh has gradually emerged as one of the foremost novelists of diasporic disruptions that occurred during the expansion of Western empire in the modern age. Massive displacement of colonized populations created new political and economic developments, creating a highly affluent West and the extremely impoverished and "fatally fractured" (Punter 36) rest of the world. The displaced people underwent equally massive cultural disruptions and transformations: they were hybridized and translated in ways that they did not always welcome or value. Ghosh imagines these "historically situated" people, using Appadurai's term for some of the diasporic writers (297). He excavates India's past, which leads him to travel to ancient cities like Egypt and the silk route, and the journey of cotton in 1500 BC. He also illuminates the links of trade and cultural exchanges that were forged between many countries in the past before the modern global economy emerged when Indians traveled across the seas escaping political and economic pressures. This historical fact has gradually been forgotten in the public mind and history. This past diaspora has given rise to a focus on modern diaspora of educated professionals to the advanced, materially developed locations like the USA, Europe, and Canada. A recent statement by V.S. Naipaul on the Indian diaspora that "it does not have the edge of oppression, the culture of oppression, and the people now think of it as the middle-class movement" (77) suggests not only the continuous concern for the issue of diaspora but also the necessity to examine Ghosh's take on Indian diaspora which had begun much earlier, even before the large scale mass transportation managed by the British rulers.

Ghosh has looked at some of the phases and experiences of modern diaspora in the novels like *The Circle of Reason* (1986), *The Shadow Lines* (1988), *The Glass Palace* (2000) and *Sea of Poppies* (2008) and his non-fictional work like *In an Antique Land* (1992). In his works Ghosh has looked into the lives of a large number of common men and women and drawn to light the suppression and hardship these unsung and unrecorded countrymen went through, when they lost their mooring on their own home lands and society. As he suggests, the loss of one's native homeland moulds his/her mode of self expression, giving birth to songs, rituals and behaviors through which the displaced try to preserve his/her connection with the origin. Deterritorialized, Ghosh's characters from diverse parts of the world seek to reclaim the territories by constructing imagined communities and homelands.

"House" or "home" in this respect becomes a significant trope in the writings of several diasporic writers because a sense of belonging to the territory is one of the deepest inner attachments human beings have. As Margaret Atwood says, "Birds sing for the same reason trucks honk—to proclaim their territory: a rudimentary language" (35), it has a primeval quality that connects a human being to the world he/she lives in. Dispossession and deterritorialization thus often cause a trauma or an anxiety, which has in itself the hidden aspect of deep longing and search for the mode of language that can express the anguish of the displaced. Unfortunately, such anxiety do not always contain the optimism of obtaining "a special insight, a vision not available to the insider" (Kanaganayakam 213) or a "sublime hope" of "future visions" (Farah 5). Ghosh is not an exception in representing this sort of unresolved anxieties and constant yearning of the displaced. Depicting the complex problems of entering into the adopted home in the lives of travelers, exiles, refugees and indentured labor class of the colonial period, he has imagined their painful journeys in search of new homes. At the same time, as one of the few writers who have dealt extensively with the 'Bengal diaspora' and the shifting locations of the economically deprived class, he has articulated the emotional and cultural experiences accompanying the forced or voluntary travels across land and seas.

In particular, Ghosh, through his fictional and non-fictional writings, has not only explored the contexts in which slaves or indentured laborers who were forcefully transported across different British colonies but also depicted the plight of voluntary refugees who have been displaced through several different political regimes whether colonial or postcolonial. In drawing one's attention to the history of India and the fragmentation of geo-political space of India, Ghosh seems to ask whether it would be possible ever to "remember a postcolonialist map properly, ever to put together a coherent account of a world where histories are mysteriously over-laid?" (*The Shadow Lines* 30). In a postmodern country where histories are overlaid upon one another, Ghosh tries to extricate, through a careful excavation, the diasporic experiences of the poor, the situations of exploitation and finally the possible forms of resurgence of human dignity.

Let's take a look at *The Circle of Reason* first. The novel portrays the social turmoil in the villages of Bengal and Bihar when the Indo–Pak War of 1971 caused a new mass exodus and illegal immigrant class. The making of a new nation is accompanied by a violence that perhaps contains the seed of birth. However, the macro-level violence gets carried away to the several levels, as the fleeing refugees face both the hatred within the place of origin and the distrust in the new areas of settlement. In *The Circle of Reason*, thus, Ghosh makes detailed portrayals of the economic and social disturbances caused by these newcomers in the places where they made unwanted guests and their attempts to slide underground as a survival strategy. Having lost their original home in East Bengal, these migrated hordes have no energy for participation in the new war: they are burdened with "memory" or "a longing for a land where the grass was greener, the rice whiter, [and] the fish bigger than boats" (*The Circle of Reason* 59). He then captures poignantly their inconsolable longing and nostalgia which all migrants (whatever the variety) probably have in common.

In *The Shadow Lines*, as in *The Circle of Reason*, Ghosh raises important issues of national identity and a sense of belonging to a nation while dealing with the issue of constant re-drawings of the national maps. In this complicatedly structured novel built upon the memories of a large number of characters and the young (unnamed) narrator's memories of his adoring uncle Tridib, Ghosh spreads his canvas wide enough to contain the characters traveling between India and England and at the same time governed by unconscious longings and desires. At the outset, the young narrator's family is presented as divided when part of the family migrated to the developed West, seeking better prospects there at the time of independence. The young boy, however, remembers all the tales his uncle Tridib used to recount to rapt the audience at the street tea shop, a typical *adda* of Indian towns in the 1950s. Bringing together the recollections of almost a century through telling the life experiences of three generations of people, Ghosh represents the postcolonial society as caught up in its varying degrees of imitativeness, mimicry, and the *angst* of the young generation's search for a new, modern, internationally valid identity. He represents that young men and women are also framed within the shadows of colonial desires for the White: Ila loves Nick Price, and Tridib does May Price. The young narrator follows these two—whom he endears very deeply and suffers with them as they experience un-relinquished love. He, too, travels to the West, mainly to London where he, like Ila and Tridib, seeks a fulfillment that eludes all of them eventually.

However, the eruption of violence on the grounds of religious sentiments and the consequential waste of lives shock the young narrator when he was a school-going child in 1964. It is much later that he reflects upon the simultaneous outbursts in cities like Srinagar, Calcutta and Dhaka, and wonders how hatred has been binding these communities, although they lay in two countries. He takes out a map and tries to ascertain their geographical distances. Their physical separation, he realizes, did not matter because below the surface of apparent reality, they were bound together in the strong links of shared history, memories, and faith. Logical reasoning fails to explain the emotional forces that govern, divide, and put together these mobs in different countries and the "indivisible sanity" that bound the "people to each other, independently of their governments" (*The Shadow Lines* 230).

The death of Tridib as he tries to protect his beloved May during the mob riots in Dhaka gives a final revelation for the young narrator. He has tried, like Tridib, to look beyond the conflicting inheritance of colonial past and its consequential division of the space, culture, and history of the nation. This young narrator, then, experiences a moment of schizophrenic split of subjecthood as he looks at the figure of Nick Price within his own subconscious self. The novel not only articulates this split of the subject formation of the postcolonial self but also attempts to explore some mode of transcendence of such split. R. Radhakrishnan comments on this psychological conflict presented through the recurrent images of "mirror" and "window." He argues that there is in *The Shadow Lines* a concern how to realize a critical and mutually transformative relationship between "mirrors" and "windows" (104–05). He writes that such questions as "under what circumstances do mirrors that reflect the self back to itself become the windows that open out to the others outside, and when do windows that provide a vision "outside" for the self become the surface of self-recognition?" are critical in understanding the dynamics of the post-modern self-formation (104–05). As he sees, Tridib's personality represents a class of utopian-cosmopolitan Indian intellectuals who emerged in the nineteenth century. His love for May, though cut short by his violent death, can be viewed as an attempt to override the asymmetrical positions of their colonized-colonizer past. He suggests that "the historical traces and unevenness will not allow any attempts to universalize or allegorize the meaning of their love" (108). Downplaying the conflicting postcolonial background, Radhakrishnan asserts that Ghosh has tried, through Tridib, to focus on "possibilities of persuasion and understanding across and beyond boundaries" (109).

The formation of the identity is certainly an important theme for Ghosh. The impact of colonial aggression which "fatally fractured" the Indian subcontinent becomes the region fit for the excavation of the history of the expansion and strengthening of the empire over India and Burma. Ghosh's observations and researches into the centuries of expansion of the Western empires in India, China, Burma, Middle East, and Mauritius are meticulously recorded through these two epic novels *The Glass Palace* (2000) and *Sea of Poppies* (2008). In *The Glass Palace* Ghosh shows how the Indians, who had to leave Burma under Burmese nationalist movement, harbor a similar reminiscence about the wealth and grandeur they had left behind. Alur, a young refugee boy, is unable to find a new home in the place he has arrived, which is Lalpukur, a small village. Unknowingly he incurs the wrath of the local Police officer and has to run away once again from Lalpukur to avoid being persecuted on false allegations of being a terrorist. He then travels to Kerala and from there to the fabulous city of Al-Ghazira, a haven for all kinds of travelers. There he encounters many companions traveling on frail vessels and finds that they risked their lives as they escaped unfavorable conditions of their homeland and traveled "To the West!" Nonetheless, Alur and his companions (an assorted group) are willing to travel and face such a risk.

In *The Glass Palace* Ghosh also narrates in a slow-moving and yet very detailed manner the lives of different classes within the colonial societies of Burma and India. His world includes the last Burmese King and Queen, and their family, who were sent to India in exile in 1885, just as the last Indian Emperor, Bahadur Shah Zafar, was sent in exile and imprisonment to Rangoon, in Burma. These lines were drawn upon the ancient nations' bodies, which were constantly in use as more people were transported from one land to the other. Then, Ghosh presents a multi-checkered South Asian society where several nations, religions and communities co-exist, and interact with one another under changing circumstances. He introduces King Thebaw, the last of the Burmese monarch, and depicts how his whole political system collapses under the hard-hitting of the British military and how street tea-shop owner Ma and her friend Saya John, Rajkumar, and an orphan drifting on a raft, come to travel from Chittagong to the port of Rangoon a day or two before the deposition of the King. Through King Thebaw's eyes and experiences Ghosh portrays a wide range of events, encompassing a great deal of historical and social developments.

Another important theme investigated in this epic portrayal of the colonial period is the devastation caused by the two World Wars and the consequential emergence of a new political consciousness in the entire region. Ghosh particularly emphasizes on the link between the capitalistic economic pulls and the expansion of empire. The whole political setup was inextricably tied up with the expanding market and appropriation of raw material which England and other countries urgently required for their industrialization during the eighteenth and the nineteenth centuries. In fact, the dependency of the West upon India, China, Africa and other locations was so great that it is appropriate for Ghosh to present the imperial enterprises in this context. Marxist economic scholar Sreeram Krishnaswami examines the "Colonial Foundations of Western Capitalism," arguing that "capitalist accumulations and development as occurred in Western Europe had its material basis in the dynamics of colonialism" (PE-86). Krishnaswami critiques that the theories and explanations of industrialization in the West have been made only in the context of the West's innovative entrepreneurial and scientific spirit by many western scholars. Yet he believes that the rate of exploitation of slave labor and the use of colonies as free market where the English traders earned more than 100 per cent or 200 per cent profits were among the reasons bringing unprecedented level of wealth to the ruling countries. According to him,

> Under colonialism, the overall rate of exploitation could be increased substantially by using slave-labor with its almost infinite rate of exploitation—or super-exploited labor in the colonies while keeping the rate of exploitation constant in the core or even allowing it to decrease it (i.e., allowing real wages to increase. (PE-88)

Thinking in the grain of the "infinite level of exploitation" of slave labor, Krishnaswami points out, one also becomes aware of the painful fact that Reform movements in the metropolitan cities or in England provided better wages and living conditions to their own poor class when exploitation surpassed all norms of human tolerance in the colonies. Each of Ghosh's novels thus depict some of the modes of colonial control and economic exploitation executed by those who held the policy of free trade and employed worst forms of coercion for their benefit. In particular, he looks into how the colonies were treated as free-markets, substantially increasing the gains of the traders who turned into cruel rulers.

In *Sea of Poppies* Ghosh, foregrounding the human figure, builds up the elaborate political game British traders deployed during the early part of the nineteenth century and describes a greatly moving account of Indians who found themselves being transported as indentured laborers or prisoners. His extensive research into the social world of Calcutta during the whole century reflects the training he has had as an anthropologist. However, it is his ability to create the subalterns who played different roles, working in the fields, opium-factories, and on the ship. His presentation of half white American and British tradesmen also makes this novel so profoundly meaningful.

Of course, Ghosh has already revealed his humanist concern for subaltern characters who struggle against the oppressive circumstances in *The Glass Palace*. In this slow-moving narrative he portrays such characters as Rajkumar, Dolly, and Arjun with more depth than the others. The awareness levels of these characters may vary, as their interests are different. Responding individually to the social and economic pressures, they emerge as fully developed human beings. For instance, Rajkumar is one of the central characters whose movements across India and Burma hold the narrative together from the opening section to its end. Although the end of the novel describes the last few days of Rajkumar's life, the incidents are narrated by one of the grandchildren who belongs to the third generation. Dolly, a beautiful handmaid of the Queen Supayalat and three princesses in India, goes through several life-exchanging experiences. Her story moves along with other narrative strands, in which Rajkumar makes his way up to the new economic structure in the colonial Burma. Indian middle class characters like Beni Prasad Dey, Uma Dey, and Arjun are those who represent the new political consciousness that had swept across the colonies during the period of two World Wars. As I have argued in another context,[1] the relationship between Arjun and Kishen who are in the Imperial British Army reflect the moral crisis that was experienced by the younger generation. Ghosh describes that "Arjun echoes the colonialists' claims that the Indians in British Services are the first true Indians, for they have left behind the considerations of caste, religion and orthodox rituals in their food habits, etc." (*The Glass Palace* 221). However, it is not apparent to him that he was simply a mimic man "with not real identity of his own" (*The Glass Palace* 221). Fighting on the battlefield, he experiences a major crisis in himself when he realizes his complete immersion in and brain-washing by the British colonial discourse. He becomes conscious that as a colonized he has become a tool of the British system, perpetuating injustice upon those against whom he is fighting. Arjun now understands that he has been acting out the will of his masters, having no free will of his own (*The Glass Palace* 429). His attendant, Kishen Singh, a lower level soldier, brings to him the historical awareness of colonial subjugation as he tells Arjun of the extreme rule of terror carried out by the British upon the natives after the war of independence in 1857. Arjun comes to recognize his own helplessness through a visionary hallucination in which he sees himself and Kishen as "lumps of clay, whirling on the potter's wheels" (*The Glass Palace* 431). He finally realizes that he has been molded like a lump of clay by the ruler's discourse, which has given him an entirely wrong understanding of words like "modern," "freedom" and being an "Indian." It is after a great deal of self enquiry that he comes to obtain a sign of his own thinking. Arjun's hard decision to desert the British Army, thus, has severe repercussions. The large scaled rebellion in the nationalist movement becomes an important form of psychological turning point. Through resistances at an individual level Arjun, Uma Dey, and other characters gain both a renewed sense of identity and freedom and a sense of agency coming to the colonized individuals.

Whereas Ghosh merges history, fiction, and economic data one another and dissolves the borders of genres in order to create his distinct narrative style in *The Glass Palace,* the political significance of national interest and sovereignty becomes more important in *Sea of Poppies*. Just as in *The Glass Palace,* the characters in *Sea of Poppies* constantly travel across national borders, making national borders insignificant. Yet, in this novel Ghosh makes arguments of free trade and free markets in the same breath as the talks of national characters and interests. During the eighteenth and the nineteenth centuries when foreign traders made their entry, the trades between the industrialized European countries and the regions in Asia were recognized as a central issue by the Indian

Kings. Girish Karnad in *The Dreams of Tipu Sultan* (1999) foregrounds Tipu Sultan's perception of the mercenary goals of the conquests by the British and how Tipu Sultan tried to thwart them by building up his own financial resources. Novels by Indo-English writers of the nineteenth century either dwelled upon the political aspects of the spread of the empire or romanticized the encounter between the native and the White individual man or woman. Few Indian writers have focused on the great significance of the economic enterprises of the British in the colonial period. *Sea of Poppies* is one of the few novels, although written in the recent times about the colonial period, which foregrounds the vast structures built by English colonial rulers to manage production, collection, and marketing of opium in the late eighteenth and early nineteenth centuries.

Sea of Poppies moves around the various jobs involved around the highly commercial crop opium and its impact not only on the farmers, their lives and village economy but also on the British policies in India and China. Beginning with the simple peasant woman, Deeti (full name Aditi), the novel then moves into the social lives and the business deals of English tradesmen, who had amassed great wealth from their legal and illegal business practices. In the discussion carried among British characters, the market in China is described to be closed as the Qing rulers of China resisted the import of opium. Mr Burnham, Mr Justice Kendalbushe, and Mr Doughty all express their unhappiness at the prospect of losing their expected profits in case Qing-China actually bans the opium trade. The irony of their approach lies in their profession of "benefits of free trade" (*Sea of Poppies* 259) because they also consider waging a war with the Chinese in order to impose opium on their market. India and China are important to them as vast markets, so that they are prepared to take any measures to retain them intact. When one of their colleagues, Captain Chillingworth, speaks a little of the impending battle bluntly calling it "butchery," the Judge very calmly says, "I am sure there will be no more killing than is strictly necessary. There is always a price, is there not, for doing good?" (*Sea of Poppies* 262).

In the meantime, Calcutta during the early nineteenth century saw the sudden emergence of new British *nabobs,* whereas the Bengali aristocrats were losing their wealth, position, and grandeur. In Neel Dhari Haldar's careless business deals and subsequent failures, one finds a complacency and self-confidence, accompanying guaranteed social and economic privileges. It was the British invasion that pulled the rug under the feet of all those privileged Indians, which treated them with contempt and sharpness. Neel undergoes the imprisonment when he is unable to pay the money he owes to an Englishman and loses all the certainties of his life. He is shamed and humiliated constantly by the prison officials who enjoy vindictive pleasure in his suffering. Like other novels of the decline of the aristocracy in India by writers like Prem Chand (Hindi: *Godan*) and Bimal Mitra (Bengali: *Sahib, Bibi and Ghulam*), Ghosh shows a swift displacement of this class from its privileged position.

In *Sea of Poppies* Ghosh, with cleverly organized narrative strokes, brings the varied groups of the Indians and British officers together on board the ship "Ibis." Again, there appear several classes functioning in a strictly enforced hierarchy: the indentured labor class, prisoners like Neel and a Chinese who is his cell-mate and is deported to Mauritius for life imprisonment, a French girl Paulette, running away from a forced marriage to an elderly English man, guardsmen who belong to the village from which Deeti and Kalua have run away, and finally a big group of sailors and lascars who came from different countries. These groups are bound together in an equally strict and rigid hierarchical division of space within the ship. The lower part of the ship holds the indentured "girmitiyas" tightly in an inadequate space, while the prisoners are kept in an adjoining cell. On the main deck, two guards keep a watchful eye on the sailors, prisoners, and laborers. It becomes an extended metaphor of a colonial territory, since the oppression is reproduced here on the basis of caste, class, and gender as it had been on the mainland.

Ghosh's brilliant depiction of the vast array of characters explains his consummate skills in etching a clearly recognizable character with distinct personality in minimal strokes. The saga of peasants and aristocracy losing land and possessions and being forced to go through transportation and unrelenting cruelties is described in detail on the basis of verifiable factual information and data. Yet, the great quality of human compassion arises from Ghosh's controlled and detached authorial tone which avoids any excessive emotional emphasis or decorative rhetoric. Ghosh also balances the cruelties and the atrocities committed by British officers with equally horrifying or repelling acts of indignity imposed on the discriminated human bodies. In the painful saga of colonial oppression the actors are not only the outsiders: their inhumanity becomes less outrageous when put against the acts committed by the village's upper caste men such as Thakurs and Bhyron Singh and the acts by family members upon a helpless young subaltern woman. The extent in which Indian men and women could go to rub in their power or social position is witnessed in the novel and makes one reflect upon the already existing forms of social oppression and injustice in the pre-colonial India. *Sea of Poppies* portrays equally the shortcomings and the evil tendencies rooted in human psyches when they enjoy social and political privileges and when they overuse their power over subaltern groups. In Ghosh's portrayal there are no extremity or dehumanization but unrelenting honesty and truthfulness.

Further, Ghosh incorporates in his novels the immense range of dialects of Indian social groups, which is the pidgin that takes shape as people using different languages interact with one another on land and on sea. In the business and social circles of Calcutta, the English pick up words from Urdu, the local Bengali dialect, just as the Indian gradually learn new English words. Ghosh presents these hybrid cultural formations and also depicts how the lascars—the seamen, who came from all the different ports on the Indian Ocean—mix their languages to communicate successfully. The American sailor Zacharay learns quickly these shades of dialects as he converses with Serang Ali, a lascar and Mr Burnham, a senior British officer. In the group of indentured laborers, too, the new changes of language and behavior give rise to a sense of hybridity that later grows fuller when they landed on their destined places. When a marriage ceremony is performed in the small enclosed space of a cabin, they make creative reinterpretations of the rituals. The songs of marriage celebration and the marriage rituals are all improvised. The way how these new ways hold over the crowd is really impressive and hilarious. Bending the traditions to existential needs becomes the guiding principle for these displaced people, who are caught in the process of becoming hybridized and translated into new cultural patterns.

Ghosh's novel *The Hungry Tide* (2004) examines further the significance of language in communicating the deeper truths of one's experience. Although the novel is about Kanai Dutt's uncle (now dead) and aunt who had moved away from Calcutta some thirty years ago to a small village, it brings together some very important issues of exile, cultural transformations, and the people's struggle to have their own land. Nirmal is a Marxist by belief and gets sent away by his own Party at one occasion in order to keep him out of meddling with the Party affairs when it comes to power in West Bengal. He is involved with a local people's uprising in a small island called Morichjhapi, where hundreds of displaced refugees were first given some land to settle down. This event becomes a turning point in his life because he sincerely wants to help those who were victimized by the government's inability to rehabilitate them.

Actually, Morichjhapi uprising and the Leftist government's cruel handling of the poor men and women trying to save their cottages has left a trail of unwelcome criticism. It has also become a black spot in the history of the government that claims to represent the masses of poor people. *The Hungry Tide* looks closely at the difficulties of perceiving in correct perspectives the lives of the marginalized social groups living on the very margin of land itself and constantly being threatened by extinction even when they wage a struggle for survival. The threats to their lives and livelihood are manifold: the extremely difficult terrain of Sunderbans is full of mangrove forests where land melts into water, as it were, and where man-eating tigers prowl and snatch away human bodies as food. In such a setting comes Kanai Dutt, a Delhi based translator who knows six languages and earns a living with his language skills. Piyali Roy also arrives, who is from the USA where her parents had migrated several years ago. She now works as a cetologist, a marine biologist, and comes to the Sunderbans region to study Asian river dolphins. Both meet at a railway station and reach Lusibari village where Kanai's aunt Nilima has called him.

Their different objectives in traveling to this remote village come together at one point, and they become friendly.

In this novel Ghosh also presents the lives of poor fishermen, their families, and their harsh natural environments, which eventually make the outsiders gradually recognize the great courage and personal strength of the main characters and the forbearance of simple village folks. Piya is attracted towards Fokir, a poor fisherman, who takes her to see the dolphins in their natural habitat. In a sudden storm he dies after he saves her from being drowned by the waves. Ghosh illuminates how the displacement disturbs all ecology including the tiger, the dolphin, and human beings. The refugees who were beaten by the state police have scattered to different areas and try to gain a foothold somewhere. The two, Kanai and Piyali, came as travelers but witnessed the plight of the poor fishing community. In trying to organize some aid system for them, they return to the village and hope to build a foothold or a new home through shared work, knowledge, and sympathy.

In conclusion, Ghosh's novels suggest that human suffering has been worsened by a series of the inhumane political and economic policies of state governments and the self-interests of domestic and international power wielders. Ghosh shows his humanist concerns by laying bare the systems that exploit less privileged groups in the society, especially when they are driven away from their homeland to new places, new cultures, and new societies. At the same time, with his natural talents and artistic skills he tells the stories of miseries that put millions of migrating hordes under the grip of uncaring authorities with rational objectivity and compassion. Each of Ghosh's novels depicts with great concern the lives of the downtrodden, forgotten, and unrecognized people. And, each novel comes up with a better narrative than the earlier ones and directs his readers' attention more to the marginalized people, geographically fragmented areas, and forgotten periods of Indian history.

Indeed, a wide range of powerless and suffering characters and humanist themes Ghosh represents in his novels reflect his deep understanding and compassion of human beings and thus puts him in the tradition of great humanistic Indian writers like

Rabindranath Tagore, Prem Chand, and Mulk Raj Anand. Further, his profound understanding and artistic sensitivity manifest in representing the diasporic experiences of the masses suggest that he has been writing in the tradition of those great twenty first century writers who have articulated the sufferings of the silenced and marginalized masses like Orhan Pamuk, Salman Rushdie, Mahasweta Devi, and Toni Morrison. Ghosh's humane, polyphonic and multi-hued works are worthy of being called great world literature that will enrich readers with acute understanding of the human values of the minority people.

NOTE

1. Santosh Gupta, "Self within the Shadows of History: Amitav Ghosh's *The Glass Palace," Literary Constructs of the Self*. Ed. Santosh Gupta and Mini Nanda (Jaipur: Rawat, 2010).

REFERENCES

Appadurai, Arjun. "Disjuncture and Difference in the Global Cultural Economy." *Theory, Culture and Society* 7 (1990): 2–3.

Atwood, Margaret. *Surfacing*. New York: Simon and Schuster, 1973. 35

Farah, Nuruddin. "Homing in on the Pigeon." *Brick* 48 (1994): 4–9.

Ghosh, Amitav. *The Circle of Reason*. New Delhi: Roli Books International 1986.

——. *The Shadow Lines*. 1988 New Delhi: Oxford UP, 1995.

——. *The Glass Palace*. New Delhi: Ravi Dayal, 2000.

——. *The Hungry Tide*. New Delhi: Ravi Dayal, 2004.

——. *Sea of Poppies*. New Delhi: Penguin, Viking, 2008.

Gupta, Santosh. "Self within the Shadows of History: Amitav Ghosh's *The Glass Palace*." *Literary Constructs of the Self*. Ed. Santosh Gupta and Mini Nanda. Jaipur: Rawat, 2010.

——. "Translating Silence: The Limits of Language in Amitav Ghosh's *The Hungry Tide*." *Contemporary Interrogations: Language and Literature*. Ed. Sunita Agrawal. Jaipur: Book Enclave, 2008. 255–261.

Kanaganayakam, Chelva. "Exiles and Expatriates." *New National and Postcolonial Literatures: An Introduction*. Ed. Bruce King. Oxford: New Clarendon, 1996.

Karnad, Girish. "The Dreams of Tipu Sultan." *Two Plays by Girish Karnad*. New Delhi: Oxford UP, 1999.

Krishnaswami, Sreeram. "Colonial Foundations of Western Capitalism." *Economic and Political Weekly* 27, 30. (July 1992): PE-81–89.

Naipaul, V.S. "Diaspora." *India Today*. The Millennium Series 2. June 2000.

Punter, David. *Postcolonial Imaginings: Fictions of a New World Order*. New Delhi: Atlantic, 2000. 30.

Radhakrishnan, R. *Theory in an Uneven World*. UK: Blackwell, 2003.

Steiner, George. "The Mind in Winter: Reflections on Life in Exile." Manjit Inder Singh, "Between History and Cultural Politics: Reflections on Punjabi Writing of the Diaspora." *Diaspora: Theories, Histories, Texts*. Ed. Makarand Paranjpe. New Delhi: IndiaLog, 2001. 107.

CHAPTER 6

The Burden of History

Ko Un's Poetry as a Political and Philosophical Act

Jihee Han

KO UN'S PLACE IN THE HISTORY OF MODERN KOREAN POETRY

Ko Un (1933–) is probably the most widely known Korean poet to international readers as well as to domestic readers. His books of poems have been translated in Arabic, Chinese, Czech, English, French, German, Italian, Japanese, Norwegian, Polish, Spanish, Swedish, and Vietnamese. He was not only awarded with major domestic prizes but also garnered some international recognition with such prizes as Bjornson Order for Literature (2005), Swedish Literary Cikada Prize (2006), Lifetime Achievement Prize by Canada (2008), and The American Awards for a Lifetime Contribution to International Writing (2011). Recently many world-famous poets have recognized him as "one of the most important poets of our time" (Robert Hass), "a magnificent poet, a combination of Buddhist cognoscente, passionate political libertarian, and naturalist historian" (Allen Ginsberg) and appreciated "his Zen insights" (Gary Snyder) and "his language with the intensity" in poetry reading (Michael McClure).[1] In addition, many world-wide literary magazines and newspapers published articles on Ko Un's literature.

Despite his international recognition as well as domestic fame, however, there still remains some hesitation among Korean critics about giving Ko Un full credit to his poetic achievements. Some acknowledge his literary significance as a *Minjung* poet (poet of the masses), but others still imply that his literary recognition was formed based upon his political activism in the turbulent periods of Korean history: they find his voice too emotionally charged and also his poetic messages too didactic. The dual assessment surrounding Ko Un's poetic achievements becomes more apparent when investigating two recent books dealing with the history of Korean poetry from the 1950s to the 1990s, which are *The History of Korean Poetry* (2007) and *Modern Korean Literature* (2008). In these books Ko Un is described as one of the representative poets who warranted visionary anger for the masses and explored the sociopolitical grounds of 'Engagement Literature.' Nevertheless, he is placed behind the highly esteemed group of engagement poets such as Shin Dong-yeop, Kim Ji-ha, Kim Nam-jo and Shin Kyeong-nim in terms of representativeness in Korean *Minjung* poetry.

To take a more detailed look at the critical receptions of Ko Un, in the 1950s when Ko Un just started his poetic career, Pak In-hwan, Jeon Bong-geon, Song Wuk, and Shin Dong-yeop had already been leading the literary community with aesthetic nihilism, cynical social criticism, or nationalist vision for the unification of two Koreas. In the 1960s when Ko Un was inclined toward pessimism and aesthetic nihilism of his predecessors, Kim Su-young and Kim Chun-su, as Nam Ki-hyeok and Lee Gwang-ho evaluate, introduced Western philosophies and Anglo-European avant-garde poetry. They were already setting the new theoretical stage for Korean modernist poetry, publishing highly aesthetic and intellectual poetry. In the 1970s, when Ko Un was noticed as a *Minjung* poet, his contemporaries Kim Ji-ha, Shin Kyeong-nim, and Seo Jeong-ju, whom Lee Hye-won notes as representative *Minjung* poets, were making creative poetic experiments and ground-breaking *Minjung* poetry in terms of poetic subjects, forms, and themes. For instance, Kim incorporated traditional folk oral genres such as *Pansori* and *Minyo* into his poems and explored the new potential of Korean long narrative poem based upon the traditional folk communal sensibility. Making a similar poetic experiment, Shin focused more on representing the uprooted, displaced lives of poor tenant farmers and under-privileged low class people and tried to creatively modernize the unique rhythm of traditional folksong genre *Minyo*. Most significantly, Seo, absorbing Western poetic theories and techniques and incorporating his mythic imagination into modern temporality, extended the range of Korean poetry. In the book of poems entitled *The Myth of Jilmajae* he created a pre-modern mythic space, called *Jilmajae,* and manifested his critical meditation on modern Korean life. He not only assimilated regional dialects and vulgar slangs in his poetry but also represented the simple lifestyle and manners of lowly villagers, unsophisticated but warm folk humanism, and finally a unique Korean communal sensibility which gradually came to dissolve in the fast pace of industrialization and urbanization in the 1970s. In the 1980s when Ko Un was finally named as one of the representatives of Korean poetry, he was still less seriously taken than other leading poets such as Hwang Ji-wu and Kim Nam-jo in terms of resistance spirit and revolutionary pathos. For instance, Yu Seong-ho acclaims Kim, instead of Ko Un, as "the most outstanding warrior-poet," saying that Kim's language is charged with "anti-foreign intervention, vision for the unification, and democracy" and has "a voice range of the most accomplished base singer in Korean lyric poetry" (197). In the 1990s when Ko Un continued to write *Ten Thousand Lives* he had started in 1986 and kept pursuing the *Hwaeum* vision of life, Korean poetry was at a turning point in terms of poetic representation. A young generation of poets such as Yu Ha, Lee Seong-bok, and Kim Hye-sun were not interested in exploring the socio-political ground for poetic engagement any more. Instead, they started to experiment with the fantasy world, viewing it as a post-modern poetic medium to explore the isolated self or split subjectivity in the face of urbanization, commercial capitalism, and individualism. Looking over the poetic changes in the history of Korean poetry, Ko Un seems to have always been a little late in terms of catching the zeitgeist of the times as well as of challenging the poetic tradition of previous decades.

Furthermore, even when it comes to the assessment of his poetic excellence, Ko Un's misfortune seems to continue. Often critics would read his engagement poetic voice negatively as "howling," "empty shouting," "sentimental sobbing," "venting out," and so on. Lee Sung-won, regardless of acknowledging the fact that Ko Un "ardently poured out his passionate engagement spirit and wrote resistance poetry," maintains a cynical view that as is evidenced in "the radical, empty catch phrase-like lines" of "Arrows" and "The Road at Dawn," his poetic artistry leaves much to be desired and remains "an incendiary propaganda wearing a suit of poetry" (459). Pak Hyeon-su, although complimenting *Ten Thousand Lives* for manifesting "the new horizon of *Minjung* poetry" (485), reveals the ambiguous attitude of the current critical community toward Ko Un's poetry: he neither makes an in-depth analysis of individual poems nor tries to illuminate Ko Un's real innovations and tribal imagination. These somewhat cursory and often unfair assessments of Ko Un's poetic achievements haven't much changed so far. His poems after 1993, thus, are virtually waiting to be analyzed and estimated from a more balanced perspective. At the same time his last poetic phase after 1993 needs to be identified and addressed in connection to the previous ones in his whole poetic career. Therefore, this essay makes an attempt to re-examine Ko Un's literary significance as a *Minjung* poet and then to make a due critical approach to the literary significance of *Ten Thousand Lives* while illuminating his unique Korean *Minjung* poetics.

KO UN'S POETRY AS A POLITICAL ACT[2]

Given the continuous political upheavals that unfolded throughout Korean history in the twentieth century, Korean writers have never had a chance to stand outside history. They went through the colonial period, the Emancipation, the Korean War, and the Partition of two Koreas, and the almost-three-decade military dictatorship. They also witnessed how the masses of *Mincho* (the grass roots) who had always been regarded as the foundation of Korea continued to be oppressed under the discourses of the powerful without having their voices heard. *Mincho* subjects had little means to claim their human rights before the powerful *Yangban* rulers in pre-modern Joseon-Korea. In the Japanese colonial period, with their mother tongue politically suppressed, they had to give up their own native names and live as subjects of Japanese empire; in the 1950s with their families divided and disconnected due to the Korean War and the consequential Partition, they had to restrain themselves and put most efforts in surviving in the rubble and ruins of their home towns; in the 1960s, the 70s and the 80s with their freedom of speech completely suppressed under dictatorial regimes, they held back their angry tears to witness a series of brutal suppression of civil rights' movements and supported democratic groups in silence; since the 1990s under the government's discourses of geopolitical threats and capitalism they found their little voices easily dubbed as dangerous to the sound economic development of the country.

At the center of political turmoil Ko Un has also witnessed the woeful state of *Mincho* people and the waste of young lives in anti-dictatorial demonstrations. However, it seems to be the tragic death of Jeon Tae-il that left an indelible mark on his mind. Jeon Tae-il was one of the factory laborers, who committed a public burning of himself in 1970 as a way of protesting against the Park regime's suppression of laborers' human rights. His final cry, "We are not machines. We want a proper labor law. Do not brush off my death," moved the whole nation and truly Ko Un, s he confesses in an interview. He recalls Jeon's noble self-sacrifice shattered him so thoroughly that he had to take some time for probing into his conscience and reassessing the strategy of intelligentsia-led, ideology-driven political resistance. This deep introspection, as he looks back, virtually catapults him from the state of intellectual torpor to a radical awakening to the necessity for connecting his poetry to political activism. Since 1971, thus, he decides to stand at the forefront of political protests and becomes a major force in establishing the Council of Korean Civil Rights Movement.

Further, Ko Un breaks from his previous lyrical poetry predominant with pessimism and aesthetic nihilism and begins to write *Minjung* poetry, appealing to general readers to restore the lofty *Minjung* spirit of the past. In fact, *Minjung* literally means the masses of the people, but in Korean historical, cultural, and political contexts *Minjung* means those downtrodden people who are socially disadvantaged and economically exploited and yet have political agency to organize protests and be willing to sacrifice their lives for the cause of Justice. Generally, their political agency is traced back to the late Joseon-Korea through Jeon Bong-jun's

Donghak Uprising. In 1894 about ten thousand poor farmers oppressed by heavy taxation and ruthless treatment armed themselves under the leadership of Jeon Bong-jun and engaged in armed struggles against the rotten regional governors and the corrupt officials. They spoke up their voices of anti-feudal system, anti-Japanese colonial ambition, and the freedom of their indigenous religion *Donghak*. Although the *Donghak Uprising* was soon suppressed with the execution of Jeon Bong-jun, it has been recognized as one of the most significant historical events in which illiterate farmers proved their own capacity to put their subjective thought into action in times of severe oppression and national emergency. From then on, there have been many common heroes who sacrificed their lives fighting for Justice, and Jeon Tae-il would be rightfully honored as one of *Donghak* farmers' descendents. Therefore, having a deep meditation on factory laborer Jeon Tae-il's self-sacrifice and the plight of the masses of contemporary working class people, Ko Un decides to seriously pursue the poetic task of re-imagining Korean *Minjung* and also to call for their political agency to rise up against *Yushin* autocracy. "Arrows"[3] is one of the famous *Minjung* poems written in this period:

> Let's become arrows
> Charge our bodies and
> pierce through the air.
> Charge our bodies
> Charge and never come back.
> Plunge our bodies deep
> [into the flesh of the enemy],
> Choose to be rotten there and
> never come back.
>
> Let's hold our breath tight and
> dart from the bowstring.
> What we have achieved
> for many decades
> What we have enjoyed
> for many decades
> What we have constructed
> for many decades
> Happiness or

> What not
> Let's leave all behind like tatters
> and charge our whole bodies
> as arrows.
>
> The void roars out
> Let's charge our whole bodies and
> pierce through the air.
> In the dark midday
> our target dashes at us.
> Until it stumbles spitting blood,
> only once [in our lifetime]
> let's all become arrows
> and bleed as such.
>
> Let's never come back!
> Never come back!
> Oh, arrows, the nation's arrows, fighters, Souls of the fallen heroes! ("Arrows," *A Wind*, 74–75)

In this poem Ko Un compares the monstrous power of *Yushin* autocracy to "the dark midday" whose oxymoronic phrase strongly suggests the absurdity of the 1970s' reality. Seemingly urging *Minjung* citizens to become "arrows" to end the political monster he himself makes a sincere pledge to dedicate himself to the process of building a new democratic government despite the fact that he might "never come back." Finally he commemorates those who would sacrifice their lives as "the nation's arrows" and "souls of the fallen heroes," reminding readers of *Minjung*'s resistance spirit in Korean history. Although the poem's diction sounds propagandistic, it still resonates with the austere protest/resistance spirit of the 1970s. Choi Won-shik finds the significance of this poem in Ko Un's truthful dedication to the cause of protest literature of the 1970s. Though "not having literary sophistication," Choi sees Ko Un's "Arrows" as responding to the political manifesto of Jang Jun-ha, a representative revolutionary leading the 1970s democratic movement. In "The Road of a Nationalist" (1978) Jang once challenged the conformism of academia and the passivity of the intelligentsia:

> Is any form of unification good? I think so. There is no higher cause than unification. ... If all my ideas, ideologies, social

> positions, material wealth, honor do not add up to result in the nation's unification but result from the partition, I think I have to give up my privilege. Without self-sacrifice, the unification of two Koreas will never be realized. This might be another form of treason. ("The Road of a Nationalist," qtd. in Choi 81, my translation)

In the dim, gloomy reality of Yushin autocracy Jang pointed out the necessity for self-sacrificing leadership which would open a new democratic future of Korea. Ko Un seems to respond to his call by pledging his dedication to political activism as well as by summoning *Minjung*'s civil disobedience to end the dictatorial regime. Combining his bold announcement of self-sacrifice with his propagandist purpose, thus, he stands out as a *Minjung* poet and lifts his voice up to urge common readers to participate in taking collective responsibility for nation-building.

As he started to carve himself out as a *Minjung* poet, however, Ko Un was initially viewed as getting an easy ride in '*Minjung* Prostest Poetry' thanks to the turbulent political situations of the day. As some critics indicate, in this period his poetry seems to sound like howling charged with raw emotions, and his poetic messages seem to be very didactic and propagandistic. However, critics paid little attention to the spiritual and poetic evolution he has achieved since he publicly took up the role of *Minjung* poet. It is true that for years Ko Un ranted and raved about human rights of urban laborers and rural farmers and tried to have his political messages crossed over to both the masses and the powerful. However, when he was put on the black list of the Korean CIA due to his political activism and finally was arrested for the charge of high treason in 1980, as he confesses later, he could review his own *Minjung* poetry in retrospect while waiting for the death sentence. Although he actually received a life-in-prison sentence, and after serving six year imprionsment, he was granted the Aug. 15th Emancipation Day special amnesty with due to his weak physical condition, he recalls that his prison experience changed his idea of *Minjung*. Soon afterwards, he gets released and after spending some time recuperating from the long period of imprisonment, he moves to a small, peaceful rural town called Anseong and resumes his writing. Here, just as he once had self-examination triggered by Jeon Tae-il's death, so he gets to have another deep, serious soul-searching, which he reveals in "I Walked through a Birch Grove." In this poem Ko Un becomes his own protagonist and writes out of his own transcendental experience of becoming one with Nature and then describes the successive awakening of an ecological mode of existence in a calm but passionate voice:

Before reaching the hillside of
Mt. Chilhyeon
in Yiwol village, Gwanghyewon,
I set foot by chance
in the large grove of birch trees.
I looked behind to see
if someone had pushed me
to come here.
No one was there
except for the looming hill
with snow flurries.
There, indifferently,
naked birch trees stood,
showing the world as it is.
Yes, only winter trees
do not know corruption.
There is no falsity in sorrow.
Who has never cried
over living?
For a long, long time,
crying has been women' job,
They've consoled themselves
by crying out loud.

Birch trees have been standing
here by themselves.
[Yet] They've willingly accommodated a visitor like me as one of them.
Not all could come out here
but they'd have welcomed
if they had come.
How beautiful they are,
embracing each other
and those who couldn't come as well.
Looking at the trees, the boughs,

and the trembling of the treetops
under the dark sky
I wished to carry a load of firewood
on my back, showing it off to myself and to the world.
No, I liked to live, obeying myself
to the principles of Nature
just like snowflakes falling in complete stillness in this cold place or
like soft steamed pork sold at a humble café in the three-way intersection.
For I've led such a dogmatic life, even picked up a fight with a breeze.

How long has it been
for us to visit such grove?
It's been almost ten years
that I set foot in this power-spot.
The strong spirituality!
It seems to transmit its divine energy not just to me but also to the world.
I can feel it in my overwhelmed heart.
There'll be time for everyone to see
that one should live in unison
with the many.
I had myself already grown old
in my youth.
Coming out here
I wish I could be born again,
I wish I could feed myself
on the natural gift of winter birch trees and grow up as someone's only child
so endeared by all neighbors
who want to take a bite [of its cheek.]

Forgetting about the initial trail
down to Gwanghyeone,
I headed without hesitation
toward the rugged track of
Chilhyeon hill in the winter wind.

("I Walked through a Birch Grove," *A Wind*, 86–88)

In the birch grove, the speaker, while looking at the naked birch trees as if embracing each other in the cold winter wind, is reminded of the strong pulsation of life that Korean *Mincho* (the grass roots) have so long preserved: just like birch trees, *Mincho people* haven't lost their generosity and warm natural hospitality toward others even when dedicating themselves solely to living itself in the maelstrom of Korean history. Recalling their tenacity to life and inspired by their simple humanism, he realizes the democratic potentials of the *Minjung* spirit in the minds of Korean *Micho* and determines to put behind the dogmatic Realism of 'Proletariat Literature.'

Thus, Ko Un, entering the 1980s, clearly starts walking on a new path, challenging the intellectual literati's equation of *Minjung* poetry with literature of 'the Proletariat' and explores the ways to manifest the essence of Koreanism in his new *Minjung* poetry based upon simple humanism of *Mincho*. As for his overt change in literary direction, Ko Un was criticized severely for having lost a sense of ethical duty to produce labor poetry or '*Minjung* Proletariat Poetry.' He was even viewed as having not only lost his previous poetic fire but also regressed to naive humanism. However, he considers this change not as a regression but as a necessary transition. In an interview he talks about his own opinion of "doctrinaire Realism":

> I like to incorporate "what is," "what must be," and "what can be" in order to enlarge the boundary of Realism which has been limited so far to doctrinaire Realism or a kind of literary trend. … I think today's Realism should include psychoanalysis and even Romanticism so that it can function as something that can extend the width of the real world and the depth of human potentials. … We have to think about why Realism gets prosaic since the advent of Postmodernism. ("Interview with Ko Un: His Literature and Life" 29)

By liberating Realism from the frame of ideology and abstruse speculation, Ko Un asserts that literary Realism can be re-configured as a flexible perspective to reflect the real lives of the masses of Korean *Minjung* grass roots.

Interestingly, Ko Un's re-configuration of literary Realism of *Minjung* can be understood more effectively in the context of his life-long pursuit of *Hwaeom* Buddhist vision in life and the world. He had been a Buddhist monk before becoming a poet and once published a short story "A Young Wanderer" (1971). Since then, he continued writing his Buddhist novel *Hwaeomgyeong* (the Avatamska Sutra) for about thirty years and finished it in 1991. To this extent, he kept walking on the road of *Hwaeom* Buddhism even if taking a side road from time to time. Generally, the *Hwaeom* Buddhist vision of life includes everything animate and inanimate in the ecology of the universe. *Hwaeom* Buddhist thinkers, thus, emphasize the notion of interdependence, as is stated in *Majjhima Nikaya*:

1. When this is present, that comes to be
2. from the arising of this, that arises.
3. When this is absent, that does not come to be
4. on the cessation of this, that ceases. (Abe 97)

According to Masao Abe, we can replace the demonstrative pronouns 'this' and 'that' with 'bigness' and 'smallness' in order to understand the statement. Then the first two lines of the statement can be rewritten as follows:

1. When bigness is present, smallness comes to be
2. from the arising of bigness, smallness arises
3. when smallness is present, bigness comes to be
4. from the arising of smallness, bigness arises. (Abe 98)

This interchangeability of 'this' and 'that' or 'bigness' and 'smallness' or 'one' and 'the many' suggests a Buddhist mode of thinking fundamentally different from the Western Hegelian dialectic notion of 'thesis,' 'anti-thesis,' and 'synthesis.' The Hegelian dialectic takes place step by step in a linear manner because the synthesis of the first and second steps become a thesis in the next step and then gets unified with another antithesis. There is no thesis without antithesis, no 'one' without 'the many,' and vice versa. This is the characteristic of Hegelian *Becoming*, that is, a process which essentially involves temporality. Contrary to this unidirectional nature of relatedness in the Hegelian dialectic, the *Hwaeom* Buddhist process of *Becoming* involves non-temporality. As is revealed in the reversibility of 'this' and 'that,' 'one' becomes 'the many' and vice versa in a completely reciprocal manner and without temporal succession. To put it another way, 'one' and 'the many' arise and perish at one and the same time. This "co-arising and co-ceasing" is called "co-dependent origination" (Abe 94) and signifies a non-lineal, non-unilateral, non-unidirectional, non-temporal nature of *Hwaeom* interrelatedness in Buddhism. Thus in explaining the relationship between 'one' and 'the many,' the proper term to use would be 'one in the many' instead of 'the many in one.'

This notion of *Hwaeom* interrelatedness, then, liberates the duality of the Holy and the Secular, Self and the Other, the Creator and the Created, and One and the Many. There is no primacy of the former over the latter. The former arises together with the latter as a dynamic whole, endlessly giving birth to and negating each other reciprocally. For instance, one's Self appears only in the relationship with the Other; if the Other disappears, one's Self also disappears. A poet as the creator, then, becomes 'a poet' and maintains his identity as such only in so far as the reader engages him as 'a poet.' This non-temporal recognition of one's identity naturally leads to the awakening that the ground of our existence is "nothingness," which is, as Abe explains, the expression a Buddhist uses to mean something that cannot be objectified temporally (64). If the ground of one's self is nothingness, the ultimate reality of the unified whole is also nothingness. This is the *Dharma* truth that Buddhists themselves strive to reach and at the same time try to teach to laymen.

On the basis of *Hwaeom* Buddhist meditation on the relationship between 'one' and 'the many,' Ko Un does not present his poetic self as the Creator, Truth, the representative Korean Self, in other words, *Being*. Rather, as any *Hwaeom* Buddhist thinker would do, he presents himself as a Truth-effect of the poetic self or Becoming-in-relationship, which constantly emerges and then disappears in the relationships between him and the others in the rise and fall of Korean history. In particular, in *Ten Thousand Lives* Ko Un puts this *Hwaeom* paradox of Becoming into practice, incessantly making and undoing his poetic self in the act of continual naming and cataloguing various lives of Korean *Minjung* grass roots. Most importantly, unlike Western inclusive poets such as Walt Whitman, he would not presume the 'absolute substance' (Being) of Spirit, whether immanent or transcendent, at the outset. He would not create one hero's journey through meeting many people toward the final Truth. He would focus on representing 'many' forms of life that manifest the 'one' nature. Just like Buddha taught "sharing rice is sharing life" and tried to enlighten and save all people, he would apply the Buddhist notion of 'all people' to the once-politically charged class name '*Minjung*' and expand its boundary large enough to contain all *Minjung* grass roots. By calling out the name of each grass root character in each poem, he would restore the beauty of each spear of *Minjung* grass roots from the amorphous mass of nameless grasses scattered on the cold ideological domain of 'Proletariat Literature.' By 2010 he has completed presenting 5,600 characters in 4,001 poems in thirty volumes. Just as a Buddhist disciplinant continues making one miniature Buddha after another as part of his discipline, he would continue to present *Minjung* grass roots to infinity, as 'ten thousand' symbolically suggests the 'numberless number' in *Hwaeom* Buddhism. In this respect it is only proper to call *Ten Thousand Lives* a literary sutra, in which Ko Un, as a Buddhist disciplinant-poet, commemorates and deifies numberless *Minjung* grass roots as Bodhisattvas.

KO UN'S POETRY AS A PHILOSOPHICAL ACT: *HWAEOM* HABITUS IN *TEN THOUSAND LIVES*

With new Realism combined with the *Hwaeom* Buddhist vision of interrelatedness, Ko Un now redefines the role of a poet as a *Gokby* instead of *Eoreun* (a social leader). In Korean cultural tradition *Gokby* is a designated female servant who is supposed to weep on behalf of a high-born master. Like a female servant, he desires to weep unspeakable pain and sorrow for those who survived bloody suppressions and endured insurmountable tragedies in the poem "Gokby" (1988):

> In Joseon period a Yangban fella,
> a poor thing,
> was accomplished in putting on airs.
> He'd consider showing tears
> as lowly manners
> He'd mask his sorrow

by clearing his throat loudly.
Even when his father died
he'd make a short sigh "Ah-y"
and let his female servant cry out loud
all day on his behalf.

Today's high class, those five, six, or seven arch-enemies, too,
give orders without feeling any sorrow.
"Throw away crying
to the crowd, not to dogs
It's their job to wail out
Ah-y-go, Ah-y-go
Not our job to care about this vulgarity or that nuisance."

When sorrow stops
being something basic to humans,
When crying belongs
only to the lowliest,
When sorrow and crying are despised as vulgarity,
Poet, you alone go out there
to the folks,
become a gokby,
become a gokby,
and weep their sorrow on their behalf. A prison inmate serving
a life sentence asked me
"Sir, please sing my life"
If I forget his words
I am not a poet, I am no poet.

("Gokby," *Stars of My Homeland* 33)

In the nineteenth-century Joseon-Korea's *Yangban* class, accomplished with pompous upper class manners, regarded showing raw emotions like 'crying out loud' as a sign of weakness inappropriate for their manly high class code of conduct. Thence they would often hide their sorrow in public even when a family member died: instead, they would hire a female servant to perform a role of wailing out loud so that all neighbors would know that the dead was truly beloved. The speaker compares the present day privileged few ruling class to those pretentious Yangban "fella[s]" and denounces their aloofness and indifference toward the immense pain of the masses of poor citizens. As he criticizes, they view those who cry over the death of innocent lives as simpletons who deserve less care than "dogs." They even treat them as inanimate things by calling them "vulgarity" or "nuisance" and without any mercy they express their sense of annoyance and impatience about doing their duty to protect such vulgar things. Appalled by the bleak reality in which basic human rights are denied and such humane feelings as sorrow, sympathy, and compassion are despised as abject vulgarity, the speaker awakens himself to one inmate's sincere request to tell his life to others and makes a strong resolution to become a *Gokby* who is hired by the masses of common *Minjung* grass roots to weep on behalf of them.

In this respect it is quite powerful and impressive that Ko Un announces his poetic intention to represent the real lives of *Minjung* grass roots instead of promoting the class ideology of 'Proletariat Literature' in the poem "Inscription," which is the opening poem of the first volume of *Ten Thousand Lives*:

> Here between you and me
> arrives the star's light million years away
> In thousands of acres of
> the Buyeo kingdom
> In fifty four villages of
> the Mahan kingdom,
> In each village of the Byeonhan
> and the Jinhan kingdom
> you and I had been interconnected,
> you and I had been in one mind and
> you and I had sung ten thousand songs
> until one song was diffused
> into so many melodies.
>
> In this ancient land
> living in division is
> none other than living in torture.
> In one's whole life there are days
> that have no meaning
> if disconnected from the others.
> Oh, a man can be man
> only among man and men.

("Inscription," *Ten Thousand Lives*, Vol. 1, 17)

Poised between a separate individual and a poet for the masses of common people, the speaker calls out the names of the ancient kingdoms, *Buyeo, Mahan, Byeonhan,* and *Jinhan* from the third century BC and imagines a mythical space in which "I" could be "interconnected" with "you" and "I" and "You" could be united in one song which later gets "diffused into so many melodies." Nonetheless, wishing to inherit that 'one' song of Korea and sing it into "ten thousand songs" of Korean people, he presents his poetic identity not as a prophet or a seer but as "a man" who can be "man only among man and men." And his vision of Becoming-in-relationship continues in all thirty volumes of *Ten Thousand Lives.*

Ko Un's naming and cataloguing also reflects his poetic vision of Becoming. Through his act of identifying each weed's indigenous name, each nameless weed in turn comes into being as a lively Korean plant named *"Myeongaju, Barangyi, Soybirum, Myeonurissikye,"* and so on. Likewise, through his act of calling out the names of each nameless peddler, servant, woman, and so on, he/she in turn becomes a real Korean named *"Daegil, Oh Geum-dok, Kim She-kyu,"* and so forth. By just appellating so far ignored grasses and unrecognized people, Ko Un shows all the animate and the inanimate and all the powerful and the powerless constitute the genealogies of Korean flaura, fauna, and people. In addition, by letting readers recognize a native Korean name of each grass and leading them to have a sympathy for each weed-like human life, he transmits a Whitmanesque message that "who degrades or defiles the living human body is cursed" ("A Woman at Auction," *LG* 123). It seems that what Ko Un realized in the birch grove gives his version of the Korean epic a substantiality which dogmatic Realism and 'Proletariat Literature' could not provide. His poetic gift is, after all, to perceive everything as it is and appreciate the temporary moment in which Being is transmuted into Becoming-in-relationship.

In the Western intellectual context, Ko Un's *Hwaeom* poetic vision manifested in *Ten Thousand Lives* could be understood in terms of what Wittgenstein indicates in *Philosophical Investigations,* that is, "a mode of investigation" that "cannot have a beginning, middle, and end" and that "cannot have organic unity, a casual, logical, sequential structure, an underlying theme or master plot" (Perloff 65). Making a comment on Fraser's detailed recounting of the prayers to rain gods in early African culture in *The Golden Bough*, Wittgenstein pays close attention to the limitations of any given description: it may tell something but simultaneously cannot actually tell anything to readers. He suggests that if Fraser's description can tell anything, it would be the fact that Africans' knowledge of nature is fundamentally different from ours. Then, also feeling that his own description of Fraser as well Fraser's description of the Africans was only fragmentary and provisional for the same reason, Wittgenstein intimates that it would be impossible for him to produce a 'finished' book. What he felt about the nature of his philosophical deliberations can, according to Perloff, only be supposed in his remark, "one can only describe and say: this is what human life is like" (qtd. in Perloff 121).

Wittgenstein's awareness of the limitation of philosophical descriptions, regardless of his original intention, could provide a platform to understand a long narrative poem that contains philosophical insights of life. For it leads readers to muse on the compatibility between philosophy and poetry, as Wittegenstein says "philosophy ought really to be written only as a form of poetry" (*CV* 24). In other words, when he states that "thoughts … proceed from one subject to another in a natural order and without break," his philosophical descriptions read like poetry, or in Perloff's words, "alternately anecdotal and aphoristic, repetitive and disjunctive, didactic and jokey, self-assertive and self-canceling" (66). In addition, as is suggested in the end of his preface, "I should not like to spare other people the trouble of thinking. But if possible, to stimulate someone to thoughts of his own" (*PI* vi), his concern in *Philosophical Investigations* seems, to a large extent, similar to a modernist poet's concern to create a new language in which the collective dream to be-in-the-world can be realized. Thus, when he meditates on "the works of great masters" in *Culture and Value* and suggests that the greatness of a work of art can only be intuited in fragmentary and provisional states without being analyzed and assembled into a logical whole, it seems, as Perloff notes, that he himself *becomes* a modernist poet who struggles with the metaphysics of modern art, history, and culture.

Understanding the poetic nature of Wittgenstein's philosophical investigation, then, yields an interesting metaphysical ramp for following the trajectory of Ko Un's poetic imagination since in *Ten Thousand Lives* Ko Un resonates with Wittgenstein's philosophical insight on the impossibility of achieving a logical whole. In more than four thousand poems in thirty volumes he "cannot have a beginning, middle, and end" and "cannot have organic unity, a casual, logical, sequential structure, an underlying theme or master plot" (Perloff 65). For one thing, the symbolic number of "ten thousand" suggests Ko Un's grand philosophical design not only of representing the universe but also of letting the disjunctive, anecdotal, and insignificant lives of Korean *Minjung* grass roots be-in-the-world. Calling out lowborn servants, peddlers, laborers, vagabonds and prostitutes, common fathers, mothers, sons and daughters, as well as highborn heroes and generals, famous Buddhist monks, dictators and presidents domestic and international, historical figures living and dead, historical places, events, even flora and fauna, Ko Un shows their 'being-in-the-world' and in a sense constructs what Pierre Bourdieu calls *Habitus* or a particular set of dispositions that are acquired through experiences based upon particular ethnicity, nationality, class, gender, and so on. Through imagining many forms of life and carrying out disjunctive philosophical speculations, he suggests that the meaning of life can be intuitively captured in each fragmentary anecdote of life. In addition, just as the *Hwaeom* vision suggests that the one seems to exist separate and independent but actually comes into 'being' in the endless cycle of "co-dependent origination" (Abe 94), he describes 'one' life after another in an unending record of 'the many' lives of Korean *Minjung* grass roots and in doing so, meditates on the beauty of ever-arising lotus flowers of Vairocana Buddha on the muddy surface of Korean history. Then, the greatness of *Ten Thousand Lives* can only be intuited in a fragmentary and provisional philosophical nature of Ko Un's poetic investigation of Becoming that resists being analyzed and assembled into one logical 'Whole' or 'Being.'

Let's take a look at "The Well" for instance and see how Ko Un uses historical, cultural, social subtexts to produce the *Hwaeom Habitus* for Korean *Minjung* grass roots characters.

> There's a well
> in the front yard of the cottage,
> a well more than ten fathom deep.

In the house filled with thick flowery scent,
Bullye's mother, glowing like
a white magnolia,
and little Bullye like a long-lasting lily
just the two of them live,
those two and a flower,
these three live all together as a family.
She is a young widow,
discreet in every word,
never takes a night-shower at the well,
even in the mid-summer's heat.
If I go on errands there,
Bullye's mother would offer
a gourd bowl of water
pulled up from her deep bottomless well.
The bluish-black water,
The water of stillness and anxiety,
whenever taking one sip,
I would feel my body tingling,
my heart pounding.

("The Well," *Ten Thousand Lives*, Vol. 2, 190)

In the original Korean poetic text, Ko Un tries to transmit a feeling of anxiety of an adolescent speaker standing in front of an attractive woman through the incantatory rhythm of his speech. For instance, even if it cannot be felt in the English translation, he uses the rhythmic repetitions of the end rime "-eoyo" so that he can suggest the young speaker's excitement as well as his efforts to maintain polite manners towards Bullye's mother. In addition, by repeating "b" sound in three consecutive lines and "Bullye's mother" in one line he reflects the psychosomatic modality of the adolescent speaker who clearly lost his wits by Bullye's mother's attractiveness. However, his tense feeling had already begun when he entered Bullye's cottage "filled with thick flowery scent": there he used to be dazzled by beautiful young widow Bullye's mother and her daughter. He used to compare each of them to "a white magnolia" and "a long-lasting lily" and this time, as if fatally lured by these luscious female flowers, he falters his voice and blurts out a grammatically wrong sentence in one breath "just the two of them live, those two and a flower, these three live all together as a family." By adding "a flower" to "those two," Ko Un reveals the adolescent speaker's boyish wish to live with these women even in the form of a natural object, "a flower."

Interestingly enough, however, the young speaker's psychosomatic anxiety has a set of socio-cultural contexts, with which Ko Un can unfold a semiotic mesh of uniquely Korean *Habitus* throughout the whole tense situation. When Bullye's mother pulls up a gourd-bowl of water from the well and offers it, the young speaker watches her bodily movements and says to himself that she seems to have "never tak[en] a night-shower at the well/even in the mid-summer's heat." And the moment he imagines the white skin of her naked body, he instantly feels his heart pounding faster. In a Korean cultural context, a well is a symbolic space where a man and a woman supposedly exchange an intimation of attraction. As the legendary love story of the first king of Joseon-Korea who fell in love with his second wife at the well testifies, the act of handing over a bowl of water has been used as a literary device as common as Western cliché of 'falling in love at first sight.' In another context, the well is also considered an intimate place where a woman reveals her affection toward her man: in the Summer a woman makes an offer to her man to cool down the summer's heat by throwing cold water to his upper body, and then the man gladly removes his shirt and takes a push-up pose beside the well. In the last but not least important literary context, the name "Bullye" contains a set of ethnic connotations that can be easily grasped by Korean readers: as the name signifies 'the feces,' she is an archetypal character of a poor but beautiful woman abused by violence, rape, and abduction. She is 'the abject being' who is shunned by neighbors because of being a defiled being or the dirty 'Other' who thus has to be shunned, far away from decent, ordinary people. Effectively using these cultural, social, ethnic contexts, Ko Un builds the ethnic *Habitus* in which the young speaker's psychosomatic responses, including trilling of his voice, his palpitating heart, dry mouth, repetition of same sounds and words, and so on, work together to create a tense atmosphere.

Nevertheless, a well also carries a universal connotation since both in Western and Eastern literary traditions it suggests a woman's genital organ, which in turn can be associated with a little boy's complicated castration fear as is narrated by Freud and Lacan. A boy recognizes the difference of his mother's body from his own and feels the fear of castration by his father. In order to overcome this fear, the boy identifies himself with his father and accepts the Law of the Father and in the process successfully develops his masculine gender identity and becomes a speaking subject in the symbolic system. Besides, as is recognized in many rites of initiation, the adolescent boy, fearing that he might be castrated in the adult world and remain a boy forever, has to enter the hole of woman's body and die in the water of woman. By successfully going through this rite of 'death by water' he can get reborn as an honorable man in the adult world.

Given that a well is associated with both the fear of death and the rebirth through death, the young speaker's expression of "bluish-black water" carries double meanings. On the one hand, he is fearful of the Father's (the community) chastisement when he sips a gourd bowl of water offered by Bullye's mother which he feels as if being pulled up out of her body that he describes as "deep bottomless well." On the other hand, he wishes to die inside the "deep bottomless well" by quenching his bodily thirst with a gourd bowl of water. Being in conflict between the fear and the desire, the boy speaker finally decides to drink cold water and deal with "the stillness and anxiety" that the young widow provokes. Every sip of "the stillness and anxiety" melting in the water, therefore, gives this adolescent boy goose bumps all over his body and makes his heart pound faster. Ko Un stops the poem here, but readers, aware of the ethnic contexts, can continue to imagine this young speaker to get reborn from an adolescent boy to a young man. Using a simple universal motif that a boy meets a girl, Ko Un weaves historical, cultural, social contexts together into such an intricate Korean poetic screen.

Ko Un adds more humanism to the lowly, abject character Bullye in "Blind Bullye," which is perhaps one of his most outstanding lyrical poems.

> Over in Chaetjonji, Mun Chong-an's daughter
> went blind when she was two.
> Twenty-six now, she hasn't been courted.
> All day long wiping narrow parquet floor

or guarding the old cottage
with nothing to lose.
She would stay at home while her old parents
worked in the field with their bent backs.
Sometimes little scallywags caught a beetle
and came in ask:
"Want some rice-cake? Open wide!"
They'd toss the beetle into her mouth
and run away.
Other times, lecherous neighbors sneaked in
and made advances to blind Bullye.
Saying "Oh my, how pretty you are,"
they'd go on fondling her breast or
fumbling around the hem of her skirt.
Startled, she'd block off the worst
while putting up with this and that.
But she'd suppress a cry
in complete silence.
When those adults,
those brutes, rather,
felt sore and went back home,
only then, alone, she'd shed tears.
From her blind eyes down came
a single tear drop, which is dangling
like a spider spooling down
and hanging still at the tip.

("Blind Bullye," *Ten Thousand Lives*, Vol. 4, 90)

In this poem Ko Un brings in an ethnic character "Bullye" to imagine a mode of Korean woman's life filled with predicaments and sorrow. Yet he adds a universal motif of blindness to the already shared negative socio-cultural associations the name "Bullye" carries, so that he could present this ethnic female character not only as a universal human being who goes through physical hardships but also as a symbol to suggest a painful irony between seeing and being blind. Twenty-six year old Bullye, although blind since the age of two, tries to prove her usefulness by doing her best in living, always "wiping narrow parquet floor" and "guard[ing] the old cottage with nothing to lose." Without any adults who can protect her, however, she has been harassed psychologically as well as physically by brute neighbors, blinded by their cruel and lustful desires. In the first half of the poem, thus, blind Bullye is presented as doubly tormented: she is not only socially disgraced but also sexually disadvantaged. However, in the latter half of the poem Ko Un reveals how she can see everything with her mind's eye and also judges that those adults are only "brutes" below the level of human beings. At the same time, he lets readers see with their mind's eye that she is strong enough to put up with every humiliating act of neighbors by "suppressing a cry in complete silence" and that only when all those brutes disappear, "alone, she'd shed tears." By contrasting the abject being Bullye with the powerful neighbors, Ko Un ultimately questions what it means to 'see' and who is really blind: even if she survives long years of unspeakable harassment and pain and sometimes sheds tears over her unchangeable conditions of being, she must have reached a mature perspective on life, so that she can see through such painful experiences and stoically accept her fate of living among 'blind' neighbors. Finally, overlapping the image of mature Bullye with a spider which spools out a thread from its own body and acrobatically hangs at the tip of the thread, Ko Un gives readers an intimation of Bullye's Becoming-in-relationship: now she is not just a blind ethnic girl but a true artist of life who knows how to control her innermost emotions and sheds only one tear drop instead of many.

In "Tip-Taker Mun Gae-pyong" Ko Un shows another poor, abject character in an affectionate but humorous tone.

> Tip-taker Mun lives in the first of
> three small villages comprising Kaesa-ri.
> In every gambling place
> and at every card-table
> set up on straw mats at funerals
> and even in a betting on an acorn-curd,
> he always showed up,
> just as Sir. Blowfly would buzz up
> the moment you squat bare-bottomed
> on a hillside crack.
> He'd stay up all night,
> yawning and even enduring
> words of contempt and disdain

until he earned a meager tip
from a big winner.
Then off he went home
and would tell his wife:
"Sorry, I got so little a tip last night."
Then his wife would reply:
"Good job, tip-taker Mun Gae-pyeong.
This'll do."

("Tip-Taker Mun Gae-pyeong," *Ten Thousand Lives*, Vol. 2, 191)

In Korean culture 'gae-pyeong' means a meager tip which is usually handed over by the winner to the participants in a stick-throwing game, a card-game, or any kinds of betting games. As Ko Un describes in the poem, common folks would play a stick-throwing game in every occasion, even in the backroom at a funeral parlor and would bet anything, even a bowl of acorn curd. Due to its gambling nature, some participants used to stay up all night and lose their temper as well as money. Thus, the winner who earned the most money on the day was expected to show his generosity toward the biggest loser by giving away a small amount of money with which he could drink away his misfortune. As time passes by, this practice of tipping comes to include any bystanders as well as players.

In this cultural context, when Ko Un calls the folk character by mixing his last name "Mun" with a small tip "gae-pyeong," he introduces this pathetic man in a very humorous light at the outset of the poem. Probably, the humorous part of the poem is the way Ko Un describes how "tip-taker Mun Gae-pyeong" appears in any game scene at any place. Comparing him to a blowfly that feeds on the feces and thus calling him "Sir, Blowfly," he mockingly praises his sincere diligence to find out all betting games and to attend them without fail. Yet in imagining that the blowflies would gather around out of nowhere, bother one with their buzzing sounds and then never disappear whatever measures one would take, readers can imagine the 1970s' socio-cultural *Habitus* of Korea in which "tip-taker Mun Gae-pyeong" lives: he has no other way to make a living except for making an uninvited visit, staying till the end of a game, even sitting up all night, and enduring all disdain and contempt to get a meager tip. Finally, at the end of the poem Ko Un sheds an endearing light on this petty, pathetic folk character so that he can draw readers' sympathy and compassion: despite the lowliest out of lower class gamblers, his tip-gathering act has been all that he could do to support his family. Thus, instead of a sentimental ending, Ko Un simply adds the wife's short response "good job, my man Tip-taker Mun Gae-pyeong. This'll do" to her husband who says "Sorry, I got so little a tip last night." By doing so, Ko Un reveals the affection of the wife who fully appreciates her man since she knows he did his best to take care of the family. With her merry tone of acknowledgement, then, readers can probably cheer up for him and also say, "Good job, Tip-taker Mun Gae-pyeong." What more is it needed other than a wife's simple, endearing remark here to compensate for all the humiliation a husband has to go through outside? This simple ending intimates Ko Un's masterly insight of a happy relationship between a husband and a wife.

Along with Bullye and Tip-taker Mun Gae-pyeong, servant Daegil is also one of the most memorable characters in *Ten Thousand Lives* because Daegil embodies what Ko Un finds one of the most conspicuous essences of Koreanness, which is Korean cultural sensibility called *Jeong* (affection). Maintaining Confucius cultural traditions, the Koreans have long placed a high value on *Jeong*, human affection, or caring heart. They would often extend the boundary of family and kinship to strangers, outsiders, and even foreigners and easily embrace them as one of them by calling them "sister," "brother," "aunt," or "uncle." Even though they have no intention to assimilate them into the family, they are going to treat strangers as if they were part of family or kinship because they share, after all, one Korean history and one Korean cultural identity despite the many modes of living. Thus, they offer their hands first, share joys and sorrows among neighbors, help out a man going through hardships of life, and even form communal networks such as *Durye* and *Pumashi* to exchange labors in the busy season as well as to patrol the community. All these customs and conventional practices constitute a natural sense of social mores as any Korean would be willing to carry out: therefore, he who doesn't know how to share *Jeong* would be severely criticized as a despicable being and often be positioned below the level of animals. Given such cultural *Habitus* surrounding the sensibility of *Jeong*, servant Daegil is probably the most decent servant in Korean history:

In Saeteo Gwan-jeon's servant Daegil
passed for a seasoned farmhand.
Picking up a brown pig and shoving it
to a pigsty was a snap for him.
Indeed, it was done
in one short squealing of a pig.
He would not complain of late meals.
At dawn he'd shake off dewdrops and
brush the road, neatly as parted hair.
Yet his clear black eyes would
twinkle more at night than by day.
By lamplight at the servant's quarter
I learned *Ga-Gya-Geo-Gyeo*
from him
and read the story of
Janghwa and Honglyeon
as fluently as the rain comes down.
He let my adolescent eyes
open to the world [as well].
After thirty-six year Occupation,
I was the only one
who knew *Ga-Gya-Geo-Gyeo*.

. . . .

He used to say
"If a man lives in luxury,
he cares only about himself.
We depend on
one another in this world."
Uncle Daegil,
He was a light to me
A bright light burning all night.
I could see it
still there
whenever I opened my eyes.

("Servant Daegil," *Ten Thousand Lives*, Vol. 1, 20–21)

Here it is important to take a note of the perspective that Ko Un represents Daegil as someone who unconsciously senses a Buddhist notion of *Hwaeom* interdependence instead of presenting him as a Proletariat who talks about a propagandistic political message. Daegil first appears as a servant with a sensuous muscular body and a genial spirit toward others, two of which are attractive enough to leave a strong impression on young Ko Un's mind. Despite being a servant, Daegil not only helps him to learn the Korean language and read a fairytale of two girls but also leads him to the enlightenment of the interdependence between man and nature as well as between man and men. Thus, Ko Un calls him as "Uncle" Daegil and presents him as a model Korean *Minjung*-subject in whose strong body *Hwaeom* perception of 'the one' in 'the many' is aesthetically represented. Transforming Daegil's identity from a servant to a teacher, to an uncle, and to a guiding light, Ko Un honors Daegil as a unique, irreducible Korean character sharing *Jeong* regardless of class and simultaneously as a decent citizen of the world beyond Proletarian ideology.

In conclusion, there is no doubt that Ko Un is a national poet who has been respected as "the greatest poet in the history of modern Korean literature," "the greatest nationalist poet," or "the highest peak of critical realism" (Lee Gyeong-su 91). Ko Un's greatness, however, should be evaluated in the whole poetic journey he made since the 1950s to the present because he is one of those who would carry modern Korean poetry forward in terms of his epic purpose and new *Minjung* poetics. As literary critic Yom Moo-woong once acclaimed Ko Un's consistent passion to speak up for Korean grass roots, saying "the trickle of Ko Un's humble resolution forms a little pool, then a river in *The Poems of the Pastoral,* and finally reaches the vast sea in *Ten Thousand Lives*" (136), Ko Un's constant seeking for *Minjung* seems to have led him to achieve something specifically grown out of nucleus Korean *Minjung* experiences in his poetic career. That 'something' might be called the authentic Korean epic, since he has called out the name of each individual from the amorphous masses of *Minjung* grass roots, has given each character a literary form and thus a form of life, and then has weaved their lives together into a cultural history of Korea in *Ten Thousand Lives*. Nevertheless, that 'something' is not limited only to the Koreans. Just as Buddha sent forth universal messages of life in *Hwaeomgyeong* (the Avatamska Sutra), Buddhist monk-turned-poet Ko Un has sung the universal epic for all people, tackling the problems of 'five desires and seven passions'[4] of human beings in *Ten Thousand Lives*. In his grand literary sutra a local individual Korean is transformed into an active universal agent who would accept his own fate, trace the footsteps of the previous generations, and project his future in the universal principle of Becoming-in-relationship.

NOTES

1. All these quotes are from Ko Un's official homepage <http://www.koun.co.kr/korea/>.
2. Part of this essay has been published in online journal, *IMPACT: The Journal of the Center for Interdisciplinary Teaching & Learning* (Winter, 2013).
3. All poems in this essay are my translation.
4. In Buddhism human beings live in bondage to five desires (wealth, fame, appetite, sleep, and lust) and seven passions (joy, anger, sorrow, pleasure, love, evil, and desire).

REFERENCES

Abe, Masao. *Zen and Comparative Studies*. Ed. Steven Heine. Honolulu: U of Hawaii P, 1997.

Choi, Won-shik. "Ko Un, Thirty-year Career as a Lyric Poet." *The Poetic World of Ko Un*. Ed. Shin Kyong-nim and Paik Nak-chung. Seoul: Changbi, 1993. 63–90.

Kim, Taehyun, Kwon Seong-woo, and Choi Won-shik. "Interview with Ko Un: His Literature and Life." *The Poetic World of Ko Un*. Ed. Shin Kyong-nim and Paik Nak-chung. Seoul: Changbi, 1993. 10–34.

Ko, Un. *Ten Thousand Lives*. Seoul: Mineumsa, 2009.

——. *The Dialects of the Universe*. Seoul: Mineumsa, 2007.

——. *The 1950s: Literature and Man on the [War] Devastation*. Seoul: Hyang-yeon, 2005.

——. *Stars of My Homeland*. Seoul: Cheongha, 1988.

——. *A Wind: Selected Poems of Ko Un*. Seoul: Changbi, 2002.

Kwak, Hye-ran. "A Comparative Research: The Reception and Influence of Whitman." *Hyundai Munhak Yeongu* 2 (2009): 91–103.

Lee Gwang-ho. "Poetics of Freedom and Aesthetic Modernism." *Modern Korean Literature*. Vol. 2. 334–357.

Lee Gyeong-su. "The Centerless World and the Beauty of the Emptiness." *The Poetic World of Ko Un*. Ed. Shin, Kyeong-nim and Baek Nak-cheong. Seoul: Changbi, 1993. 91–106.

Lee Hye-won. "Formal Features of Narrative Poetry in the 1970s." *Modern Korean Literature*. Vol. 3. 90–116.

Lee Sung-won. "Poetry in the Age of Industrialization: 1972–1979." *The History of Korean Poetry*. Ed. Oh Se-young. Seoul: Mineum, 2007. 395–472.

Nam Ki-hyeok. "Poetics of Laughter and Post-Modernity." *Modern Korean Literature*. Vol. 2. 190–215.

Oh Se-young et al., eds. *The History of Korean Poetry*. Seoul: Mineum, 2007.

Pak Hyeon-su. "The Era of Minjung Revolution: 1979–1991." *The History of Korean Poetry*. Ed. Oh Se-young. Seoul: Mineum, 2007. 473–532.

Perloff, Marjorie. *Wittgenstein's Ladder*. Chicago: The U of Chicago P, 1996.

Shin, Kyeong-nim and Baek Nak-cheong. *The Poetic World of Ko Un*. Seoul: Changbi, 1993.

Song Ki-han. "Aspiration for Democracy and Frustration: 1961–1972." *The History of Korean Poetry*. Ed. Oh Se-young. Seoul: Mineum, 2007. 337–394.

Whitman, Walt. *Leaves of Grass*. Ed. Sculley Bradley and Harold W. Blodgett. New York: Norton, 1973.

Wittgenstein, Ludwig. *Philosophical Investigations*. Trans. G.E.E. Anscombe. London: Blackwell, 1968.

——. *Culture and Value*. Trans. Peter Winch. Chicago: The U of Chicago P, 1984.

Yom, Moo-woong. "The Depth of Life and the Pride of National Literature." *The Poetic World of Ko Un*. Ed. Shin Kyong-nim and Paik Nak-chung. Seoul: Changbi, 1993. 123–138.

Yu Seong-ho. "Minjung Sensibility and Exploration of Being in the 1980s's Poetry." *Modern Korean Literature*. Vol. 3. 184–205.

CHAPTER 7

Literature of the Arabian Peninsula and Transcultural Literary Exchange in the Post-Oil Era

Saddik Gohar and Doris Hambuch

Literature of the Arabian Peninsula and Transcultural Literary Exchange in the Post-Oil Era within the category of Middle Eastern Literatures the least discussed are generally those of the Gulf Cooperation Council (GCC) members: Kuwait, Bahrain, Qatar, United Arab Emirates, Oman, and Saudi Arabia. The fact that the literary history of this region has been explored to a much smaller extent than that of, for example, Iran, Lebanon, or Egypt, allows for the assumption that its literary lifeline may be the shortest in this part of the world.[1] Closer analysis demonstrates that, disregarding the region's oral traditions, this fact is particularly true for the narrative genres. Even a recent comprehensive study such as Joyce Moss's *Middle Eastern Literatures and Their Times* (2004) does not include a single writer from the above listed countries, and the only texts included which use the Gulf region on the Peninsula as setting are Abd Al-Rahman Munif's *Cities of Salt* (1984 in Arabic, 1987 in English) and Ghassan Kanafani's *Men in the Sun* (1963 in Arabic, 1978 in English). In 2010 the Saudi writer Abdo Khal won what is referred to as the Arabic Booker Prize. Khal emphasizes in the interview with Loay Mudhoon that "this award represents a milestone for literature in the Gulf region, writing that has long been virtually ignored by the rest of the Arab world,"[2] and, one may add, by the world in general. One aim of this essay is to highlight the ways in which literature from the GCC countries contributes to a canon of World Literature, an area of literary studies which has continuously enjoyed re-definition but which may currently be changing more rapidly yet. The increasingly transcultural and cosmopolitan societies of the Arabian Peninsula are indicative, in this context, of themes favored by contemporary authors, which aim to reconcile collective memory and modernization. When taking a closer look at the importance of translation for literary exchange, the present study singles out the United Arab Emirates for its extraordinary effort to make texts from local authors available abroad.

Due to the transcultural and multilingual nature of the GCC communities the contemporary Gulf Country writer is no longer the speaking voice of the tribe but s/he becomes part of the regional transformations and the international challenges which left their imprints on the geopolitical map of his/her country. A scrutinized analysis of scholarship on the literary works by writers from the Arabian Peninsula reveals the limitations of narrow critical approaches which ignore the intricate relationship between the past and the present, between tradition and modernity in contemporary texts from the GCC communities. These texts reflect various aspects of life in the respective countries since the post-oil era. Investigating the significant intricacies and overlaps in Gulf Country literature between tradition and identity on one hand and modernity and globalization on the other, the present research project explores the attempt of writers from the Arabian Peninsula to navigate the complicated intersections between two eras (the pre-oil/fishing and pearl-diving era and the post-oil era). Such an investigation articulates national narratives which are integral to the ambitions of local communities and rooted in the geopolitics of modernized countries. The process of rapid modernization in the GCC countries has significantly and expansively engaged different fields such as education, economy, industry, tourism, culture and media, leading to complicated consequences (positive and negative) which captured the imagination of Gulf Country writers who came to occupy the literary scene at a critical moment in the modern history of the Arabian Gulf region.

Since the early 1970s, after the economic boom overwhelmed the GCC countries due to the exploitation of its oil resources, the entire region has been gearing toward an era of modernization which implied radical socio-political and cultural developments and transformations. The new economic and technological conditions accelerated the process of urbanization, paving the way for the rapid shift from a traditional to a more complicated life-style. This process of rather fast-paced transitions necessarily inspired the imagination of many promising writers in the region who found themselves in a limbo of cultures. Attempting on the one hand to hold on to and celebrate traditions and the collective memory of the past, these writers were also proud of the new strategic status acquired by their countries and their more significant places on the world maps of education, economics, politics, tourism, and the arts. These writers emphasize local perspectives, deploying domestic narratives which depict the confrontation between the culture of the sea and desert, at the same time that they represent the culture of the new urbanized city in their texts. Entangled in the labyrinth of the modern metropolis, a product of the process of urbanization, and threatened by the invasion of foreign cultures and the forces of globalization, contemporary Gulf Country writers, since the post-oil era, have been concerned with the reconstruction of national identity and indigenous traditions in their literary works. A close analysis of Abdo Khal's *Tarmi Besharaaren Kalqasr/Spewing Sparks as Big as Castles* shall serve as an illustration of the ways in which themes related to post-oil socio-economic transformations are represented in the literature of the Arabian Peninsula in general and of Saudi Arabia in particular.

In his highly controversial novel *Tarmi Besharaaren Kalqasr/Spewing Sparks as Big as Castles* (2010) Khal attempts to underline significant socio-political issues rooted in the moral infrastructure of Saudi society. Khal emphasizes that the mutual alliance between corrupt politicians and opportunistic businessmen who monopolize national wealth and economic resources leads to the impoverishment and marginalization of the great majority of people in Saudi Arabia. Unlike writers who celebrate the economic, industrial and technological accomplishments resulting from modernization in the GCC region, Khal expresses his doubts and fears concerning the threats and challenges integral to the politics of post-oil changes jeopardizing native existence, traditional culture, indigenous heritage and local identity. Khal introduces in his novel an agonizing narrative which exposes the victims of the process of post-oil urbanization and modernization in the coastal city of Jeddah, a microcosm of the Saudi society.

Spewing Sparks as Big as Castles explicitly reveals the absurdity and inequity of power and authority in the post-oil era in Saudi Arabia. Throughout more than three hundred pages, the novel creates the inner world of a new palace and narrates the fate of those who are destined to become its puppets and victims. Khal's explosive novel condemns the corruption and immorality of the dwellers of palaces, who turn their backs on the socio-economic problems of the surrounding impoverished neighborhoods. Along with grotesque satire of power and authority, the novel exposes the palace and its owner as symbols of abuse and exploitation. Set in a destitute Jeddah neighborhood, the events alternate between the poor district and the palace which has recently been built, depriving the community members of access to the sea shore: "And the last task our exhausted sun undertakes each day—after it has cast off its searing heat—is to descend towards the palace in complete peace."[3]

The novel then explicitly explores the contradiction between the poor class located in the "Hell" district and the inhabitants of the palace ("Paradise") living in an ivory tower. The intruding class which emerged in the post-oil era monopolizes the stock market and the state economy, accumulating unlimited wealth through illegal and crooked methods. Instead of devoting their massive wealth to the welfare of their society, they utilize it in perverted ways to satisfy their egos, often in violation of fixed moral codes. The immoral behavior of this hegemonic class leads to the victimization and dehumanization of the lower classes, tearing apart the national unity of the local society.

For instance, the owner of the palace is a well-connected gambler with many allies helping him to keep monopoly over investments funded by the government. He owns "an army of consultants" whose main job it is to dig deep holes and set traps for other potential bidders and rivals in order to "drown them in the lake of greed and subsequent bankruptcy".[4] The owner of the palace commits heinous crimes against his rivals. On several occasions, he sets traps which involve prostitution, bribery, slander, and the employment of owners of fake projects in order to drive his enemies to bankruptcy. When Hatem Tarabi, for example, flirts with Maram, the seductive favored mistress of the palace owner, he attracts the latter's malice. Tarabi is lured to accept a fake economic transaction. As a result he has to declare bankruptcy.

Rumors constitute an integral part of the palace world. It is said, for example that Maram is the ex-wife of a greedy businessman who traded her in the process of a big transaction.[5] Others say she is the daughter of a well-known merchant who left her in the hands of the palace owner in return for major loans.[6] There are also rumors about the family members of the palace owner. Shahla, the aged wife is said to have had a first lover who spent his life dreaming of marrying her and remained a bachelor because of this unfulfilled dream.

There is no doubt that Khal's masterpiece is a painfully satirical work which depicts the damaging impact of power and money on the lives of the down-trodden classes. The novel's incidents oscillate between an old impoverished quarter of Jeddah, the Saudi city on the Red Sea, and a neighboring luxurious palace. Through the eyes of several narrators the reader is introduced to the horrifying realities of the palace, symbolizing the intruding rich class in Saudi Arabia, and its victims, the members of an indigenous fishing community in the old city of Jeddah. Because the novel, in revealing the bitter realities of life in the post-oil Saudi metropolis, touches on taboos it achieved success on the popular level.

In this context, it is important to point out that the novel's popular and local success has exposed the disparity between the conservative Islamists and the advocates of free speech in the Arab world in general and in Saudi society in particular. The local success of the novel uncovers the double standard of life in the Saudi society as it depicts a deeper divide, a wide gap between what is officially sanctioned and what is privately watched, read or talked about behind closed doors. It is noteworthy to mention that in Saudi conservative communities, *Spewing Sparks* is accused of celebrating immoral behavior because it challenges the fixed moral traditions of the Saudi society. But in educated circles, the novel is highly appreciated because it denounces despotism and hypocrisy. It reveals abuses of power considered taboo for decades. As a brilliant exploration of the conflict between the individual and the state, the novel alludes to the sacrosanct triangle of taboos in the Saudi community—politics, sex and religion—and is therefore officially banned in Saudi Arabia.

Spewing Sparks depicts the interactions between two contradictory worlds represented by the residents of the palace and the downtrodden dwellers of the area surrounding the palace. It shows how the latter are often attracted by promises of glamour and extraordinary wealth. After the palace's master, a business tycoon, whose origins are not fully disclosed, claims the sea shore to build his enormous construction replete with gardens and swimming pools, young men from the fishing community are longing to explore the unknown world behind the palace walls.

In the beginning of the novel the central narrator describes a world where people are crammed into a shabby and dirty district: "The name of our quarter is The Pit, or The Salt Mine, or The Bottom of Hell, or Inferno; all are terms that reflect torment, and our lives." The destitute district, which is reminiscent of the first part of Dante's *Divine Comedy,* has been situated in the old city of Jeddah since the pre-oil era. The narrator captures activities in this poor quarter prior to the building of the palace by saying, "The quarter awakens before the sun's rays penetrate the windows of the huddled houses to the contented lapping of the satiated sea. It awakens to the racket of boys preparing to set off down twisting lanes on their walk to school."[7] Khal further describes the early morning rituals and habits of people in the traditional fishing community with an emphasis on their appreciation of the surrounding landscape: "The raucous banter of fishermen returning with fresh catches from trips began the previous night, and songs on the radio exuberant in the dewy morning air. Songs that soothe the soul, refreshing like the drizzle of summer rain, they pierce the breast, and lungs expand to receive life's refreshing air." He also subtly provides minute details about the simplicity of life in a pre-oil Jeddah delineating the routine movements in the neighborhood's alleys, describing "The alley awakes to the rattle of padlocks on shop doors as the owners open up, and the cries of street hawkers calling after young school children, tempting them to purchase a sweetie [sic] or a poorly manufactured toy or a snack that begins with the mouth and ends up with a runny tummy for whoever's bowels have not been previously fortified." Khal's description, it appears, recalls his own childhood memories in the city of Jeddah after his family moved from Jizan, in the Southern part of Saudi Arabia.

The novel narrates the life history of three young men from a poor background who left their miserable environments to work for a rich authoritative businessman, the infamous owner of the palace. They are enticed by the affluent, but corrupt, lifestyle in the palace. When the palace was built, nobody among the members of the fishing community near the sea shore dared to confront the rich palace owner regardless of the ecological and economic disasters brought upon them by the construction project. Instead, Uthman Kabbashi, a builder of fishing boats, cancels all the contracts for new boats. Though the fishermen are angry with him he does not want their money to be lost in the purchase of boats which "will not find water to sail in" (Khal 164). The sailors, along with Uthman Kabbashi are seen weeping after they lose their only source of income, saying "In place of the waves of the sea lie blocks of iron and cement" (Khal 163). Hamed Abu Jalambo, the leader among the sailors and fishermen, reacts with peaceful resistance in the form of popular lyrics and elegies that lament the disappearance of the sea to the community's radically changed reality. His ballads look like farewell songs "written by a lover to his departing beloved" (Khal 162). Nobody among the members of the fishing community openly challenges the owner of the palace who destroyed their source of living.

Due to his authority and wide relationships, nobody dares even to mention the name of the palace owner. Throughout the novel his name remains unknown but called "the master" (Khal 160). Regardless of the negative consequences that resulted from the construction of the palace, most of the surrounding community is eager to enter its gates and meet the owner. Such an ambivalent attitude toward the palace, the implied wealth and corruption, punctuates most of the events in the novel. For example, Mohamed al-Rekabi depends on the palace for his livelihood and is therefore not able to leave it anymore, despite the fact that he hates its rotten atmosphere tainted by prostitution, deception, intrigue, perversion and gambling. Al Rekabi criticizes the immoral behavior of the master and his friends who spread corruption and debauchery in the surrounding society, and yet he is unable to distance himself from them.

Belonging to the emerging commercially successful class that determines the fate of the Saudi people, the rich and authoritative palace owner is able to seize an extended area of land on the sea shore of Jeddah to establish his luxurious palace. The inhabitants of the surrounding poor district called "Hell" are not allowed to have direct access to the sea shore after the building of the palace. However, young people from the poor neighborhood are attracted to the opulence and inner secrets of the decadent construction. Eissa al-Rudeni, a young man from the district is able to save the palace owner's elder son from drowning. As a result the gates of the palace are opened for Eissa, who falls in love with Moudi, the spoiled daughter of the palace owner. Eissa treats Moudi as his wife though in reality the two develop an illicit love affair. Eissa makes love to Moudi inside the palace, jeopardizing himself to the wrath of the master. Furthermore, Eissa paves the way for two of his closest childhood friends to enter the world of the palace—Tarek Fadel, the psychologically disturbed central narrator of the novel, and Usama al-Bishri.

The three young friends are being dominated by the owner of the palace and used to serve his vicious purposes. The palace owner is a ruthless and sadistic tycoon who tortures his opponents in many ways. Tarek Fadel, the bisexual protagonist is forced to carry out his master's evil orders, including rape and other forms of physical torture. Tarek is shown as a sadistic monster commanded to take revenge on the male rivals of his master. Raping rituals are video-taped in order to increase the victim's intimidation and to enforce silence in fear of scandals. The inside of the palace symbolizes an epitome of the rich and corrupt class that emerged within Saudi society in the post-oil era. The three young men from the Hell district meet with abusive politicians, parasitic businessmen and decadent tycoons who control the money market. They also meet with a great number of female servants and poor girls who are transformed into prostitutes and sex slaves to entertain the master and his entourage. Many of these girls initially came to the palace looking for work or help with administrative services.

The three young men—Eissa, Usama and Tarek—remain in the palace for decades but fail to become part of the master's social class regardless of the enormous wealth they accumulate. For example, Eissa attempts to bridge the social gap between himself and his beloved Moudi by using Khaled Banan, a psychology teacher, to help him obtain the Master degree as well as a PhD in International Law from Arab universities. Denied the kind of social mobility which would make him suitable for Moudi, Eissa does succeed in increasing his wealth through deceptive ways and becomes one of the biggest share-holders in several companies. However, after the palace owner's death and the succession of his elder son, whom Eissa once rescued from drowning, the new master decides to Eissa financially to prevent him from proposing to the sister. The elder son continues the father's legacy. Finally, Tarek is forced to rape his friend Eissa in the presence of the new master of the palace. Eissa, as a result, becomes insane, is seen walking in the streets of Jeddah completely naked, and then shot dead when he returns to the palace.

Usama al-Bishri, the third young man to enter the palace, is emotionally attached to his maternal cousin, Tahani. But his sentiment is not reciprocated because Tahani is attracted to Tarek, whose virility becomes notorious. Instead of appreciating Tahani's love, Tarek breaks into her house at night and brutally rapes her. Her father, Saleh Khaybari, enters Tahani's bedroom after the heinous act but fails to arrest or recognize the attacker who jumps out of the window. Tahani tells her father that she was raped by an unknown "human wolf." She denies any prior relationship with the rapist. To remove the shame that has fallen upon the family's honor, Saleh takes Tahani to an isolated village where his tribal folks live and kills her without mercy. After burying her body in a secret graveyard, he tells the neighbors in Jeddah that Tahani was married to one of his own relatives in a remote region of the country. Usama, the desperate suitor now deprived of Tahani's presence, does not believe the fabricated story about her marriage and spends most of his life waiting for her return. Usama never finds out that it was his friend Tarek who instigated Tahani's pre-mature death. When he learns about her murder, however, he starts to roam the country searching for and eventually finding the graveyard. In his misery he finds solace in visiting Tahani's grave and regularly planting roses and other flowers around it.

Tarek, the monstrous anti-hero of the book, is cut off from his family and social roots after he enters the palace. Like Usama and Eissa, Tarek is involved in illicit sex affairs. Unlike Usama's and Eissa's, Tarek's affairs are with different women and men inside and outside the palace and serve to prove his manhood and masculinity.[8] Tarek believes that man is destined to live without a chance to redeem himself from sin: "falling in sin is the law that governs man's life since primitive times" (Khal 176). He adds, "Life is filthy business. It starts off clean and seductive with encouraging words of advice, but truth be told, you have to commit sins to be a human being" (Calderbank's translation 4). When he reaches his fifties he tries to repent and seek salvation but fails. His suffering reaches a zenith when his younger brother Ebrahim, a devout person, rejects him. When Tarek tries to give Ebrahim some money, the latter turns him down because "rotten money has a rotten smell" (Khal 178). Tarek is also turned down by the Imam when he enters the mosque to perform prayers.

Tarek is psychologically disturbed as a result of his upbringing in a dysfunctional family. Tarek's vicious aunt, Khayriyya, is shown to have encouraged his sadism. During his adolescence, she caught him while he attempted to have sex with one of her sheep. Catching sight of his enormous penis, she spreads disturbing rumors in the neighborhood and even pushes him to have sex with one of her neighbors called Souad. This relationship at such an early stage in his life has a destructive effect on Tarek's development, and the sensationalism revolving around his virility appears as most obvious criticism of the chauvinist nature of the palace's abusive oppression. Due to his miserable life in the impoverished fishing community, Tarek calls the palace "Paradise" while referring to his own district as "Hell." The palace owner uses Tarek, originally a victim of economic dispossession, to sexually abuse his rivals. The aggressive anti-hero, a native and notorious bully of the fishing community, becomes a pawn in the hands of the palace's owner. It is important to point out, however, that Tarek is the central narrator and not a mere instrument but a participant in the violence, an agent of political oppression. Inside the palace, the victims of the master are stripped of their dignities.

Eventually, Tarek hates all women including his mother, Saniyya. He believes that his mother is a sinful woman who remains faithful to Geith, her first lover, even after her marriage to his father.[9] When Tarek's father dies in an accident, Saniyya marries Geith. Tarek's misogyny is, for example, expressed when he states that "all women look like sponges. They are able to absorb any liquids whether blood or water" (Khal 210). The most monstrous among the narrators, Tarek is also the one driven to terminate the abusive and decadent system. By the end of the novel he decides to assassinate the owner of the palace: "Tarek carries the corpse of the master in his own imagination" (Khal 181). He fails to accomplish his mission. A final horrible discovery, by the end of the novel, is that Mariam, one of the palace's prostitutes is Tarek's own half sister. Because Tarek does not know about his father's other wives he is not aware of the origins of Mariam. Like Oedipus, Tarek commits the sin of incest due to ignorance but unlike the Greek hero, Khal's protagonist does not punish himself for the dreadful act.

Using the postmodern technique of collage, Khal added two appendixes at the end of the book. The first one is titled "The Palace Women" (Khal 192). In order to create an illusion of reality the author provides names and pictures of the prostitutes and sex slaves from the palace in addition to a copy of a love letter written by Tahani to Tarek Fadel. The fake message carries Tahani's signature. The second appendix is called "The Barrier" and includes extracts from local newspapers and websites which reference many of the events described in the novel. Khal also utilized (post)modernist narrative strategies like flashback, juxtaposition, and intertextuality in addition to allusions to *the Quran, the Bible, Hamlet, Othello* as well as novels by prominent Arab authors such as Najuib Mahfouz's *The Thief and The Dogs* and Ala' al-Aswani's *Yacobian Building*.

Poststructuralist critics such as Roland Barthes and Jacques Derrida have marginalized the role of the author removing him/her from the center of the text production process, claiming that language has no communicative function. In this context, Barthes introduced the idea of "the death of the author" while Derrida considered the concept of writing as "an orphan." Taking into account the non-existence of transcendental/universal reference (dismantling of paternity), poststructuralists like Barthes and Derrida argue that all texts refer to one another, intersect and interrelate with one another randomly and infinitely. The term "intertextuality" was introduced by Julia Kristeva in the 1960s. In *Desire in Language* Kristeva discusses the appearance of texts or parts of texts in other, newer texts. She points out that several utterances from other texts "intersect and neutralize one another in the space of a given text" (36). Kristeva's concept of intertextuality can be traced back to the structuralist works of Saussure, as well as to Bakhtin's theories. Underlining the rational nature of language, Saussure argues that signs are not referential since they acquire their signification from different kinds of relationships with other signs, particularly opposition. Bakhtin focuses on the social context within which words are exchanged. He observes that all utterances are either dialogic/double-voiced or polyphonic/multiple-voiced and this notion incorporates intertextuality. Advocating Bakhtin's concept which signifies that all texts contain within them society's ideological struggles and tensions, Kristeva argues that texts do not present stable meanings. To her, texts reflect society's ideological conflict over the meaning of words. For example, words like "wealth," "power," "corruption," "poverty," and "death" that frequently appear in the text of *Spewing Sparks as Big as Castles* carry society's conflict over their meaning.

Like Kristeva, Barthes believes that a text is an inter-textual construct which is woven with citations, references, echoes, cultural languages—antecedent or contemporary—which cut across it through and through in "a vast stereophony." He adds that the text's inter-texts (which include other works/texts) are themselves inter-textual constructs and therefore cannot act as the signified of the text's signifiers because they themselves are signifiers. Barthes also argues that the origin of the text is not a unified authorial consciousness but a plurality of voices, of other words, other utterances and other texts. In *Image-Music-Text*, Barthes states that the modern author does not release a single "theological meaning," what he calls "the message" of "the author-God" but produces "a multi-dimensional space in which a variety of writings—none of them original—blend and clash" (146). Thus, the text is a "tissue of quotations drawn from the innumerable centers of culture." In the light of the theories initiated by Derrida, Kristeva, and Barthes, *Spewing Sparks* is partly a post-modern text due to its inter-textual peculiarity. Linda Hutcheon argues in *A Poetics of Postmodernism* that postmodern literature is typically inter-textual as it combines forms and styles from both high culture and popular culture. She points out that parody is "a perfect postmodern form, in some sense, for it paradoxically both incorporates and challenges that which it parodies" (11).

It is relevant to argue here that *Spewing Sparks* fulfills the above-mentioned criteria to a great extent in the sense that it is a text which is born out of other texts and that it shows a strong parodist quality. However, Khal's novel, which is based on the author's experience in the city of Jeddah and in which the author appears as the consciousness of the central character cannot fulfill the French poststructuralist premise of writing "as an orphan" which indicates the death of the author. It is, however, noteworthy to argue that Barthes's theories shift the emphasis from text to reader and thus constitute several binary oppositions including "work" versus "text," "readerly text" versus "writerly texts," "text of pleasure" versus "text of bliss," and "doxa" versus "paradoxa." Within this context, it is clear that French poststructuralist theories have removed the author out of the hermeneutic circle which makes it difficult to apply these theories literally to a book like *Spewing Sparks,* based on the life experience of the author/narrator. Thus, it is more appropriate to refer to the poststructuralist theories of American critics such as Harold Bloom and Hillis Miller who agree with the French poststructuralists, to some extent, on the issue of intertextuality and reject "the death of the author" hypothesis.

Susan Friedman reveals that the emphasis on the agency of the author represents a characteristically American redefinition of intertextuality. According to her, "many American critics from Bloom to Miller have refused to let the author die as they forged various intertextual methodologies" (159). For example, Bloom agrees with the French post-structuralists that all texts are inter-texts and a single text has only part of a meaning: "it is a synecdoche for a larger whole including other texts. A text is a relational event and not a substance to be analyzed" (qtd. in Allen 136). Applying this theory to poetry, Bloom presents a map of misreading and psychological defense mechanism developed by poets to disguise the influence of their precursors. Nevertheless, it is significant to reveal that Bloom agrees with French poststructuralist critics in advocating an open intertextuality but he disagrees with them in excluding the social and cultural contexts from the open intertextual domain. He insists on the crucial role of the author. Further, Bloom uses the term "facticity" to indicate the unavoidable influence of certain writers within Western tradition, such as Shakespeare and Eliot, on modern writers, even those who do not read them.

Taking into consideration Bloom's approach to intertextuality, it is relevant to state here that in contemporary literary theory, the term "intertextuality" has replaced the term "influence" which is associated with traditional influence studies. Jay Clayton and Eric Rothstein argue that contemporary critics prefer to use the concept of intertextuality in their studies because the term "influence" is elitist and concerned only with major works. Dealing with a greater variety of works as social products, the notion of intertextuality comes to replace the more limited concept of "influence." It is interesting to argue that *Spewing Sparks* reveals its inter-textual side as a post-modern text that is also characterized by an authorial presence. Intertexts in Khal's novel are drawn from different domains and disciplines. Khal's text interrelates with other texts but does not at random as the French poststructuralists argue. Most texts that appear in the novel are carefully chosen to serve the novelist's vision. A variety of texts stemming from a variety of sources are manipulated by 'a talented author' to create a post-modern text which is a mosaic of other texts.

Finally, in Umberto Eco's words, "the already written and the already said threaten to turn one's narrative and narrative voice into a mere repetition of previous utterances and previous texts" (qtd. in Allen 194). In his treatment of local motifs, Khal uses many external texts. The novel's title *Spewing Sparks as Big as Castles* is chosen in reference to the Holy Quran's line, "Indeed it throws about sparks huge as forts/As if they were a string of yellow camels" (Surah/chapter LXXVII, "Those Sent Forth").[10] The

Quranic narrative, used as an inter-text, refers to hell and its dwellers. Delineating Jeddah as a hell Tarek muses, as quoted above: "The name of our quarter is The Pit, or The Salt Mine, or The Bottom of Hell, or Inferno; all are terms that reflect torment, and our lives." The novelist alludes not only to Islamic holy texts but also draws from Biblical sources. Jeddah, and in particular the microcosm of the palace, is depicted as a sinful city analogous to Sodom and Gomorrah.

Other borrowed texts belong to a variety of sources ranging from popular Saudi folklore, historical studies and contemporary Arabic novels, to documentaries and allegorical prose works. Khal's novel is equally punctuated with erotic texts from ancient and modern sources, as well as realistic descriptions of the city of Jeddah, particularly the Hamra district.

> There were two directions we used to take so we could plunge our bodies into the sea: the beach which stretched along the coast south of Jeddah, but which had deteriorated suddenly so that taking the road there was no longer desirable. And there was Al-Hamra district that had sprung up as the destination for those heading for a day out after Engineer Muhammad Sa'eed Al-Farsi (The Mayor of Jeddah) reshaped the sea front as a series of inlets and lined them with pieces of art by some of the world's greatest artists, deploying hundreds of workers to spruce up the entire length of the Corniche. (8)

In addition to distinguished realistic figures like the mayor of Jeddah, the author himself and some of his childhood friends appear as characters in the text of the narrative. Thus mixing fact and fiction, Khal incorporates intertextuality as a postmodern technique and captures life in the city of Jeddah at a transitional stage, ushering in the new prosperous post-oil era. Numerous flashbacks are reminiscent of the pre-oil years when the city depended on fishing and pearl diving and followed traditions integral to the patriarchal nature of conservative Saudi society.

> My grandfather on my mother's side came here carrying his wares: Indian fabrics, Javan incense and mi'zars (male clothes) from the Hadramoot (a region in South Yemen). He built himself a large house which he planned from the beginning to

> fill with his offspring, for there his lust had so overflowed that he acquired four women and put each one in a corner of the wide courtyard whereupon he proceeded to indulge with them his carnal desires every night. His pleasure intensified whenever he came to my grandmother (my mother's mother). She was of Turkish extraction and the beauty in her face had erupted and flowed all over her body. (4)

Khal's story of the people in Jeddah is as critical of the ugly and corrupt practices that undermine the traditional, pre-oil foundations of Saudi society as it is of post-oil corruption and greed. The central narrator reveals the macho mentality of his grandfather who lived in a society in which women's foremost purpose was to satisfy men's desires and produce offspring. The narrator exposes the false concepts of masculinity deeply rooted in the collective consciousness of a society that abuses the concept of polygamy.

> In his morning session he (my grandfather) would be bursting with pride as he told his companions how he had been able to see to his four wives without recourse to the potions of Abu Rasheed, the herbalist. Abu Rasheed was a herbalist of Indian origin who claimed some knowledge of herbs and their properties that enabled a man to behave like a crocodile and satisfy ten women without his passion waning. He was the subject of much veneration by those men whose strength had diminished and who were in urgent need of his services so that their manhood would remain erect in the boudoir. (4)

As a challenge to the religious and social taboos that dominate Saudi society, Khal's postmodern novel attempts to disrupt what Jean-Francois Lyotard calls "the grand narratives" of traditional societies or what Derrida labels as the discourse of a "totalized system." "Totality," according to Lyotard, is maintained through the means of "grand narratives" or "master narratives" which are stories a culture tells about its practices and beliefs. Lyotard observes that every belief system or ideology has its grand narratives. It might be argued that grand narratives are kinds of meta-theories or meta-ideologies that explain an ideology; a story that is told to explain an existing belief system. Lyotard argues that all aspects of traditional societies depend on grand narratives and postmodernism is a critique of these grand narratives because of its awareness that such narratives serve to mask the contradictions and instabilities that are inherent in any social organization or practice.

Moreover, Lyotard points out that postmodernism rejects grand/master narratives and favors "counter/mini" narratives or what he categorizes as "legitimate narratives" (19) which are stories that aim to deconstruct conventional and conservative narratives. In rejecting the grand narratives of conservative Saudi culture, Khal seeks to introduce his postmodern counter-narrative throughout a novel which uncovers the negative sides of a backward tradition that hides beneath a veneer of religious hypocrisy. As a whole, the novel delineates the downfall of a poor district in Jeddah as it illuminates the ambitions, dreams, frustrations and miseries of the disenfranchised members of society. The marginalized inhabitants of the impoverished community are given voices which have not been heard for centuries.

> Our generation inherited hopes. As young men we consoled ourselves by stealing glances at everything we set eyes on; stealing a glance at some delicious food, some smart clothes, fast cars, and the money that flowed through the trades' shops, and women on their way to the market that lay between the houses and the narrow winding lanes. Our eyes would pick up everything and this is what trained us to dream, and be satisfied with what was suspended in our imaginations. (6)

The novel uncovers hidden secrets of urban life in Saudi Arabia in the post-oil era emphasizing local perspectives and deploying domestic narratives which depict the confrontation between the poor and the rich, between the traditions of the sea and desert on one hand and the exploitative politics of the decadent palace dwellers on the other. Capturing the complicated intersection between past and present, the novel illuminates the raving impact of unlimited authority upon an emerging society in that it depicts the opulent life of an ultra wealthy class living in palaces while the surrounding society is inflicted with abject poverty. In other words, the novel spotlights the juxtaposition of a world poisoned by decadent wealth with a world suffering from poverty, with people stripped of their human rights and even their dreams.

> We would dream simply to sit in a restaurant and eat delicious food, or that this shop or that was ours, or that our evening would be blessed by the company of some women or other. A life in which we wore our dreams until they got dirty and then threw them into a bin for collecting dirty clothes and changed them for another dream. This was the life of poverty and hardship. A life suited to wearing dreams, and to be constantly changing them for, at any rate, they were unseen garments.

The English translation of Khal's novel has not been completed, but the fact that it is in progress and will join a growing list of translated Gulf Country texts is an obvious indication that the literature from the Arabian Peninsula is becoming more widely acknowledged and discussed within a context of World Literature. While selected stories and poems from across the region were already included in Salma Jayyusi's 1988 collection *The Literature of Modern Arabia,* there are now collections such as Denys Johnson-Davies's *In a Fertile Desert: Modern Writing from the United Arab Emirates* (2009) devoted entirely to one specific Gulf country. Local publishing houses support their writers' efforts to reach foreign audiences or even audiences within the GCC countries in which large numbers of residents do not speak Arabic. The Emirati Mohammad Al Murr had, for example, not only his *Wink of the Mona Lisa* (1998) but also *Dubai Tales* (2008) published by the Dubai based Motivate Publishing.

In "Naguib Mahfouz and the Cruelty of Memory" Edward Said remembers his attempt in the 1980s to convince a New York publisher who was then looking for 'Third World' books of Mahfouz's relevance for the planned project. Said's attempt remained unsuccessful. He "was told (with no detectable irony) that Arabic was a controversial language." Mahfouz has since become a Nobel Prize winner and one among only three Arab writers, all three Egyptians, included in *The Norton Anthology of World Literature*. Much like Mahfouz has mapped his native Cairo, Al Murr is representing Emirati topography, especially Dubai in his stories. Al Ain, the UAE's third largest city, in the interior of the country and bordering with Oman's Buraimi, is the setting of Mariam Al Saadi's "Like the Others," a story included in this author's first story collection *Mariam and the Fortune*, a collection which became available in German translation in the same year it was first published. In an effort to make cultural background accessible to foreign audiences, Al Saadi's as well as Al Murr's translated collections include glossaries in which Arab artists are referenced alongside unique terminology.

An even greater effort to introduce foreign readers to the stories and traditions of her home, its topography as well as its past, is made by Maha Gargash who wrote her debut novel *The Sand Fish* in English. Although Harper Collins advertises this text on the cover as "a novel from Dubai" this specification relates primarily to the origin of the author rather than the settings of the story. The novel tells of various rural and mountainous areas in the North of the country during the early onset of the oil boom. Having grown up in a poor community in the mountains the protagonist moves to the coast as the third wife of a much older pearl merchant. Unable to admit to or even suspect and be informed of his own infertility this man is searching for the woman who will finally deliver his long desired child. The first wife arranges, unbeknownst to the protagonist Noura, for a romance with one of the merchant's servants and leads her husband, after Noura conceives with the servant, to believe that he is indeed to be blessed with an heir after all. Noura rejects the servant's plea to elope with him and thus complies with the first wife's deceptive plot. Like Khal's novel Gargash's text thus grapples with patriarchal traditions, with family structures and class difference. Unlike *Spewing Sparks* it paints a picture mainly of the pre-oil era and references the onset of the oil boom only in a few passages. The merchant does sense that he will have to move his business away from the pearl industry in the near future, but Gargash's novel ends before post-oil transformations become tangible.

As the in-depth analysis of Khal's novel and the brief discussions of translated texts, as well as Gargash's *Sand Fish* from the Arabian Peninsula show, themes currently represented by Gulf Country writers relate largely to their assessments of the transitions brought forth by the development of fairly recent new industries. These transitions include, generally speaking, changes to natural landscapes as well as to their inhabitants and communities. They entail the merging of clan- and class-oriented with more transcultural societies, as well as feminist challenges of traditional patriarchal structures. They furthermore scrutinize the rapid growth of metropolitan areas along with the changes brought forth by increasing tourism. Current socio-political transitions engendered by what is referred to as the 'Arab Spring' will no doubt inspire many literary works from the region.

NOTES

1. Attention should be drawn at this point to the invaluable resource provided by Keren Dali, Juris Dilevko and Glenda Gerbutt in *Contemporary World Fiction: A Guide to Literature in Translation*, whose second chapter on "The Arab World" includes texts from Saudi Arabia, the UAE and Yemen.
2. Loay Mudhoon, "The Discovery of Arabic Literature in the Gulf: An Interview with Abdo Khal," trans. Nina Coon (http://en.qantara.de/webcom/show_article.php/_c-310/_nr-738/i.html).
3. Anthony Calderbank, trans. "Extract from *Tarmi Beshararen Kalqasr/Spewing Sparks as Big as Castles,*" *The Best of the New Arabic Fiction* (Abu Dhabi: Emirates Foundation Publications, 2010), 3.
4. Abdo Khal, *Tarmi Besharaen Kalqas/Spewing Sparks as Big as Castles.* (Beirut: Aljamal Press, 2010), 166.
5. Ibid., 168.
6. Ibid., 169.
7. Calderbank, trans. "Extract from *Spewing Sparks as Big as Castles,*" 3–11.
8. Abdo Khal, *Tarmi Besharaen Kalqas/Spewing Sparks as Big as Castles.* (Beirut: Aljamal Press, 2010), 185.
9. Ibid., 189.
10. Yusuf Ali, *The Translation of the Meaning of the Holy Quran* (Beirut: Alaalami Publications, 2001), 882.

REFERENCES

Ali, Yusuf. *The Translation of the Meaning of the Holy Quran*. Beirut: Alaalami Publications, 2001.

Allen, Graham. *Intertextuality*. New York/London: Routledge, 2000.

Al Murr, Mohammad. *The Wink of the Mona Lisa*. Trans. Jack Briggs. Dubai/London: Motivate Publishing, 1998.

——. *Dubai Tales,* trans. Peter Clark. Dubai/London: Motivate Publishing, 2008.

Al Saadi, Mariam. *Mariam und das Glück*. Trans. Bashar Humeid and Evelyn Agbaria. Basel: Lisan, 2009.

Barthes, Roland. *Image-Music-Text*. Trans. Stephen Heath. London: Fontana, 1977.

Calderbank, Anthony, trans. "Extract from *Spewing Sparks as Big as Castle.*" *The Best of the New Arabic Fiction*. Abu Dhabi: Emirates Foundation Publication, 2010.

Dali, Keren, Juris Dilevko, Glenda Gerbutt. *Contemporary World Fiction: A Guide to Literature in Translation*. Santa Barbara, CA: Greenwood, 2011.

Friedman, Susan. "Weavings: Intertextuality and the (Re)Birth of the Author." *Influences and Intertextuality in Literary History*. Ed. Jay Clayton and Eric Rothstein. Madison, WI: U of Wisconsin P, 1991. 146–180.

Gargash, Maha. *The Sand Fish*. New York: Harper Collins, 2009.

Hutcheon, Linda. *A Poetics of Postmodernism: History, Theory, Fiction*. London/New York: Routledge, 1988.

Jayyusi, Salma Khadra, ed. *The Literature of Modern Arabia: An Anthology*. London/NY: Kegan Paul Intl. and King Saudi U, 1988.

Johnson-Davis, Denys, ed. *In a Fertile Desert: Modern Writing from the United Arab Emirates*. Cairo/NY: The American U of Cairo P, 2009.

Khal, Abdo. Tarmi Bishararen Kalqasr/*Spewing Sparks as Big as Castles*. Beirut: Aljamal P, 2010.

Kristeve, Julia. *Desire in Language: A Semiotic Approach to Literature and Art*. Trans. Thomas Gora. New York: Columbia UP, 1980.

Lawall, Sarah, et al., eds. *The Norton Anthology of World Literature: Vol. F – The 20th Century*. 2nd edition. NewYork: Norton, 2002.

Lyotard, Jean-François. *The Postmodern Condition: A Report on Knowledge*. Trans. Geoff Bennington and Brian Massumi. Minneapolis, MN: U of Minnesota P, 1991.

Moss, Joyce, ed. *World Literature and Its Times: Profiles of Notable Literary Works and the Historical Events That Influenced Them. Vol. 6: Middle Eastern Literatures and Their Times*. Detroit/London: Thomas Gale, 2004.

Mudhoon, Loay. "The Discovery of Arabic Literature in the Gulf: an Interview with Abdo Khal (2011)." Trans. Nina Coon. <http://en. qantara.de/wcsite. php?wcc=9157>. October 2011.

Said, Edward. "Naguib Mahfouz and the Cruelty of Memory." <http://www.counterpunch.org/mahfouz.html>. April 2009.

CHAPTER 8

Ikezawa Natsuki as a Conscientious Witness to Japanese Society and History[1]

Hajime Saito

Undoubtedly, to name one Japanese novelist who is the most popular and the most widely known in the world, it would be Murakami Haruki (1951–). His novels in Japanese and translations boast of international as well as domestic selling power. Interestingly, as he gains a wider renown, Murakami begins to turn his interest to the society and history he has been part of. In "Always on the side of the egg,"[2] his acceptance speech for the Jerusalem Prize for literature (2009), he referred to the divided situations in Gaza and set forth active debates.[3] In 2011 he "slammed" Japan's nuclear energy policy, addressing the catastrophic damage that the Fukushima nuclear disaster brought about.[4] Certainly, Murakami is now willing to take on a role of an intellectual though in the late 1970s and early 1980s he seemed to avert his literary gaze from social and historical issues.[5] Particularly, since 1995 when the great Hanshin earthquake (17 January) and the sarin gas attack on the Tokyo subway by Aum Shinrikyo cult (20 March) shook the Japanese society, Murakami has actively been raising his voice as a concerned intellectual.

However, when it comes to discussing Japanese writers' political engagement, it would be against reason not to mention Ikezawa Natsuki (1945–). Ikezawa, who is a poet, novelist, essayist and translator, has 33 years of literary career under his belt. Yet surprisingly, he is little known in world literature as well as holds an insignificant place in the history of Japanese novel. Of course it would be not true to say that Ikezawa is a total stranger to world readers. Two of his novels have been translated: the Akutagawa Literary Prize winning novel *Sutiru Raifu* (*Still Lives* 1984) and a less popular novel *Hana o Hakobu Imōto* (*A Burden of Flowers* 2000) are available in English translation.[6] However, in comparison with active Murakami studies, it is disappointing that no single international monograph on Ikezawa has been published. It is even more so since *A Burden of Flowers* which garnered the Daily Publishing Culture Award deals with a cosmopolitan theme, "the clash between Europe and Asia, life and death, and desperation and salvation" set in one of the most famous resort island, Bali,[7] and strongly reveals Ikezawa's lifelong commitment to raise an intellectual voice about socio-historical issues. Given this neglect of Ikezawa in the literary history of Japanese novels as well as in world literary studies, it is time to re-estimate the pertinence of Ikezawa's conscientious voice and his literary significance. Particularly, it will be refreshing for world readers to know how cosmopolitan attitude he has held toward Japanese society and history as a concerned intellectual and what unique representations he has made for minority races as a responsible writer.

Ikezawa's first novel, *Natsu no Asa no Seisouken* (*The Stratosphere in the Summer Morning* 1984), features Yasushi Kimura, a Japanese writer of a local newspaper in Shizuoka. One day, he goes missing while conducting a research into Japan's deep sea fishing industry in the Pacific. He finally finds himself on a shore of a Pacific island and starts living like Robinson Crusoe. After a while he meets an old American actor Myron Cunard who lives a retired life in the island next to the one Kimura lives, and he forms a strange friendship with the actor. The story ends tragically, raising a consciousness of not only the existence of the US military force in the island but also of the historical relationship between Japan and the US.[8]

In the second novel *Mashiasu Giri no Shikkyaku* (*The Fall of Macias Guili* 1992) the cultural, financial and military relationships between the US and Japan form the main conflicts of the story. Guili, dictator of a fictional Micronesian island state called Nabidad, is a native Nabidad man who has adopted a Japanese life style. In fact, he got education under the Japanese Occupation in the 1940s and has since developed his commercial and political career maintaining a close contact with Japanese politicians and merchants in the post WWII era. Even when he could take his own ways as a dictator, he continues Japanese way of life, eating rice every morning as a Japanese would. Throughout the story, however, Guili keeps being torn by three political powers: firstly, Japan for which Guili has been performing a kind of agent; secondly, USA with which Guili's political enemies has collaborated; lastly, his islands' traditional and spiritual power. He finally commits suicide, as if wishing to escape from the impasse of the power triangle. This ending can be said to be one of the most remarkable achievements of the 1990s' Japanese literature in that Ikezawa materialized his postcolonial insights into the entangled histories among political powers in and around the Pacific in such a subtle, sophisticated way.[9]

Entering the 2000s, Ikezawa's sense of social responsibility becomes even stronger. *Iraku no Chiisana Hashi o Watatte* (*On a Small Bridge in Iraq* 2003) is a collaborative work, putting out Ikezawa's severe criticism against America's unreasonable intervention into Iraq with a famous photographer Seiichi Motohashi's photographs of Iraqi people and landscapes side by side. *Mukudori Tsûshin* (*Reports of a Starling*) and its sequels are collections of essays written during his stay in Okinawa Island (1993–2005), southernmost part of Japan, in which he raises a very critical voice against the violence that both the US and mainland Japan wield on the people of Okinawa. Through these novels and essays, it is clearly shown that Ikezawa has put his commitment to society and history into practice.

Ikezawa's social and historical consciousness is manifested otherwise. *Tanoshii Shûmatsu* (*Happy Ends* 1993), whose title plays a pun intended to have an ironic effect—in Japanese "shûmatsu" means both "weekends" and "(apocalyptic) ends"—includes an essay addressing the Lucky Dragon 5 incident in 1954. A small fishing boat Daigo Fukuryû Maru (Lucky Dragon 5) from Yaizu chity in Shizuoka Prefecture, Japan, was operating near Bikini Atoll. Unexpectedly, the crew members of the boat were exposed to the nuclear fallout from a US hydrogen bomb test called "Bravo Castle," which saw the beginning of anti-nuclear movements in Japan.[10] Ikezawa ends this collection of essays with the following remarks: "if the world ends tomorrow, would you plant apple seeds?" This apocalyptic vision is supplemented by his continuous search for alternative ways of living: the wind-power electricity, for example, is one of the main topics in *Subarashii Shinsekai* (*Brave New World* 2000). His anti-nuclear vision in these works poignantly echoes against the tragic accident of Tokyo Electric Power Company's Fukushima No.1 nuclear plant on March 2011.

In a way Ikezawa's sense of social responsibility for those who get to suffer under the macroscopic power games seems only natural when we consider his biographical background. Ikezawa was born in Obihiro, a city in eastern Hokkaido, northernmost part of Japan, in 1945. His father Fukunaga Takehiko was a famous novelist and scholar of French literature (1918–1979). Evacuated in 1944 from Tokyo under bombardment to Obihiro, he met Ikezawa's mother Harajō Akiko (1913–2004) who was a poet. Their marriage, however, broke in five years, and Harajō moved to Tokyo with his son, Natsuki, in 1950. In his youth, he dropped out of the Saitama University [Department of Science and Engineering] in 1968 and became a translator traveling around the world. In 1972 he got married and stayed in Greece from 1972 to1975. After returning to Japan, he published his first book of poems, *Shio no michi* (*The Road of Salt*). In 1984 he made his debut as a novelist with *Natsu no asa no seisou-ken* (*The Stratosphere in the Summer Morning*). While he stayed in Okinawa from 1993 to 2005, he journeyed through the island and published numerous works. Mostly staying at the edges and outside of Japan in his entire life, he has had experience of displacement, which seems to have led him to be keenly conscious of the histories of minority people who have long been unfortunate victims of mainland Japan's power games.

Ikezawa's sympathy for the minority is most remarkably represented in *Shizukana Daichi* (*A Quiet Land* 2002). In the novel of Ikezawa, who is a descendant of the Wajin people in Hokkaido—the grandparents of Ikezawa's mother, Harajō Akiko, were emigrants from Awajishima (Awaji Island: an island between the islands of Honshû and Shikoku) to Hokkaido in the early Meiji era (around 1870)—addresses directly the tragic history of Ainu people, one of the indigenous race of Hokkaido. To speak briefly of a not-peaceful history between the Ainu and the Wajin, the Wajin people came from Honshu (the mainland of Japan) to Ainu moshir ["the land of mankind" in the Ainu language] around 15th century and began to expand their territory in Hokkaido region for the pursuit of commercial profits and for the defense particularly against Russia. After winning victories from the Battle of Koshamain (1456) and the Shakushain War (1669–1672), the Matsumae clan, the most powerful group among the Wajin people, and the Tokugawa Bakufu in Honshu (the Tokugawa *shogunate*, a feudal regime of Japan established by Tokugawa Ieyasu and ruled by the shoguns of the Tokugawa family [1603–1868]), colonized and exploited the Ainu people. The situation hardly changed after the end of the Tokugawa Bakufu and the consequential establishment of the Meiji government in 1868. Although things begin to change nowadays, there still exists a slur of racial discrimination which makes the Ainu people to be hesitant about revealing their racial identity and heritage.[11]

Given this racial history between the Ainu and the Wajin, *A Quiet Land* tells a story inspired by Ikezawa's maternal ancestors in the early Meiji era. The story is centered on the relationships between the Munakata family (Wajin) and their Ainu friends. Munakata Saburō, along with his younger brother Shirō, immigrated from Awajishima to Shizunai, a village in the southeast Hokkaido, in 1872. In the village, Munakata boys met and made friends with Oshiankur, an Ainu boy. Despite the Wajin tendency to look down on the Ainu as lesser beings, friendship between Munakata brothers and the Oshiankur family grew stronger as the years went by. In 1880, they decided to open a horse farm together. Soon, the farm bred excellent horses, and the cooperation between the Wajin and the Ainu seemed to be a success. This success doesn't last long because of a series of tragic incidents: a Wajin capitalist obstructed the farm; Saburo's wife, Ekarian, died after abortion; Saburo killed himself with his rifle; the farm finally went to smash. Since few Japanese novelists have ever dealt with this racial topic, Ikezawa's novel deserves a favorable attention for the fact that it contains the history of the complicated relations of two racial groups in Hokkaido. In addition, Ikezawa should have received even higher acclaim for his artistry that he transforms a record of a painful history into an epic romance in which universal human values such as cooperation and friendship between two antagonistic groups are celebrated.

Nevertheless, *A Quiet Land* is also a problematic novel in terms of affiliation of the Other. For example, the novel strangely lacks descriptions of Ainu/Wajin marriage. Saburō gets married to Ekarian, an apparently Ainu woman, but she is in fact a Wajin woman who grew up with an Ainu family. When Saburo asks Ekarian's father, Benzō Akiyama (his Wajin name: his Ainu name is Tukiante), to allow him to get married to her, the following conversation carried between the would-be father-in-law and the son-in-law conveys a bit of surprise to contemporary readers.

> "Ah, could I ask you to allow me to get married with Ekarian?" Benzo looked at Saburō with a wondering face.
>
> "No, it's not natural that a Wajin man like me would like to get married with an Ainu woman. I know that the yukar [Ainu epic verse] suggests that gods get married with gods and Ainu people get married with Ainu people, but I can hardly find anyone who could be my wife among Wajin women, and I know no woman but Ekarian whom I would like to marry.
>
> "Wajin people in Shizunai village would often meddle in or talk too much about this, but I will do my best to devote my entire life to love Ekarian."
>
> (*Shinzukana Daichi* 308–309, my translation)

Then, Benzō answered to Saburō, with the yukar's wisdom in mind.

> "Gods have to get married with gods, Ainu with Ainu, then Wajin with Wajin. Truth is, Ekarian, my daughter, is a Wajin woman like you, Saburō."
>
> Saburō looked at Benzō's face with a look of astonishment.
>
> (*Shinzukana Daichi* 309, my translation)

This sudden reinstallation of the boundary between the Wajin and the Ainu is surprising not only because no clear reason of shying away interracial/ethnic marriage is given but also because the story of Ainu/Wajin cooperation that dominates the first half of the novel naturally leads readers to expect that Saburo is going to marry an Ainu woman. Why could Ikezawa not have inserted a final inter-racial/ethnic union in this novel?

A clue can be found in Ikezawa's intensive fourteen lecture series delivered during seven days at Kyoto University (2005) about what he believes to be masterpieces of world literature. In the 12th lecture, while talking freely about *A Quiet Land* for a change, he touches on a dilemma he struggles with as a writer and an individual. As a descendant of a Wajin family in Hokkaido, Ikezawa feels responsible for the tragic history of the Ainu people. Explaining the main reason why he made a decision of writing a novel on the Ainu/Wajin history, however, he makes, rather in a straightforward manner, it clear that he feels little sympathy with proletarian literature, although he has a high regard for its earnest and deep concern with history and society. Having two of most famous Japanese proletarian novelists Kobayashi Takiji (1903–1933) and Tokunaga Sunao (1899–1958), in mind, Ikezawa asserts that his priority is given to "literary grace."

> [Proletarian literature] is written merely for the purpose of accusation and is instrumentally subject to politics. That is, thought comes before literature. [...] Then, a kind of splitting takes places in my mind. On the one hand, I do feel that I would like to write an entertaining story, a good story of literary grace. On the other hand, I would like to put social issues into my writings—factors that would put our society under accusations.
>
> (*Sekaibungakuo Yomihodoku* 348, my translation)

He goes on to elucidate on why he could not imagine a happy union between the Ainu and the Wajin history.

> It seems impossible to write a story involving Ainu people of Hokkaido in the Meiji era with happy endings—it can be hypocritical and fake. In fact, there might have been "happy"Ainu people you could find in history, but you must describe their unhappiness as a whole as long as you would write about Ainu people in this [Meiji] period. There shouldn't be any case of "all is well that ends well." In this sense, this novel is a kind of Greek tragedy that proceeds under the

> pressure of the god, History. The ending must therefore be "apocalyptic." [...] Writing up this novel, I now think and feel: "this is too dark and serious, after all." I feel I have overloaded on myself and I still have a kind of pain.
>
> (*Sekaibungakuo Yomihodoku* 356, my translation)

Considering his remarks, it is understandable why Ikezawa felt the theme of Ainu/Wajin marriage "too serious" to be put into the plot of *A Quiet Land*. It is important, however, that he acknowledged the fact that the lives and histories of the Ainu and the Wajin people have intersected and created such characters who, despite hard and discriminatory surroundings, tried their best to lead a harmonious life with the minority race.[12]

Despite his hesitation about the interracial union, Ikezawa takes a consistent step forward in representing history and society from a cosmopolitan perspective. For example, *Kadena* (2009) is a novel, one of whose main characters has a mixed American–Filipino racial background. Its setting is Okinawa, whose history provides Japanese readers with basic socio-historical knowledge of the characters. Still in Okinawa there is the Kadena Air Base, an extraordinarily huge US Air Force hub base in the Pacific where, in times of emergency and war, F-15s and B-52s take off and land.[13] Okinawa people living around the US bases, one of which is the Kadena Air Base, have ambivalent feelings toward them: some of them believe that they cannot but live with the US bases, and others feel annoyed by the incredible roaring sound of jet fighters and bombers and mostly resentful at US soldiers' violence against nearby dwellers.[14] However, it is necessary for readers to understand the history of Okinawa people who have been forced to live their difficult lives under military pressure in order to have a full appreciation of *Kadena*.

In the Edo period (early seventeenth century to 1868), Okinawa, originally a kingdom, was called Ryûkyû. However, the Ryûkyû people were intervened and exploited by the Satsuma clan of the Edo Bakufu for its desire to increase sugar production. As the history of Okinawa from the Meiji restoration (1868) to the Pacific War (1941–1945) shows, the Tokyo bureaucrats had carried out unbelievably inhumane discrimination against Okinawa Prefecture. For example, Okinawa people had been prohibited from speaking their own dialect. Most tragically, many of them—at the lowest estimate—42,000 Okinawans were victimized during the Battle of Okinawa (1945).[15] From 1945 to 1972, under the US Occupation, they had led unstable lives: the Koza Riot in 1970 in which about 5000 Okinawans clashed with about 700 US MPs is regarded as an extreme expression of their resentment toward the US presence in their abode.[16] Even after the return of Okinawa to Japan in 1972, the US bases remained, mainly due to the Japan–US Security Treat. This complicated history explains why the situation in Okinawa has not been improved among the US, Japanese government and Okinawa people.

Given this historical background, *Kadena* can be understood as a story of extraordinary cooperation of people with various backgrounds and of their resistance against the Vietnam War in which Japan played a role directly as well as indirectly. One of the most famous demonstrations in the midst of active anti-Vietnam War movements in late 1960s was carried out in Kyushu. In 1968 Kyushu city Sasebo residents and thousands of protesters came out to the streets and showed their rage against the USS Enterprise, a nuclear powered aircraft carrier.[17] The novel apparently models its plot on the basis of the Beheiren movement (*Betonamu ni Heiwa o Shimin Rengo* "Citizen's League for Peace in Vietnam"), a famous coalition of a few hundred anti-war activists to assist US soldiers to run away.[18] In this novel, too, four characters—Mr Annam (a Vietnamese spy whose real name is a mystery), Freda Jane Miller (a Filipino–American woman and a US master sergeant in the Kadena Air Base), Chōei Kadekaru (a middle-aged Okinawan man who has survived the famous Battle of Saipan that took place between USA and Japan in 1944) and Takahiro Taira (a young Okinawan who has experienced high-school education in USA)—incidentally form a team of resistance to help young US soldiers to escape from the battlegrounds. The team concocted a scheme to assist young American soldiers including Leutenant Patrick Beehan, chief pilot of a B52 bomber *Saigon Bride* (and a lover of Frieda Jane), with the help of Okinawa people who had their own age-old resentment against the US intervention. By amalgamating real histories in Okinawa with his literary vision of international cooperation, Ikezawa seems to try to compensate for what he failed to dramatize in *A Quiet Land*.

In conclusion, Ikezawa, though not widely known to world readers and been under appreciated by Japanese critics and readers, is truly a unique novelist who has explored innovative ways of representing the hidden histories of the Japanese minorities in his entire life. *A Burden of Flowers, The Stratosphere in the Summer Morning, The Fall of Macias Guili, On a Small Bridge in Iraq, Reports of a Starling, Happy Ends, Brave New World, A Quiet Land, Kadena,* all these novels and essays deal with a theme of clashes between the West and the East, life and death, desperation and salvation. Representing a heterogeneous space on the basis of real histories of Japan, Ikezawa has tried to awaken readers to see the cracks of seemingly homogeneous Japanese society and history and to speak up the necessity to practice active affiliation of the Other. It is time to give due attention to Ikezawa's cosmopolitan gaze that comprehend the East and the West, the Majority and the Minority, and Art and Politics and to his intellectual courage to have held a flag of Japanese conscience up high.

NOTES

1. A part of this paper has been already published in my "Posutokoroniaru Merankoria" [Postcolonial Melancholia], *Bungei* (2011 Spring), pp. 68–71. This volume includes a special issue focusing on Ikezawa. Also, in this paper I use the Japanese order to write Japanese names. In "Ikezawa Natsuki," for example, "Ikezawa" is his family name.
2. The speech, given on 17 February 2009, is available at <http://www.haaretz.com/culture/arts-leisure/always-on-the-side-of-the-egg-1.270371>.
3. See "Novelist Murakami accepts Israeli literary prize," *The Japan Times* (20 February 2009) at <http://search.japantimes.co.jp/cgi-bin/nn200 90217f2.html >.
4. See "Novelist Murakami slams nuclear policy," *The Japan Times* (10 June 2011) at <http://search.japantimes.co.jp/cgi-bin/nn20110610x2.html>.

5. *Hitsuji o Meguru Bouken* (*A Wild Sheep Chase*), published in 1982 (translated into English in 1989), is a good example. The first chapter of the novel is '1970.11. 25,' the day when Mishima Yukio (1925–1970) committed his famous hara-kiri suicide, although it is repeatedly emphasized in the novel that the hero who calls himself Boku ("I") doesn't care about what TV news shows tell in terms of the novelist's sensational suicide and the 1970s turbulent Japanese society.
6. In France, the publisher Philippe Picquier has published some of his novels. Regrettably, there is no entry of Ikezawa in Wikipédia (fr).
7. The quotation comes from the following JPPP (Japanese Literature Publishing Project) at <http://www.jlpp.go.jp/jp/publishers/jlpp_2010_ai_sheet_german.pdf>.
8. In the novel Kimura works in Shizuoka, where a small fisher-boat Daigo Fukuryû Maru (Lucky Dragon 5) set sail for Bikini Atoll (and was exposed to radiation fallouts) in 1954. Some readers might remember this famous incident.
9. Nonetheless, while German translation of this novel was published in 2002, no English translation has yet been published.
10. Already in 1982, Ikezawa translated Peter Goodchild's critical biography on John Oppenheimer, and in "Translator's Note" Ikezawa clearly states that Goodchild's criticism on Oppenheimer is inadequately critical on the Manhattan Project and USA's nuclear policy in view of the only people on whom USA dropped A-bombs twice (pp. 290–291).
11. Discrimination against Ainu people is still an issue of dispute. See, for example, Suvendrini Kakuchi, "Ainu discrimination defy the law," *Asia Times* at <http://www.atimes.com/japan-econ/BE19Dh01.html>. 19 May 2000.
12. Center for Ainu & Indigenous Studies (University of Hokkaidō) provides invaluable materials with which we can ponder upon the actualities (including inter-racial/ethnic marriage) that present-day Ainu people have to face.
13. To see how huge US military bases are in Okinawa, visit these websites: <http://www.globalsecurity.org/jhtml/jframe.html> and <http://www.globalsecurity.org/military/facility/images/okinawa-map-jp1.gif >.
14. For further information, see the website entitled "US Military Violence Against Women: Okinawa and Japan," <http://usmvaw.com/okinawa-and-japan/>.
15. On the Battle of Okinawa, see the website <http://www.globalsecurity.org/military/facility/okinawa-battle.htm>.

16. On the Koza Riot, see John Mitchel's "Koza remembered" <http://search.japantimes.co.jp/cgi-bin/fl20091227x1.html)>.
17. Not only on Sasebo Protest but also on anti-Vietnam War movements in Japan generally, see Peter Kelman's doctoral thesis, *Protesting the national identity: the cultures of protest in 1960s Japan*. Chapter 5 of the thesis is focused on the Sasebo incident.
18. On Beheiren, see Keiji Hirano's "Antiwar campaigners to donate documents to Vietnamese museum" at <http://mailman.lbo-talk.org/2002/2002–February/003886.html>.

CHAPTER 9

Shakespeare in China

Past, Present, and Future

Liu Hao

Introduced into China in the early twentieth century, Shakespeare has been read and staged in this country for about a hundred years. The reception of Shakespeare in China, including translation, criticism, and stage performance, has gone through a complicated process. Though the reception of Shakespeare in China is a history of only about a hundred years, it is difficult to make a holographic picture of Shakespeare in China, for the complicacy of political situation and cultural changes in each stage of its reception, and the broad difference between Chinese dramatic tradition and Shakespearean drama. Among the most important influences on Shakespeare in China are the social and cultural changes and consequently the ideological tendencies, and the Chinese dramatic tradition.

To sketch the outlines of some aspects of the reception of Shakespeare in China, this essay first traces the historical process of the introduction of Shakespearean drama and poetry in China from the late nineteenth century till today, setting Shakespeare reception in the context of social and cultural landscape, and attempts to sketch the images of Shakespeare in different historical phases (part I). It goes on to focus on a contemporary Peking Opera adaptation of *Hamlet* to illustrate the way Chinese people read and use Shakespeare in today's China, followed by discussion of the potentials and projections of the development of Shakespeare studies in China in a globalized cultural environment (Part II).

A BRIEF HISTORY OF SHAKESPEARE IN CHINA

Shakespeare was first introduced into China between the late nineteenth century and the turn of the twentieth century. The more than a hundred years of Shakespeare's reception in China involves general introduction, commentary, translation, performance and scholarly criticism and research. The hundred years see great progress in each of these aspects.

The one hundred years since the late nineteenth century is also a time for great changes in China in terms of social system, politics and culture. The process of Shakespeare's reception in China stretched from the late Qing Dynasty, across the period in of the Republic of China (1912–1949), the anti-Japanese war (1937–1945), to the new era after the founding of the People's Republic of China.

Since the political and cultural situation changed dramatically during the hundred years, Shakespeare's works were interpreted in different perspectives and with various theories as they became more assimilated into the developing Chinese modern culture. The history of Shakespeare in China will be reviewed in six phases: the embryonic phase (from the late nineteenth century to the turn of the twentieth century), the preparatory phase (from the early twentieth century to 1921), the initial phase (from 1921 to 1949), the middle phase (from 1949 to the 1960s), the revival phase (from 1976 to the 1980s), and the new phasc (after the 1980s).

The Embryonic Phase (From the Late Nineteenth Century to the Turn of the Twentieth Century)

Since the late nineteenth century, the Qing Empire proved to be a weak nation in terms of national defense capabilities and political strength. Chinese intellectuals turned to western culture, hoping to remedy social ills with imported ideas. Various publications were seen in China, aiming at introducing western culture to Chinese people and calling on them to open their eyes to the world. By the time of Shakespeare's first arrival, western culture was the rage in China, especially among the young intellectuals. The Renaissance spirit, in particular, was extolled by Chinese intellectuals, in hope of reforming Chinese culture. Renaissance culture was introduced to China by Christian missionaries in the late Qing Dynasty. With other writers and artists, Shakespeare was introduced to Chinese people as a famous member of English literati (qtd. in Meng 2) and the best poet ever after Homer (4).

Shakespeare was first mentioned in *Si Zhou Zhi*[1] (Records of the Four Continents), listed among the greatest British writers. He was briefly introduced in other books and journals about western culture, such as *Biographies of People from Japan and the West,*[2] a journal entitled *The Continent,*[3] and *Biographies of Sixty World Celebrities.*[4]

The earliest recorded commentary on Shakespeare by Chinese people is possibly in the diary of Guo Song-tao who served as envoy to France since 1876 and envoy to France and Britain since 1878. In his account of a printer exhibition in 1877, Guo talked about Shakespeare: "One of the most famous among the prints is by Shakespeare, an accomplished playwright some two hundred years ago in England, as renowned as Homer of Greece" (267, my translation). And in another entry of 1879 in his diary, he wrote: "The Shakespeare play I saw focused on the plot rather than the grandiose appearance" (743, my translation). Guo had also introduced some achievements of the west in the fields of philosophy and science. He seemed to think high of Shakespeare's works. So did other Chinese envoys. During the same period of time, Chinese envoys Zeng Jize, Zhang Deyi, and Dai Hongci had the experience of watching Shakespearean plays in London, Berlin and Paris respectively and they kept the accounts in their diaries too.

Among the leading cultural figures who helped introduce Shakespeare in this period, Liang Qichao, a political reformer and renowned scholar, and Wang Guowei, a political reformer and renowned scholar who had been the tutor of the last emperor, both play important roles in Shakespeare's early reception in China. Wang enthusiastically discussed the merits of Shakespeare's works, praising his broad horizon, knowledge of life and his noble ideals. Yan Fu, the translator of *Evolution and Ethics* which showed a profound influence on the world-view of Chinese people during the period of burgeois demacratic revolution (and even till now), commented on the vividness of Shakespeare's characterization in his introduction to the Chinese version of *Evolution and Ethics* (Yan 57) and the translator's notes in other works.

Besides intellectuals and envoys who were privileged to know more about the culture of western countries, some famous political figures in China spoke favorably of Shakespeare. Li Hongzhang, a leading statesman in the late Qing Empire and a controversial politician in Chinese history, mentioned Shakespeare's skillful writing when addressing his audience on an diplomatic occasion (Cai 138). Kang Youwei, a political thinker and reformer of the late Qing Dynasty, made favorable comment on Shakespeare and compared him to the ancient Chinese poet Qu Yuan,[5] the forefather of Chinese poetry. Ma Junwu, a scholar and new-democratic thinker listed Shakespeare among the Renaissance cultural figures and fiercely advocated the adoption of Western culture in China.

The Preparatory Phase (From the Early Twentieth Century to 1920 or 1921)

From the early twentieth century to 1920 or 1921 is the preparatory phase of Shakespeare reception in China, and more introductions, translations and remarks were seen, with some performances based on the incomplete translations. Chinese scholars translated western works to advocate cultural reform, aiming at spreading new ideas among the public and preparing them for a new age.

Two translations of Shakespeare based on Charles and Mary Lamb's *Tales from Shakespeare* caught much attention from the Chinese readers in this period. One is *Xie Wai Qi Tan* (*Overseas Fantastic Tale*) by an anonomous translator who rendered ten stories into Chinese. The other is the translation of twenty stories by a renowned traditional scholar Lin Shu in collaboration. It is interesting to know that both translators used classical Chinese which is more elegant but difficult than Chinese vernacular, and they adopted the style of traditional Chinese literature. Known as the "king of translators," Lin was well versed in classical Chinese literature and striving to draw the readers back to the beauty of classical Chinese through his translation. He did some rewrite to suit the taste of Chinese readers. It was based on Lin Shu's translations that the pioneers of Chinese modern theatre (the early form of which is known as 'wen ming xi'—the civilized drama) started to perform Shakespeare in China.

This preparatory phase also saw the earliest Shakespeare criticism in China. In 1905, Wang Xiaonong[6] discussed the plays in the form of classical Chinese verse (Ruan), i.e., twenty poems of four lines, each containing seven characters, with a strict tonal pattern and rhythm scheme.

In 1917 and 1918, four essays entitled "On the Poetic Plays of Shakespeare" were the earliest recorded essays devoted to serious and comprehensive Shakespeare criticism. However, there was more random commentary than serious criticism in this phase.

The Initial Stage (From 1921 to 1949)

In 1921 *Hamlet*, the first faithful translation of a Shakespearean play was completed by Tian Han. Since then scholars started their research on Shakespeare's works and with various translations and stage adaptations, Shakespeare began to enjoy a reputation among its Chinese readers and audience. The phase from 1921 to 1949 may be called the initial phase of Shakespeare in China.

Tian was a leading figure in Chinese dramatic circle for a long time. It is worth noting that he used modern Chinese rather than classical Chinese for his translation. It is also revealing that Tian's translation was published in 1922 in the eleventh issue of the second volume of a journal named *The Young China*, a name indicating its cultural and political preference in the cultural conflicts between the old and the new.

Since the publication of Tian's translation of *Hamlet*, in China were published about a dozen translated Shakespeare plays, including *The Taming of the Shrew* and *The Merchant of Venice* in the 1920s, and the translations of *Hamlet, Macbeth, The Merchant of Venice, Twelfth Night* and other plays in the early 1930s. Among the translators during the 1930s and 1940s, Zhu Shenghao and Liang Shiqiu both tried their hands at the translation of the corpus of Shakespeare's works. Zhu Shenghao's posthumous translation of *The Complete Works of Shakespeare* was a milestone, though he only finished thirty-one plays by his death in 1944. Liang Shiqiu was to finished the translation of thirty-seven plays and all Shakespearean poems by himself in 1967 in Taiwan. Besides the plays, Shakespeare's poems were rendered into Chinese after the May Fourth Movement in 1919. Both the sonnets and *Venus and Adonis* were published in Chinese.

The anti-Japanese War started in 1937, but the translation and introduction of Shakespeare never ceased. Translators like Cao Weifeng and Zhu Shenghao in particular continued their work in hardship. To perform Shakespeare's drama was in a sense a sign of the perseverence and warrior spirit for Chinese people of that age. A production of *Macbeth* in 1945 directed by Huang Zuolin was a good example of fusing Shakespearean drama and Chinese tradition.

In this period, Chinese people gradually got to know the real Shakespeare with the help of more translation and performance. More than seventy periodical essays on Shakespeare were printed in the 1920s. In the 1930s and 1940s, scholars introduced into China critical ideas from abroad. Among them the Soviet Shakespeare studies was to exert significant impact on Chinese Shakespeare studies. The leftist writer Mao Dun, for example, had refered to Marx and Engel's interest in Shakespeare and the Soviet Shakespeare studies in his essay "Shakespeare and Realism" in 1934 (Wei Ming).[7] Though independent research on Shakespeare was not yet popular with Chinese scholars, some of them contributed original ideas to this field. What's more, Chinese researchers had already attempted to make comprehensive comparison between Shakespeare and his contemporary Chinese dramatist Tang Xianzu.[8]

However, before 1949, a large porportion of the people in this country was uneducated and illiterate, and thus readers of Shakespeare were quite few compared to the large population.[9]

The Middle Phase (From 1949 to the 1960s)

With the founding of the People's Republic of China in 1949, the reception of Shakespeare strode to a new stage. The ethos in China was radically different since 1949, and Marxism and socialist culture became the mainstream of social ideology. The new government and the people were eager to refashion the culture. Not all western works were welcome in the new cultural environment. However, because Marx and Engel had made favorable comments on Shakespeare, among all the western writers, Shakespeare was the first to appear in the new China.[10] During this period of time, the Soviet Shakespeare studies showed profound influence on the reception of Shakespeare in China.

Shakespeare's plays in Chinese continued to appear in print the 1950s and the early 1960s. Some previous translations of the plays were reprinted. And translators were working on more plays. Some of them received much attention from the readers and audience. There were more than one versions of *Much Ado About Nothing* (1953 and 1962), *A Midsummer Night's Dream* (1954 and 1955), *As You Like It* (1953 and 1955) and *Hamlet* (1955 and 1956) within these years, and they remained Chinese people's favorite Shakespeare plays for a long time.

From 1949 to the 1960s, Shakespeare studies in China mainly adopted the ideological approach, especially in the light of Marxist theories. Between the mid 1950s and the 1960s, the first high tide of Shakespeare criticism was believed to come, with about a hundred and thirty theses discussing Shakespeare's works. There were also about sixty articles on the performance of Shakespeare. Another important aspect of Shakespeare studies in this period was the translation of Shakespeare criticism, namely about 80 critical essays from Ben Jonson to Bradley, with about sixty theoretical analyses and about twenty reviews of stage adaptations. The main trend of Shakespeare criticism in China in this phase was to read his works in a Marxist perspective and to follow the Soviet scholarship.

To be specific, a notion coined and advocated by the Russian critic Anatoli Lunacharsky was influential—"socialist realism," a term to "describe a theatre that should, in his view, accompany revolution." With "new realism," Lunacharsky meant that literary works "reflected the lives of ordinary people and described contemporary class-oriented society" (qtd. in Levith 29). Chairman Mao Zedong's "1942 Talks at the Yenan Forum on Art and Literature" was like a golden precept for writers and artists in this period of time, and it "came to be a guide to orthodoxy for Chinese

Shakespeareans, as well as other critics, scholars, and creative writers" (29). In Mao's view, all literature and art "should be for the masses" – that is, for "workers, peasants, and soldiers" (29). It follows that the Chinese Shakespeareans and theatre people must interpret Shakespeare's works to "serve the ideological and political objectives of the present and ongoing revolution" (30). For Chinese critics, Shakespeare should be viewed as a humanistic thinker in Renaissance, and they would also judge his characters on the social classes they belong to. Chinese critics emphasized "historical and socioeconomic issues, class relationship, and various critiques of feudalism, capitalism, and religion ('superstition')," and "Shakespeare's own ideological status and orthodoxy" was "a matter for interpretation, as Chinese critics focus on what they see as the class struggle prompting a given work during England's early modern period and/or the class struggle represented in a play or group of plays" (Levith 28).

In 1966, the nationwide Cultural Revolution broke out in China, which called halt to the studies of Shakespeare and western literatures. This period is known as the "calamity of ten years." The culture of the country didn't recover until 1976 when the Cultural Revolution was ended.

The Revival Phase (From 1976 to the 1980s)

Though there was a halt in the 1960s and 1970s due to the cultural retrogression caused by the Cultural Revolution, the revival of Shakespeare studies in China came after 1976. In the 1980s, more than one foreign scholar talked about the "Shakespeare Renaissance" in China. There was an essay entitled "Shakespeare Renaissance in China" published in *Shakespeare Quarterly* in 1988. Reviewing the period between 1976 and the 1980s, the essay described such a scene: "It is said that within hours of the death of Mao, queues formed in the streets for copies of Shakespeare's most popular play in China, *The Pound of Flesh* [*The Merchant of Venice*]" (Brochbank 197). Though the accuracy of the report is yet to be ascertained, Chinese people's passion for Shakespeare, and for western literatures that they did not have access to during the Cultural Revolution was officially revived.

One of the big events for Chinese readers was the publication of Zhu Shenghao's translation of the complete works of Shakespeare in 1978 with the missing plays supplemented by other translators, though the publishing was much delayed. This edition is said to represent the first translated complete works of any foreign author to be published in the People's Republic of China. Chinese readers and students who intended to read Shakespeare's text in English were going to get great help from a series of annotated editions of Shakespeare initiated in the 1980s. A Shakespeare Library was established at Fudan University in Shanghai by professor Lin Tongji.[11] Other academies and universities also began collecting Shakespearean materials for teaching and research.

In 1981 an exhibition was organized in Beijing—"Shakespeare's Time." Another significant event was the founding of the Shakespeare Society of China in 1984 with subsequent membership in the International Shakespeare Association. A sign of the successful reception of Shakespeare by the political mainstream was that Hu Qiaomu, a secretary who had worked for Mao Zedong and for the Chinese Communist Party, was the honorary president of the Shakespeare Society.[12]

Though Marxist approach was still the main trend in this phase, more perspectives are allowed, and the unique view of Chinese scholars was encouraged. Cao Yu, the first president of the Shakespeare Society, proposed in his "Inaugural Observations" for *Shakespeare Studies* that "we are reading the world giant Shakespeare from the point of view of a modern China involved in its own recent history ... We attempt to study Shakespeare from a Marxist perspective.... [we should] approach Shakespeare's great soul from many different angles" (qtd. in Levith 60). Though recharged with new energy after the repression of the Cultural Revolution, cautious critics mostly continued to view literature as a weapon in class struggle (qtd. in Levith 86), and Shakespeare's plays were taken to be critiques of early England (He "Chinese Eyes" 97). Social themes and heroic model characters were still the analytical focus that "in most Chinese critical essays only the 'political issues' of the play are carefully examined while its other themes are ignored" (He "Trends" 96).

In this phase, a tie was to be built between Chinese Shakespearean activities and world Shakespeare studies and performance. In 1980, Cao Yu and some other dramatists of China visited Stratford-upon-Avon. They brought with them Zhu Shenghao's translation of the complete works of Shakespeare as a gift to the Royal Shakespeare Company. The names of Chinese critics began to appear in international periodicals and conferences, e.g., Lu Gusun's essay "Hamlet across Space and Time" in *Shakespeare Survey* 36. *The Shakespeare Quarterly* began to include Chinese Shakespeare studies in 1985. The voice of more Chinese Shakespearean scholars was to be heard in world Shakespeare circles.

Because of the pressure of strict censorship, western productions were almost abandoned on Chinese stage during the Cultural Revolution. In 1979, the Shanghai Youth Theatre made a production of *Much Ado about Nothing,* which marked the flourishing new age of Shakespeare on Chinese stage.[13] In the same year, Derek Jacobi and the Old Vic gave nine performances of *Hamlet* in English in Shanghai and Beijing. This production was "the first appearance by a British company on mainland stages since the founding of the People's Republic," according to London's *Evening Standard,*[14] the televised performance on the last night reached an estimated audience of ten million viewers (qtd. in Levith 61). In the 1980s, several Shakespeare plays were staged mostly in Beijing and Shanghai, the two centers of Shakespeare performance. A production of *The Merchant of Venice* in 1980 acted by Beijing Chinese Youth Art Theatre marked the "revival of literature and art in China after the Cultural Revolution" (Li "Bard" 65). The play was performed for more than two hundred times in different cities between 1980 and 1982, and won several awards from the Ministry of Culture.[15] Huang Zuolin the director who had studied Shakespeare drama at Oxford University and tried to blend Shakespearean stories with Chinese style, enthusiastically directed *Romeo and Juliet* and the Kunqu version of *Macbeth* (known by its Chinese title *The Bloody Hands*).

The 1986 Shakespeare Festival was the most influential Shakespeare event in this phase. It took place in April 1986, organized by the Shakespeare Society of China, the Chinese Dramatic Art Research Society, the Beijing Drama Academy and the Shanghai Drama Academy. Twenty-seven playing companies, academies, universities, and studios presented sixteen plays in twenty-eight productions; sixteen of them were in Shanghai and twelve were in Beijing.[16] Lectures, seminars, and book publications were added to the stage presentations.[17]

During the revival period from 1976 to the 1980s, Shakespeare studies and performance in China were revived, and Chinese people's enthusiasm for Shakespearean drama and poetry was invigorated.

The New Phase (After the 1980s)

If the Shakespeare Festival in Shanghai was a history-making event, the next period proves to be a totally new page in the history of Shakespeare's reception in China. After the 1980s, Chinese Shakespeare has taken on new forms, advancing in every aspect, and establishing more international communications.

In this new phase, Shakespeare becomes more accessible to Chinese readers with more publications and multimedia facilities. The completion of the revised and supplemented version of the complete works of Shakespeare which was started by Zhu Shenghao dozens of years ago was a noteworthy step in 1998. This edition is till now the most complete and sophisticated translation of the complete works of Shakespeare. This phase has also seen the Chinese version of Shakespeare's works in verse—another edition translated by Fang Ping. Now a most updated Chinese edition of Shakespeare is forthcoming, by the hands of a selected group of translators.

A good chance for Shakespeare fans in college is the "Chinese Universities Shakespeare Festival" (competition) hosted by the Chinese University of Hong Kong. English majors of all universities and colleagues nation-wide are invited to enter the first round.

Shakespeare symposium has become a regular academic activity. Chinese Shakespeareans are well informed of the updated achievements in this field, and have contributed new perspectives. In the latest three Shakespeare symposia in Shanghai, Chengdu and Chongqing in 2004, 2006 and 2009 respectively, university teachers, graduate students and researchers from all over China presented their research on Shakespeare and Shakespearean culture. The range of their topics showed international horizon and unique Chinese perspectives: first, textual studies, themes and characters; second, Shakespeare's text and literary tradition, e.g., Shakespearean plays and the tradition of Greek tragedy, Shakespeare's sonnets and the tradition of sonnet, Elizabethan revenge tragedy; third, Shakespeare and historical background, e.g., the Renaissance society, the nature of royal power; fourth, Shakespeare and theories, e.g., the postcolonial reading of Shakespeare, the feminist approach to Shakespeare's plays; fifth, Shakespeare on stage and on screen (Shakespeare on Chinese stage in particular), e.g., the analysis and appreciation of Chinese adaptations of the four great tragedies; sixth, Shakespeare and cultural issues, e.g., Shakespeare's return from elite culture to mass culture, the relation between Shakespearean literature and mass media, Shakespeare and the forms of politics and culture, Shakespeare and modern Chinese literature; seventh, comparative studies of Shakespeare and Chinese literature; eighth, translating Shakespeare in China; ninth, teaching Shakespeare in China.[18] From the topics above, we may see that Chinese researchers are open-minded to adopt various approaches while trying to foster more sophisticated Chinese Shakespearean studies.

SHAKESPEARE'S IMAGES IN CHINA AND THE UNIQUE FEATURES OF SHAKESPEARE IN CHINA

In the one hundred years of reception, Shakespeare has been studied and appreciated in a great diversity of cultural environment. Ever since his first arrival, Shakespeare's name was associated with the cultural development in this country. It is interesting and revealing to see how Shakespeare appeared in the eyes of Chinese people of different ages.

The Three Images of Shakespeare in China

In the Chinese eyes, the image of the Renaissance playwright varied with Chinese people's aesthetic horizon and ideological expectations. Among the many 'Shakespeares' in the context of Chinese culture, the following three images are most representative.

First, Shakespeare as a writer comparable or similar to traditional Chinese writers. When Shakespeare was introduced into the country, Chinese people first tended to compare him with the cultural celebrities in Chinese tradition. On the one hand, his works were analogized to those of the ancient Chinese dramatists, and he was especially labeled as "you ren," which is a Chinese term for practitioners of traditional Chinese opera (Liu 341). There are other titles given to him in the early commentary of Shakespeare indicating his connection with Chinese poets, Confucian scholars, and some early critics even approached Shakespearean works in the same way as they did with traditional Chinese literary works, giving comments in the form of classical poems.[19] An interesting example is that Lin Xu, the above mentioned Chinese translator, considered Shakespeare as representative of the traditional thoughts in the west and comparable to Chinese fairy stories in his foreword to the translation of Shakespeare' plays.

Second, Shakespeare as a standard-bearer or incarnation of Western civilization. As change and revolution became the leitmotif of the age in the early twentieth century, while introducing his works and trying to maintain the "original taste," more Chinese intellectuals began to consider the Renaissance playwright and poet as the representative of western humanism that appeared to them like a remedy for the decay of Chinese culture. His position as a leading dramatist in the west was an attraction to Chinese people. As two groups of intellectuals argued fiercely on the upholding or abolishment of traditional Chinese drama, Shakespeare, together with Ibsen and Bernard Shaw, became paragon of western drama for Chinese dramatists to admire.

Third, Shakespeare as an orthodox cultural figure. The third important image of Shakespeare in China is an orthodox cultural figure who is safe to be discussed and never falls. As Shakespeare is extolled by Marx and Engels, he continued to be respected in the new cultural environment after 1949, even when the literary works were strictly censored in China. Actually since the 1920s, Shakespeare was respectfully addressed as "sha weng" (the old man Sha), and the image of senior and respected gentleman (which is implied in the title "sha weng") lasts till today.

The Unique Features of Shakespeare in China

Two unique features are evident in the history of Chinese Shakespeare: the enshrined image of Shakespeare, and the indigenization of Shakespeare in various ages.

First, the enshrined image of Shakespeare. Though Shakespeare's high cultural position in China is not an exception, a unique phenomenon in the reception of Shakespeare in China is that even before Shakespeare's works were well known to Chinese people, his reputation as a leading literary figure was established. On his first arrival, his skills were claimed by both the traditional scholars like Lin Shu and the radical intellectuals like Lu Xun. He was seen as a humanist, representative of the more advanced culture from the West. Due to the trend of westernization in the early 20th Century, he was much admired before carefully read in the embryonic, preparatory, and initial phases of his introduction in China; ratified by Marxist criticism in the middle phase, Shakespeare continued to be identified as the orthodox writer and his position as a representative of the high culture was not challenged with the political and cultural changes.

It is not improper to call Chinese people's love for Shakespeare a "Shakespeare complex" which is the result of "a tangle web of the Soviet experts" influence, traditional Chinese ethics of respecting authority (Li *Shashibiya* 227) and the admiration for western novelties in the early 20th Century. He was a great writer in the eyes of not only experts and Shakespearean scholars, but also people who have not read the original texts or even the complete Chinese translation.

Second, the indigenization of Shakespeare. Another unique feature of Shakespeare in China is the intellectual and theatrical passion to assimilate him into Chinese culture of various ages.

In the early phases of introduction and adoption, both the cultural conservatives and cultural radicals took Shakespeare as a signboard for their cultural believes and ideological claims to advocate the maintenance of the traditional literature and ethical canons or the adoption of the new culture. As is previously discussed, Lin Shu's Chinese version gave its reader a feeling of reading a series of legends written in the classical Chinese style; and the earliest recorded Shakespeare criticism was written in the form of a series of twenty classical Chinese poems. From the initial phase to the contemporary time, Shakespeare has appeared on Chinese stage in the form of Peking Opera, Kun Opera, Yue Opera and other local genres of traditional Chinese opera.

There may be three reasons for Shakespeare being so indigenized ever since his first arrival. Firstly, he was among the first group of foreign writers known to the Chinese people in the late Qing Dynasty and the early years of the Republic of China. It was a time when the radical intellectuals in China were eagerly absorbing the western cultural message. A good way to introduce Shakespeare to the mass audience was to make it as accessible and enjoyable as the Chinese works. Secondly, having been approached in various aspects, the richness of Shakespeare's text invited interpretations with Chinese characteristics when his works came to China. Thirdly, China is a country that enjoys a long history of dramatic art, which is an important element in the forming of the cultural horizon and aesthetic expectation of Chinese readers.

The above mentioned two features of the reception of Shakespeare continue to be seen in the new phase of Shakespeare in China. To give a specific example, the next part of the essay will discuss a case of indigenization of Shakespeare in recent years.

SHAKESPEARE IN CHINA: THE PRESENT AND THE FUTURE

A Case of Indigenization: The New Peking Opera Production of *Hamlet*

To give a specific example of how Chinese people interpret Shakespeare in a different perspective, this part of the essay will treat a new Peking opera adaptation of *Hamlet* in mainland China. As a showcase, the adaptation demonstrates how the Shakespearean meets the Chinese on the stage. This new adaptation of *Hamlet* which is renamed *The Revenge of Prince Zidan* has been presented both in several cities in China, and abroad in Denmark and France.[20] The Chinese director resets the story in ancient China. The plot is considerably simplified, and the number of characters minimized. With some reconfiguration, the whole play is rendered into seven acts: Act 1 Meeting the ghost; Act 2 Feigning madness; Act 3 The play; Act 4 Chastising the mother; Act 5 The girl going mad; Act 6 Joking with a skull; Act 7 A duel. The overall style of the production is Chinese aesthetics—traditional music, sketchy setting, dramatic patterns with singing and dancing. The producer—Shanghai Peking Opera Troupe—wants to draw the young Chinese people to traditional Chinese aesthetics through a familiar play by Shakespeare.

The most conspicuous change in this Chinese adaptation is the introduction of the ghost. Not assuring the audience of the true identity of the ghost, Shakespeare's original text begins with a prolonged period of mystery, uncertainty and suspense, in which the reader's curiosity is stimulated, and the tension between the reader's expectation and awareness level is built. As is said by Stephen Booth, the presentation of the ghost is "insistently incoherent and just as insistently coherent. It frustrates and fulfills expectations simultaneously" (226).

The Peking Opera adaptation, however, begins with Prince Zidan (Hamlet) meeting the ghost at night. Before the fervent prince is presented on the stage, the play devotes the opening scene to the ritual dancing of the god of justice. The god unfolds himself in the typical pattern of self-identification in a traditional Chinese opera

> I'm the god of justice in hell. Yongbo, King of Chicheng was murdered. Since he has yet sins to be purified, he is sentenced to the punishment of fire in hell in day time, and is sent out to wander in the human world at night. Come and take Yongbo's soul here. (My translation)

That is how the ghost is first introduced in *The Revenge of Prince Zidan*. The scene then shifts to Prince Zidan and Xiahou Mu (Horatio) riding fiercely to the platform, with Xiahou Mu telling Prince Zidan what he has seen in a previous encounter with the ghost.

In this Chinese adaptation, the subjective report of Xiahou Mu follows the edict of a god. The identity of the ghost is revealed by the god even before it appears on the stage or is mentioned by any characters. Different from the secret conversation between the father and the son in the original version, the Peking Opera adaptation presents the meeting of the old king and the prince with the goblins on stage, moving and dancing. And the god of justice, also on the stage, acts like an omniscient supervisor.

Two major changes are seen in the opening scene of the Chinese adaptation: a new character, and less suspense. The god of justice as a new character not only makes the play more Chinese, but introduces into the narrative mode a new point of view—the perspective of a god representing supreme justice. The narrative perspectives also make difference in judgment and values. What is special about this new view point is that the story told from the perspective of the god of justice can always be trusted and taken as objective facts, or at least in the context of traditional Chinese drama. The god of justice in traditional Chinese drama and old legends features wise judgment and just decision.

Unlike the original narrative mode in which characters are supposed to have first-person limited point of view, the god of justice acts like a third-person omniscient narrator, and is able to convey message that is taken as truth without a second thought. In this sense, the new character is a significant change, because it refashions the moral system in the play. The god appears at the very beginning as a supervising authority and the moral judgment comes before the story. We may also think that in this adaption the director draws a sharper contrast between good and evil at the very beginning.

Another major change is about the mode of message delivering. The message about the identity of the ghost and truth of the murder is delivered intermittently in Shakespeare's text. But the Chinese version prefers delivering the message without a break. The story of the murder is told at one go. If in the Shakespearean text the reader's awareness level remains low for long, in the Chinese version his awareness is raised to a considerably high level with the opening speech of the god of justice. The omniscient perspective and the dispelling of suspense are inter-related in the new version. They both point to a more explicit narrative and a sharper contrast between good and evil. Booth has commented that "the first scene of *Hamlet* ... frustrated and fulfills expectations simultaneously" (226). We may say that the beginning scene in the new version does more to fulfill expectations because of the changes in its narrative mode. And with that, less "intellectual uneasiness" is provoked (226).

With another device characteristic of the Peking Opera version, we also find the new explicitness and intensified moral judgment. The queen whose innermost working is strikingly absent in Shakespeare's text is assigned two more soliloquies by the director of the Chinese version. The first is delivered after the prince shows a play to test his uncle. The queen retreats to her chamber alone, and thinks aloud in retrospection. Another soliloquy is added when the queen happens to have overheard the king and Yinze (Laertes) plotting against the prince and she decides to sacrifice herself to save her son. The soliloquies may clear up the suspense about the queen's feeling, for they make logic depiction of the queen's mind, and give a plausible explanation of her previous state of oblivion. What's more, with the queen making up her mind to sacrifice herself, the moral message is emphasized, echoing the omniscient vision of the god of justice. If the weakness of the queen has blurred the moral vision, when she declares that she is taking the prince's side, the boundary between good and evil is re-asserted.

This Peking Opera adaptation is not an exception. Changes were seen to feature the Chinese aesthetics, to draw the distinction between the good and the evil, and to give clear moral message in the previous productions of Chinese opera, including the Peking opera version of *King Lear*, the Kun Opera and Peking Opera versions of *Macbeth*, the yue Opera *Hamlet*, etc.

The Potential and Prospect of Shakespeare Studies in China

Seeing *The Revenge of Prince Zidan* against a background of cultural comparison, we may come to three main features in the present situation of Shakespeare reception and its future projection. First, Chinese people's unique aesthetic horizon is now more evident and potentially more productive. Second, Shakespeare as a culture trend is closely tied to Chinese classical culture which is temporarily dormant but revivable in the post-modern China. Third, Shakespeare is now not only a corpus of literary works to be introduced from Britain to China, but a shared vocabulary to convey new cultural message.

Firstly, in the Peking Opera production of *Hamlet*, traditional elements of Chinese drama prevail in terms of moral theme and aesthetic form. As is said by H.R. Jauss, "the aesthetic tradition and cultural background, as well as personal preference compose the receiver's taste and requirement, known as the horizon of expectation which results in an implied expectation in receiving the literary works from another culture" (7–37). With the god of justice as a new character, the moral values of the play is adjusted to the Chinese context, and the distinction between the good and the evil is more explicit and clarified; the avenger takes a high moral position; and the edificatory force of the play is highlighted on Chinese stage. Besides the explicit moral message, the plot of the play is cut simple, the structure made more compact, and characterization sketchier. Chinese symbols are used for audience to recognize the characters, and the typical Chinese dramatic singing and dancing moved the audience and won their applause.

The over-clarification and the explicit moral evaluation were considered a great disadvantage of traditional Chinese drama when Shakespeare was first introduced into China. As Fu Sinian[21] said, "the over-explicit moral vision hindered the audience's judgment," and "the new drama should aim at enabling the audience's ability of making judgment for themselves" (61). However, through the theories of traditional Chinese drama, we may be able to view the issue in a new light. Traditional theories have laid much emphasis on the edifying power of traditional Chinese music from which drama originated. With an explicit moral vision, there is no place for any doubts as to the distinction of the right and the wrong in a play, which is an unconscious protection of the moral system in the world of the receivers, in accordance with the values in traditional families.

However, the edifying power in Chinese drama is far more than didactically imposing a world-view. The edifying and the entertaining functions are one in the tradition of Chinese drama. While making sure that all audience correctly understand the moral message, traditional Chinese drama works with intellectuals in a more subtle way, aiming at aesthetic nurturing which is the core virtue of traditional Chinese edification, believed to be able to foster noble characters. From the Chinese version of *Hamlet* and other productions, we may say that the Chinese aesthetic horizon as well as moral system is always evident in Chinese people's reception of Shakespeare, and now they show more potentials as people come to rediscover the merit of the traditional Chinese values since the turn of the 21th Century, and as Shakespeare and

Chinese dramatic culture are interacting more closely with each other in today's China.

Secondly, compared with the previous Chinese Shakespeare productions, the new production of *Hamlet* shows more cultural confidence and better complementariness of the Chinese forms and the Shakespearean themes. In our new age, more attention is drawn to the unique Chinese view on Shakespeare and Chinese directors try to infuse Shakespeare with more Chinese elements in the theatre. What's more, the production is more internationally and culturally rewarding, building a link between the international stage of Shakespeare and the domestic traditional theatre, and it is also a more sophisticated design to recharge Shakespeare with Chinese artistic symbols and mode of thinking. Shakespeare continues to go side by side with Chinese culture, especially classical Chinese culture. As is exemplified by the success of Peking Opera *Hamlet*, the fusing and symbiotic prosperity of Shakespeare and traditional Chinese dramatic culture may be a possibility and new direction of the development of both.

Though in today's China, Shakespeare and traditional Chinese drama have not been so popular with the youth as they should be in terms of their virtues and the benefit that the youth might get from them, partly because traditional literature has been underappreciated during the long period of cultural changes. However, in this we see more potentials than regret, for it is now a time to witness the rise of traditional culture with more and more young people working to re-discover its great value. Hopefully, the prosperity of traditional Chinese culture is to herald a new round of interest in Shakespeare.

Thirdly, the Peking Opera *Hamlet* and other Shakespeare productions in China show the potential of Shakespeare as a platform for more cultural exchanges in a new age of globalization. Though the adaptation was produced on the invitation of the international Shakespeare festival in Denmark, the directors stated that they were aiming at Chinese college students as potential audience. It is interesting to notice that a hundred years ago, Chinese people used the form of traditional literature and opera to introduce Shakespeare, and now, the Shanghai Peking Opera troupe is using Shakespeare to draw the young people's attention back to traditional opera.

This version of *Hamlet* is not an exception, since Shakespeare has been used as a vehicle to communicate more ideas between different groups of people on various occasions. Shakespeare's plays now convey more message about the situation of contemporary people in such productions as the post-modern production of *Hamlet* 1990 by Beijing People's Art Theatre[22] which features the mental predicament of contemporary people, the 2004 Taiwan production of *The Tempest* which involved interaction with the audience prior to the performance (Huang 191–2)[23] and the 2006 film *The Banquet*[24] which shows a loan of Shakespeare's story. With the interesting cases of 'Chinese Shakespeares,' we may say that Shakespeare is now a stage for the contemporary Chinese to express themselves and a signboard to arouse young people's interest in traditional Chinese drama.

If Shakespeare was a corpus of literary works to be translated a century ago, now it has become a shared vocabulary that is facilitating cultural translation in a broader sense—in the sense of communicating moral values and aesthetic traditions of different cultures and seeking a voice that speaks for modern Chinese people.

NOTES

1. The first print (possibly in 1841) was lost. Republished by Lin Zexu in 2002.
2. The first print was published in 1903 by Dawenshe, Shanghai.
3. *The Continent*, Vol. 10, 1904.
4. *Biographies of World Celebrities* was published first by Shanxi School Press, 1908.
5. Qu Yuan, 340-278 B.C. has been recognized as the first great poet in Chinese history.
6. Wang Xiaonong, 1858–1918, was a prominent dramatist in China.
7. First published under the pen name "Wei Ming."
8. Tang Xianzu, 1550-1616, was one of the best dramatists in Chinese history, author of *The Peony Pavilion*.
9. See Levith 23.
10. Li Ruru's *Shashibiya* 46-47.
11. I visited the library in December 2004, and felt that it was now more to commemorate than to be used. It had a good collection of

materials published in or before the 1980s, but not well updated probably since the new main library of the university was a better attraction for the students.

12. See Levith 55.
13. See Wilkinson 39-58.
14. 11 June 1979. See Levith's note.
15. See Fan 23-27.
16. See Li Ruru's "Bard" 69 and Zhang Xiayang 115.
17. Quoted in Levith 71.
18. For the 2006 conference, see Feng Wenkun's *Shakespeare in the Eyes of Chinese Scholars* (Beijing: China Wenlian P, 2007). I attended the 2004 and 2009 conferences.
19. See Liu 341-42.
20. Its premier was in 2005. The actor who has been starring in this production told me that they are invited to more countries and changes are made to the production till today.
21. Fu Shinian, 1896-1950, was a Chinese linguist and educator.
22. Directed by Lin Zhaohua. Its premier in 1990 was a sensation. The play was revived in 2009.
23. The producer of the Contemporary Legend Theatre published four versions online, and potential audience were able to cast votes for their favorite version. See Alexander C.Y. Huang's *Chinese Shakespeares: Two Centuries of Cultural Exchange*.
24. It was directed by Feng Xiaogang.

REFERENCES

Alexander, C.Y. Huang. *Chinese Shakespeares: Two Centuries of Cultural Exchange*. Columbia UP: New York, 2009.

Brochbank, J. Philip. "Shakespeare Renaissance in China." *Shakespeare Quarterly* 39. 2 (Summer 1988): 195-204.

Booth, Stephen. "On the Value of Hamlet." *Shakespeare: An Anthology of Criticism and Theory 1945-2000*. Ed. Russ McDonald. Malden: Blackwell, 2004.

Cai, Erkang. *Li Hongzhang in Europe and America*. Changsha: Yuelu P, 1986.

Fang, Ping. trans. *The New Translation of the Complete Works of Shakespeare*. Shijiazhuang: Hebei Education P, 2000.

Feng, Wenkun. ed. *Shakespeare in the Eyes of Chinese Scholars*. Beijing: China Wenlian P, 2007.

Fu, Sinian. "On Play Writing." *Essays On Chinese Modern Drama*. Ed. Jinbo Zhou. Beijing: Beijing Correspondence College P, 2003.

Guo, Songtao. *Diary of Guo Songtao*. Vol. 3. Changsha: Hunan People's P, 1982.

He, Qixin. "Shakespeare Though Chinese Eyes". Ph.D. dissertation. Kent State University, 1986.

He, Qixin. "Major Trends of Shakespeare Criticism in China." *Proceedings of the Patristic, Mediaeval and Renaissance Conference, Villanova University,* 1984. 9.

Jauss, Hans Robert. "Literary History as a Challenge to Literary Theory." *New Literary History,* 2.1 (1970): 7-37.

Levith, Murray J. *Shakespeare in China*. New York: Continuum, 2004.

Li, Ruru. *Shashibiya: Staging Shakespeare in China*. Hong Kong: Hong Kong UP, 2003.

——. "The Bard in the Middle Kingdom." *Asian Theatre Journal* 12.1 (Spring 1995): 50-84.

Lin, Zexu. *Records of the Four Continents*. Beijing: Huaxia P, 2002.

Lin, Shu. trans. *Tales from Shakespeare*. Beijing: Shangwu P, 1981.

Liu, Hao. *Hamlet in Mirror: A Chinese Aesthetic Perspective on Hamlet and Its Reception in China*. Ph.D. dissertation. Peking University, 2008.

Lu, Gusun. "Hamlet Across Space and Time." *Shakespeare Survey* 36 (1983): 53-56.

——. *Oversea Strange Tales*. Shanghai: Dawenshe, 1903.

Meng, Xianqiang. *A Brief History of Shakespeare in China*. Jilin: Dongbei Normal UP, 1994.

Ruan, Kun. "The Earliest Shakespeare Criticism in China." *Wuhan University Journal* (Philosophy and Social Sciences) (1989): 2.

Shen, Fan. "Shakespeare in China: The Merchant of Venice." *Axian Theatre Journal,* 5.1 (1988): 23-27.

Wang, Guowei. "A Biography of Shakespeare." *The World of Education*. 1907.

Wei, Ming. "Shakespeare and Realism." *Literature and History,* 1.3 (1934):

Wilkinson, J. Norman. "Shakespeare in China." *New England Theatre Journal,* 2.1 (1991): 39–58.

Yan, Fu. *Evolution and Ethics*. Beijing: Science P, 1971.

Yu, Kunshi. Dir. *The Revenge of Prince Zidan* [Hamlet]. Shanghai Peking Opera Troupe. Tianchan Theatre, Shanghai. 2005.

Zhang, Xiaoyang. *Shakespeare in China: A Comparative Study of Two Traditions and Cultures*. Newark, NJ: U of Delaware P,1996.

Index